BEYOND RESTITUTION

This open access book offers a unique perspective on the return of cultural objects by considering the aftermath of the handover processes.

While calls for the repatriation of heritage have been made since the start of the decolonisation process, it is only in recent years that the debate on returning cultural objects has gained widespread prominence. This has been followed by ongoing efforts from several countries to change the legislation, adopt principles, and invest in provenance research to turn repatriation into a more proactive mechanism.

The book tells the story of cultural objects that were housed in European institutions and returned to countries in Africa, Asia, and the Americas. In addition to in-depth analysis of relevant laws and policies, each of the case studies integrates interviews with those who were directly involved in those return processes, as well as those who were impacted by them, including museum staff, government representatives and community members. The book presents previously unheard insights into past return processes, the manifold modalities that such processes have followed, and, at times, unexpected outcomes. By doing so, it offers possible lessons to be learnt for future returns.

Volume 3 in the Art Law Library series

The Art Law Library

The Art Law Library includes books on all aspects of the law relating to art in its widest sense, including antiquities, museums, intangible cultural heritage, archives, intellectual property and human remains. Titles in the series are invaluable to those working and studying in the fields of law, museums, galleries, libraries, planning, archaeology and law enforcement. The series continues the imprint of the Institute of Art and Law.

Series Editor: Ruth Redmond-Cooper, Editor of* Art Antiquity and Law, *and founder of the Institute of Art and Law

Recent titles in the series

Volume 1: The Parthenon Marbles Dispute: Heritage, Law, Politics
Alexander Herman

Volume 2: Digitising Cultural Heritage: Clashes with Copyright Law
Pinar Oruç

Volume 3: Beyond Restitution: Exploring the Stories of Cultural Objects after their Return
Kristin Hausler and Elke Selter

Beyond Restitution

Exploring the Stories of Cultural Objects after their Return

Kristin Hausler
and
Elke Selter

•HART•
OXFORD • LONDON • NEW YORK • NEW DELHI • SYDNEY

HART PUBLISHING

Bloomsbury Publishing Plc

Kemp House, Chawley Park, Cumnor Hill, Oxford, OX2 9PH, UK

1385 Broadway, New York, NY 10018, USA

Bloomsbury Publishing Ireland Limited, 29 Earlsfort Terrace, Dublin 2, D02 AY28, Ireland

HART PUBLISHING, the Hart/Stag logo, BLOOMSBURY and the Diana logo are trademarks of Bloomsbury Publishing Plc

First published in Great Britain 2025

A catalogue record for this book is available from the British Library.

A catalogue record for this book is available from the Library of Congress.

Library of Congress Control Number: 2025936799

ISBN: HB: 978-1-50998-252-3
ePDF: 978-1-50998-254-7
ePub: 978-1-50998-253-0

Typeset by Compuscript Ltd, Shannon
Printed and bound in Great Britain

For product safety related questions contact productsafety@bloomsbury.com

To find out more about our authors and books visit www.hartpublishing.co.uk. Here you will find extracts, author information, details of forthcoming events and the option to sign up for our newsletters.

PREFACE

The question of returning cultural objects has long been a contentious issue in the heritage sector. Throughout the course of the research conducted for this book, it has become increasingly clear just how complex and unsettled this matter remains. In Europe, two sets of primary arguments have often hindered a constructive and equitable dialogue over the issue: the conservation arguments, which ranges from claims such as 'without us, all of this would be lost by now' to concerns about the lack of local infrastructure for preserving these collections; and the legal arguments, which may rest on restrictions to the de-accessioning of objects from collections, good faith acquisition, or the absence of a relevant legal regime at the time the object was removed from its context or lack of contemporary obligation to return. Often raised in combination, these arguments close the door for a resolution of conflicts over cultural objects based on ethical grounds, which means in turn that any past wrongs that may be associated with the removal of an object which should be addressed, such as those linked to colonialism, are equally overlooked. Furthermore, they perpetuate the fallacy that Europe is somehow better placed for protecting, preserving and caring for objects that may rightfully belong to others.

This book is not designed to comprehensively cover all aspects of the topic at hand. Instead, it aims to fill a knowledge gap by addressing the following question: how have certain individuals and institutions successfully facilitated the return of cultural objects, and what has become of these objects after their return? While this exploration was driven by an aspiration for a deeper understanding of the meaning of these past returns for countries and communities of origin, it was also fuelled by a simultaneous interest in shedding some light on the impact of those returns on the European institutions involved. As we found out, not all returns were equally meaningful or impactful. In the process of addressing our research queries, this book evolved into something more: an ode to all the dedicated individuals we interviewed, on both sides of these narratives. These people have navigated considerable challenges and made courageous decisions to bring about these returns. They have recognised that conservation and legal arguments should not always be seen as unsurmountable obstacles and that ethical considerations may provide a more equitable ground for a satisfactory resolution to an often difficult situation. Thus, while this book delves into the intricacies of return processes and relevant laws and policies, it equally celebrates the remarkable individuals without whom none of the returns included herein would have been possible.

The research for this book spanned nearly three years and entailed fieldwork in different corners of the world, from Chile to Indonesia. This endeavour would not have been conceivable without financial support. We are particularly grateful to the Dorset Foundation, which provided us with invaluable time to develop the research idea and establish the foundational elements needed for the initial concept to flourish. Additionally, we extend our heartfelt thanks to the Leverhulme Trust, which recognised the importance of the under-explored questions we aimed to address. We appreciate not only its generous support but also its patience and flexibility, which allowed this research to continue while addressing the barriers imposed by the COVID-19 pandemic to our fieldwork. Our gratitude also goes to Professor Robert McCorquodale and Dr Andrzej Jakubowski, who thoughtfully reviewed our proposal to the Leverhulme Trust, as well as the anonymous reviewers who supported the project.

LEVERHULME
TRUST

Several of the case studies presented in this book could not have been completed without the invaluable work carried out by Panggah Ardiyansyah, Dino Schiappacasse and Kavenaa Tjiworo. All three have been our eyes and ears in their home countries while COVID-19 restricted our ability to conduct fieldwork in person. Their assistance has meant that we could gather data in the case study countries to complement our analysis, while at the same time enriching the narratives with a diversity of voices.

We also extend our gratitude to colleagues at the British Institute of International and Comparative Law (BIICL) for their unwavering support in getting this project off the ground, in particular Diane Denny and Professor Spyros Maniatis, as well as those who provided us with invaluable support throughout its course, including especially Victoria Wyndham, Deepa Craig, and Dr Jack Kenny. We are also grateful to our colleagues at the Institute of Art and Law: Alexander Herman for chairing a discussion at the Institute, which allowed us to test our preliminary findings, and Ruth Redmond-Cooper for having positively responded to our publication proposal. In addition, we also extend special thanks to Dr Alina Holzhausen for her extremely meticulous review as we brought the manuscript to completion, as well as to the expert editing team at Hart Publishing.

This book would also not have been possible without the steadfast support of our respective families, including those who have passed away during the course of writing. Claire, you are missed beyond words.

Finally, we extend our heartfelt thanks to all those who generously agreed to donate some of their precious time to participate in interviews for this book, whether formally or informally, and share their unique perspectives: without you, there would be no stories to tell about the return of cultural objects. After all, while this is a book about objects, it is even more about all the people who cherish them.

Kristin Hausler (London) and Elke Selter (Geneva)
July 2024

CONTENTS

1

Introduction

Looking Back to Move Forward

This publication goes 'beyond restitution' in several ways. It goes beyond the usual discussions to look at what happens to objects after they were returned, but also at the complexities of receiving an object back. It also goes beyond the narrow, legal and formal forms of restitution – those processes that often cannot take place because of legal hurdles – to look at what made returns possible in the past and how that was done. It does so because cultural objects are more than ordinary items; they all have a story with evolving meanings. Restricting a cultural object to a singular interpretation, a single desirable 'life' in the eye of a specific beholder, limits the vast possibilities, interpretations and reinterpretations that are possible. Seven cases of objects that were returned from institutions in Europe to institutions or communities in countries as diverse as Cambodia, Canada, Chile, Indonesia, Namibia, Nepal and Tanzania illustrate what it means to go 'beyond restitution' and demonstrate that, just like the story of an object did not end when it was taken, it also does not end the moment it is returned. In one way, these cases could be considered as success stories: cases where amidst numerous obstacles, the different parties involved made a desired return happen. Yet, this is not a book about successes; rather, it is about what going 'beyond restitution' allows for – looking at what happens following the conclusion of an agreement. By exploring the often complex objects' biographies, through their arrival and stay in Europe, their return and the processes that started them, to their reception back in their country of origin and their 'lives' afterwards, this book offers nuanced perspectives on the values and meanings associated with the return of cultural objects.

I. A Rear-View Mirror Perspective on the Return of Cultural Objects

Debates over the legitimacy of cultural objects in European institutions and their possible return to their countries of origin are not new. For example, whether the Parthenon sculptures could be purchased with public funds was already the object of a debate in the House of Commons in the early nineteenth century.[1] And a formal request for their return was already made by the Greek government in 1983,[2] soon followed by a passionate plea from Melina Mercouri, then Minister of Culture of Greece, calling for their return 'in the name of fairness and morality' at the Oxford Union in 1986.[3] These repeated requests, both formal and informal, as well as the countless news headlines and publications,[4] have long given the appearance of a continued stalemate in the area of restitution. But in 2017, when French President Emmanuel Macron addressed the return of African heritage at the University of Ouagadougou in Burkina Faso, the return of cultural objects truly became a ubiquitous matter of interest in Europe, which instigated meaningful developments and constructive dialogues.

Macron's speech highlighted culture as the primary means to rebuild a 'shared and future imagination' between France and Africa.[5] Affirming that 'a large share of several African countries' cultural heritage' is kept in France without 'valid, lasting and unconditional justification', he declared that African heritage 'must be showcased in Paris but also in Dakar, Lagos and Cotonou'. He added that 'the conditions to exist for temporary or permanent returns of African heritage' should be established within five years. Although this five-year window has now closed, returns, even if only on a temporary basis, remain an exception.[6] According to Kwame Opoku, former legal advisor at the United Nations, 'the only persons who do not benefit from the delay caused … are the original owners in Africa, who have been eagerly waiting for the restitution of their looted treasures'.[7]

Nevertheless, as these words had now been proclaimed by the sitting Head of State of a former colonial power, it elevated the matter to the highest political level and generated an unprecedented reaction. In France, the speech led to the commissioning of a Report (known as the Sarr-Savoy Report), which assessed the origin of African cultural objects in French public collections, offering perspectives on provenance research, cultural cooperation, their eventual return, as well as

[1] Report from the Select Committee of the House of Commons on the Earl of Elgin's Collection of Sculptured Marbles &c (25 March 1816); Note that their possible return was the object of numerous discussions both inside and outside Parliament; see House of Commons Library, 'Briefing Paper: The Parthenon Sculptures' (9 June 2017) Number 02075.

[2] This request would be officially rejected the following year.

[3] Foundation Melina Mercouri, 'Oxford Union, June 12, 1986', www.melinamercourifoundation.com/en/oxford-union-june-12-1986.

[4] See, for example, L Bursey, 'Demokratia: Will the Greek Ideal Work in Greece's Favour to Return the Parthenon Marbles under International Law?' [2024] *Journal of International Humanitarian Legal Studies* 1, who analyses in turn the following two major publications: C Titi, *The Parthenon Marbles and International Law* (Cham, Springer, 2023); and A Herman, *The Parthenon Marbles Dispute: Heritage, Law, Politics* (Oxford, Hart Publishing, 2023).

[5] Élysée, 'Emmanuel Macron's Speech at the University of Ouagadougou', 28 November 2017, www.elysee.fr/en/emmanuel-macron/2017/11/28/emmanuel-macrons-speech-at-the-university-of-ouagadougou.

[6] K Opoku, 'Do French Museums Still Need To Study Looted African Treasures?', *Modern Ghana*, 26 May 2024, www.modernghana.com/news/1315012/do-french-museums-still-need-to-study-looted-afric.html.

[7] ibid.

the applicable legal framework.[8] The Report advocated 'a new relational ethics' to overcome France's legal hurdles, which do not generally allow for the de-accession of objects housed in public collections.[9] Indeed, as this legal barrier remains in place for now, a specific law had to be passed when Macron announced the intention to return 26 objects that had been claimed by Benin in order for these objects to leave the Quai Branly-Jacques Chirac Museum.[10]

Elsewhere in Europe, the matter also became centre stage, with the establishment of committees or the adoption of new legislation or guidance,[11] some of which are addressed in greater detail through the case studies in this book. For example, in Germany, the Museums Association published practical guidance for collections gathered during the colonial era in 2018, and the various levels of government jointly adopted some framework principles in 2019, underlining a need for 'dialogue and transparency', as well as a 'general willingness to return artefacts from colonial contexts'.[12] Going beyond a legal rationale, the principles call for the identification of objects 'which were appropriated in a way which is no longer legally and/or ethically justifiable and enabling their return is a moral and ethical obligation and an important political task for our age'.[13] In Sweden, the National Heritage Board adopted detailed guidance for managing the return of cultural objects in 2020, emphasising the role and views of museums as they can adopt a 'proactive approach and identify objects … that could be returned for ethical reasons or where the museum is of the opinion that these would be of greater value to the potential recipient than they are to the museum'.[14] In another

[8] F Sarr and B Savoy, *The Restitution of African Cultural Heritage: Toward a New Relational Ethics*, translated by DS Burke (Paris, Ministère de la Culture, November 2018).

[9] To advance the question of returns, another study published in 2023 sought to provide recommendations, including for the possible removal of the legal hurdles to de-accessioning museum collections; see J-L Martinez, 'Patrimoine partagé: universalité, restitutions et circulation des oeuvres d'art. Vers une législation et une doctrine françaises sur les "critères de restituabilité" pour les biens culturels', French Ministry of Culture, 27 April 2023). The approach suggested largely follows the 'exception approach' to the inalienability of national collections adopted thus far in the UK; see K Hausler, 'Les musées nationaux de Royaume-Uni face aux demandes de restitutions, ou l'exception qui confirme la règle' in C Bories et al (eds), *Demandes de restitution et avenir des collections muséales* (Paris, Mare et Martin, 2022).

[10] This law also allows for the return of a sword to Senegal; see Loi no 2020-1673 of 24 December 2020, relating to the restitution of cultural objects to the Republic of Benin and the Republic of Senegal.

[11] For example, in Belgium, which is not considered further in this book, a law was adopted; see M-S de Clippele and B Demarsin, 'Pioneering Belgium: Parliamentary Legislation on the Restitution of Colonial Collections' (2022) 8 *Santander Art and Culture Law Review* 323.

[12] German Museums Association, 'Guidelines for German Museums: Care of Collections from Colonial Contexts', 3rd edn (2021), www.museumsbund.de/publikationen/guidelines-on-dealing-with-collections-from-colonial-contexts-2; Federal Foreign Office, 'Framework Principles for Dealing with Collections from Colonial Contexts Agreed by the Federal Government Commissioner for Culture and the Media, the Federal Foreign Office Minister of State for International Cultural Policy, the Cultural Affairs Ministers of the Länder and the Municipal Umbrella Organisations', 13 March 2019, www.auswaertiges-amt.de/blob/2210152/b2731f8b59210c77c68177cdcd3d03de/190412-stm-m-sammlungsgut-kolonial-kontext-en-data.pdf.

[13] ibid, Framework Principle 7.

[14] Swedish National Heritage Board, 'Good Collections Management. Guidance for Managing the Return of Cultural Objects', 2020, www.raa.diva-portal.org/smash/get/diva2:1433378/FULLTEXT01.pdf.

example, in England, the practical guide adopted by the Arts Council England in 2022, although not explicitly about colonial context, calls for a consideration of the 'ethical principles relevant to the particular circumstances' and seeks to empower 'museums to take proactive action' towards restitution and repatriation 'in a spirit of transparency, collaboration and fairness'.[15]

Thus, while calls for the return of heritage and the decolonisation of museums are not new, the reckoning by many European governments of the need to respond to them promptly and adequately, as well as to consider addressing the legal barriers to their return, is more recent. Yet, despite these efforts, return processes themselves seem to progress rather slowly, if at all. This may be partially due to the provenance research, often arduous and costly, that is required for returns to proceed in an appropriate manner.[16] It may also be a consequence of the broader politics of return, which tends to remain a state-to-state process that is difficult to separate from complex post-colonial relations between these states.

Considering the number of cultural objects collected from overseas, very few have so far left European institutions. Nevertheless, a few returns have already taken place some decades ago. Given the numerous initiatives being discussed, adopted and implemented to address the issues raised by requests for return and the presence of contested objects in collections generally, looking back at some of these past processes could inform contemporary and future return processes. Thus, this book offers a rear-view mirror perspective on past return processes, to assess not only the processes themselves but also their aftermaths, which has so far largely been left out of the debate. By telling the stories of completed processes, the book highlights that returning objects and receiving them back is only part of a process, not the end of the 'life' of these objects, the meanings and uses of which continue to evolve alongside the people who associate with them.

In particular, this book seeks to identify lessons learnt as to the aspects of past return processes that have been concluded to the satisfaction of the parties and to those that have perhaps been less satisfactory. It offers entirely new insights as it incorporates the views of individuals who were directly involved in the return of those objects at the time, as well as the views of many of those who are still dealing with the aftermaths of those returns. Indeed, receiving an object back, deciding where

[15] It was updated in 2023; see Arts Council England, 'Restitution and Repatriation: A Practical Guide for Museums in England', September 2023, www.artscouncil.org.uk/supporting-arts-museums-and-libraries/supporting-collections-and-cultural-property/restitution-and-repatriation-practical-guide-museums-england, 7. However, it should be noted that the Guide also calls to consider a claimant's standing to make a claim and the legal grounds for the claim itself. Indeed, the Guide does not appear to seek to rebalance power relationships, with the need for a formal claim and a decision-making body, which does not include the claimant. In addition, even in a country like Switzerland which was not a colonial power, its Museum Association has published a booklet on provenance research which focuses on the colonial context in 2022; see VMS AMS, 'Recherches de provenance dans les musées II: Collections liées aux contexts coloniaux. Notions de base et introduction à la pratique', 2022, www.museums.ch/admin/data/files/media/file_fr/424/vms_standard_provenienz_koloniale-sammlungen_f_web.pdf?lm=1700553846.

[16] See Opoku (n 6).

and how to reintegrate it in a given context, is neither a straightforward nor static matter. To allow for the analysis and findings to be relevant for a wide range of actors, objects and contexts, this book adopts a broad approach purposely. It thus presents a diverse range of case studies, not limited to a specific geographical area or historical context, and not restricted to a certain type of object or return process either. Both conditional and unconditional returns are included, as well returns to a nation, a museum or a community. Before presenting the seven case studies, this introduction provides an overview of the broader historical and legal context.

II. The Restitution Debate in the Historical and Legal Contexts

As none of the case studies analysed in this book was resolved through a judicial route, this section considers some of the barriers to bringing a restitution claim before a court. It then looks at some of the general ethical standards that have been developed to guide return processes. Finally, it points to a human rights approach, which provides another general framework that may further guide those processes.

A. Evolving Global Norms and Outstanding Gaps

Cultural objects have long been used for nation building because of their intrinsic link with peoples' identities. This is also why they are often targeted during hostilities: to affirm sovereignty over another nation's population, either through the destruction of their heritage or through its appropriation. While the seizure of cultural objects during armed conflict is now prohibited (both under treaty and customary international law), this has not always been the case.[17] It is with the adoption of the specific rules regulating the conduct of warfare that this prohibition started to crystallise at the end of the nineteenth century.[18] However, at the time, these rules were only considered applicable among the states that had adopted them, and not to wars they were fighting in their colonies. Therefore, the looting of cultural objects within the colonial context was not generally deemed unlawful. Even beyond colonial contexts, a (sometimes only apparent) lack of explicit laws protecting cultural objects from being taken away and exported meant that many of these objects arrived in Europe lawfully, at least under the rules recognised as applicable at the time by those who had taken them.

[17] See, for example, rules 40 and 41 of the International Committee of the Red Cross (ICRC) Customary International Humanitarian Law (IHL) database and their related practice: www.ihl-databases.icrc.org/en/customary-ihl.

[18] See in particular art 56 of the Regulations concerning the Laws and Customs of War on Land, annexed to the Hague Convention (II) with Respect to the Laws and Customs of War on Land (adopted 29 July 1899, entered into force 4 September 1900) 187 CTS 429.

With regard to return, while there is also an obligation to return a cultural object that has been taken unlawfully during a situation of occupation, this only became binding with the adoption of the First Protocol to the Hague Convention for the Protection of Cultural Property in Armed Conflict in 1954 before being now largely considered as part of customary international law.[19] However, in light of the principle of non-retroactivity,[20] it is not possible to apply the Protocol to historic claims as it does not explicitly allow it.[21] And beyond armed conflicts, while an obligation to return cultural objects which may have been taken in other contexts of domination may be considered *de lege ferenda* (what the law should be), it is not yet part of customary international law, even when strong moral grounds could be invoked. The absence of consistent and uniform practice is apparent in light of the existing domestic laws of several European states still barring the de-accession of museum objects for their return, as well as the continued refusal to permanently return certain objects, such as the Parthenon sculptures.

Furthermore, the evolution of these norms cannot be disassociated from the decolonisation processes and the emergence of human rights following the Second World War. With the dissolution of colonial regimes, newly created states had a need to shape national identities distinct from their former rulers; such state-building exercises were often supported with the establishment of a common national heritage. Thus, the question of the return of cultural objects became intimately linked with the exercise of the right to self-determination, as well as the need to address historic injustices.[22]

In this context, states increasingly called for their cultural objects back. With the adoption in 1970 of the Convention on the Means of Prohibiting and Preventing the Illicit Import, Export and Transfer of Ownership of Cultural Property (the 1970 UNESCO Convention), under the auspices of the United Nations Educational, Scientific and Cultural Organisation (UNESCO), the international law protecting heritage started to extend beyond armed conflicts. The 1970 UNESCO Convention was meant to put up barriers to the illegal trade in cultural objects feeding the growing demands of the art market, but it also provides for the facilitated return

[19] State parties must 'return, at the close of hostilities, to the competent authorities of the territory previously occupied, cultural property which is in its territory', see First Protocol to The Hague Convention for the Protection of Cultural Property in the Event of Armed Conflict (adopted 14 May 1954, entered into force 7 August 1956) 249 UNTS 215, art 1.

[20] Vienna Convention on the Law of Treaties (adopted 23 May 1969, entered into force 27 January 1980) 1115 UNTS 331, art 28.

[21] Note that these rules were considered in the case of the return of the Venus of Cyrene, which had arrived in Italy in 1915 and was returned to Libya; see A Chechi, 'The Return of Cultural Objects Removed in Times of Colonial Domination and International Law: The Case of the Venus of Cyrene' (2008) 18 *Italian Yearbook of International Law* 159.

[22] The United Nations (UN) Charter affirmed the principle of 'equal rights and self-determination of peoples' in 1945; see UN Charter (adopted 26 June 1945, entered into force 24 October 1945) 1 UNTS XVI, art 1(2); and also UN Charter, ch XI. In its 1960 declaration on decolonisation, the UNGA affirmed that, by virtue of the right to self-determination, 'they freely determine their political status and freely pursue their economic, social and cultural development'; see Declaration on the Granting of Independence to Colonial Countries and Peoples, UNGA Res 1514 (XV) (14 December 1960) para 2.

of stolen or illegally exported cultural property from one state party to another.[23] While it affirms nationalist interests in cultural heritage, it has two major limitations. First, and in accordance with international law, the 1970 UNESCO Convention is not applicable retroactively, which means that it does not apply to objects that have left a state party's territory before its entry into force in 1972. Nevertheless, this treaty established a benchmark year with regard to provenance which means that, in principle, reputable collectors (including museums) now only enter pieces in their collections if they have been either exported from their country of origin before 1970 or legally exported after that date.[24] Second, the 1970 UNESCO Convention is limited to return from one state to another. Hence, another convention was adopted in 1995 (the 1995 International Institute for the Unification of Private Law (UNIDROIT) Convention on Stolen or Illegally Exported Cultural Objects) to provide for the return of objects in private hands.[25] The 1995 UNIDROIT Convention also presents the advantage of including objects that have not been inventoried, another limitation of the 1970 UNESCO Convention, as well as reversing the burden of proof, which means that the possessor required to return an object has to prove due diligence at the time of acquisition to obtain compensation. However, it does not benefit from a very large number of state parties, and like the 1970 UNESCO Convention, it does not apply retroactively.

While the adoption of these treaties led to changes in the way in which the art market operates, it did not provide a solution to historic grievances, that is, those concerned with objects taken from a state's territory before the entry into force of the 1970 UNESCO Convention and sometimes even before the international recognition of that state and its contemporary borders. Therefore, ever since becoming independent, newly formed states have led the impetus for the adoption by the United Nations General Assembly (UNGA) of resolutions concerned with the return of cultural objects. Already in 1973, the UNGA requested the Director-General of UNESCO to study the 'legal implications flowing from the existence of legislation for the protection of the national artistic heritage, including problems of exchange and the voluntary return of various cultural works'.[26] The UNGA also adopted a resolution specifically dedicated to the 'Restitution of works of art to countries victims of expropriation', in which it stressed that 'the cultural heritage of a people conditions the present and future flowering of its artistic values and its over-all development' and deplored 'the

[23] The 1970 UNESCO Convention has been ratified by 141 states. For objects inventoried and stolen from a museum, public or religious monument, or a similar institution, art 7(b)(ii) provides that state parties should undertake appropriate measures to seize and return any cultural property stolen and imported. According to art 13, parties are responsible at the national level for restitution and cooperation.

[24] P Gerstenblith, 'The Meaning of 1970 for the Acquisition of Archaeological Objects' (2013) 38 *Journal of Field Archaeology* 364.

[25] The 1995 UNIDROIT Convention on Stolen or Illegally Exported Cultural Objects now counts 54 state parties.

[26] UNGA, Preservation and further development of cultural values, including the protection, restitution and return of cultural and artistic property (11 December 1980) UN Doc A/RES/35/127, para 4.

wholesale removal, virtually without payment, of *objets d'art* from one country to another, frequently as a result of colonial or foreign occupation'.[27] 'Convinced that the restitution of such works would make good the serious damage suffered by countries as a result of such removal', it further affirmed that prompt interstate restitution would not only strengthen international cooperation but also constitute 'just reparation for damage done'.[28] Finally, the UNGA explicitly recognised the 'special obligations in this connexion of those countries which had access to such valuable objects only as a result of colonial or foreign occupation'.[29] However, it did not clarify what that 'special obligation' was anchored on and, despite several similar resolutions being adopted in subsequent years,[30] the calls for return from former colonies largely amounted to a 'call into the void'.[31]

In an attempt to move the debate forward, the then Director-General of UNESCO, Amadou Mahtar M'Bow, issued a powerful plea for the return of 'Irreplaceable Cultural Heritage to those who Created it' in 1978, lamenting 'the vicissitudes of history' that had robbed many peoples of their 'inheritance'.[32] While affirming the need to return those objects to which populations attached the most importance, his address also recognised the interests of those who had now housed those objects for a long time. As it included alternatives to restitutions such as long-term loans, his message adopted a rather balanced approach, which took into consideration the internationalist approach to cultural heritage.[33]

Yet, despite multiple efforts at the international level, the legal basis for returns has so far remained inadequate. Even with regard to objects having been taken from their countries of origin after 1970, the existing treaties are often not applicable as they have not been universally accepted, as demonstrated in a couple of the case studies presented in this book.[34] Moreover, as the case studies in this book also show, it is challenging to request the return of an object located in a foreign jurisdiction based on the domestic legislation in force at the time. In addition, the circumstances in which an object left its original context may not be entirely clear and, thus, disputed. Therefore, there is a need to consider ethical (rather than solely legal) grounds when considering the possible return of a cultural object. Accordingly, alternative means of dispute resolution based on equity and

[27] UNGA, Restitution of works of art to countries victims of expropriation (19 December 1973) UN Doc A/RES/32/18, preamble.

[28] ibid, preamble and art 1.

[29] ibid, para 2.

[30] This continues to this day, with a resolution even adopted unanimously in 2021; see UNGA, Return or restitution of cultural property to the countries of origin (6 December 2021) UN Doc A/RES/76/16; see also C Scott, *Cultural Diplomacy and the Heritage of Empire: Negotiating Post-colonial Returns* (Abingdon, Routledge, 2020) p. 137.

[31] Interview with Etienne Clément, lawyer and former UNESCO official, 1 March 2023. Note that a working group was then created to advance the matter, which the non-retroactive 1970 UNESCO Convention had not addressed; see E Clément, 'Musées, collections et les translocations du patrimoine culturel' (2022) 29 *La Vie des Musées* 18.

[32] Unesco Courier, 'A Plea for the Return of an Irreplaceable Cultural Heritage to Those Who Created it: An Appeal by Mr Amadou Mahtar M'Bow, Director-General of UNESCO' (Paris, UNESCO, July 1978) 4–5.

[33] See Clément (n 31) 21.

[34] See chs 3 and 8 in this book.

what many of those engaged in the return processes presented in this book have described as the 'right thing to do' have often been the preferred avenues for returning cultural objects.

B. Alternative Dispute Resolution and the Strengthening of Ethical Returns

In 1978, the same year in which M'Bow issued his plea, UNESCO established the Intergovernmental Committee for Promoting the Return of Cultural Property (ICPRCP, also known as the 'Return & Restitution' Intergovernmental Committee), which first convened in 1980.[35] Given the limitations of the existing legal framework, the ICPRCP does not adjudicate claims, but acts as a facilitator and supports cooperation among Member States.[36] Any UNESCO Member State can make a request for a dispute to be brought before it, when no treaty is applicable and bilateral negotiations have failed. Recognising that alternative modes of dispute resolution may be a constructive way to solve challenging disputes, its mandate was even extended to mediation and conciliation in 2005,[37] with the ICPRCP seeking to establish itself as a 'space for interstate dialogue'.[38] While the ICPRCP has not yet become the go-to forum for the resolution of disputes over cultural objects,[39] it has played a role in several returns.[40] With regard to objects removed in a colonial context specifically, the ICPRCP established an expert group in 2021, in order to elaborate recommendations regarding their possible return.[41] Initial recommendations focused on cooperation, capacity building and ethical dimensions.[42]

When adopting the MONDIACULT Declaration in 2022 as part of the World Conference on Cultural Policies and Sustainable Development, UNESCO Member States further called return and restitution as an 'ethical imperative to foster the

[35] UNESCO Records of the General Conference Twentieth Session (Paris, 24 October–28 November 1978) Volume I Resolutions 20 C/Resolution 4/7.6/5.

[36] Note that state parties can also defend the interest of public or private institutes based on their territories or of their nationals. For more on the mandate of the ICPRCP, see the Statutes of the Intergovernmental Committee for Promoting the Return of Cultural Property to its Countries of Origin or its Restitution in case of Illicit Appropriation (Adopted by 20 C/Resolution 4/7.6/5 of the 20th session of the General Conference of UNESCO, Paris, 24 October-28 November 1978) CLT/CH/INS-2005/21, art 4.

[37] ibid.

[38] See Clément (n 31) 22; and interview with Etienne Clément, lawyer and former UNESCO official, 1 March 2023, in which he underlined that African nations did not insist on this issue at the time as their relations with the 'North' were focused on trade, military support and combatting apartheid.

[39] Note that para 17 of the Declaration of the UNESCO World Conference on Cultural Policies and Sustainable Development – MONDIACULT 2022 (28–30 September 2022, Mexico City) MONDIACULT-2022/CPD/6 (MONDIACULT Declaration) calls for the promotion of proactive mediation by the ICPRCP.

[40] For example, it played a role in the case study discussed in ch 8 of this book.

[41] ICPRCP, Twenty-Second Session (27–29 September 2021) Decision 22.COM/15; Initial recommendations were discussed in 2024, with a view to adopting them at the Committee's 25th session.

[42] ICPRCP, Twenty-Fourth Session (29-31 May 2024) Decision 24.COM/13.

right of peoples and communities',[43] with the activation of an ethical (rather than legal) responsibility which in turn would allow the realisation of human rights. While considerations based on ethical grounds are generally better apt at generating proactive approaches to the question of return, they also bring added complexity and uncertainty to the parties in comparison with purely legal considerations. Therefore, guiding principles should be considered for those out-of-court processes to be both 'just and fair' and resolve disputes over cultural objects in a way that may bring some satisfaction to both parties. The Code of Ethics of the International Council of Museums (ICOM) provides the following overarching guiding principles:

> Museums should be prepared to initiate dialogue for the return of cultural property to a country or people of origin. This should be undertaken in an impartial manner, based on scientific, professional and humanitarian principles as well as applicable local, national and international legislation.[44]

The ICOM Code of Ethics also calls for museums to 'work in close collaboration with the communities from which their collections originate as well as those they serve',[45] which may include diaspora groups. Just like societies evolve, museums have continuously re-invented themselves and their role(s) within them, with both decolonisation and globalisation having an impact on their functioning. The current context is not the same as it was in 2002, when 18 major Western museums signed a Declaration on the Importance and Value of Universal Museums to assert the eighteenth-century concept of 'encyclopaedic museums',[46] seeking to cement their control over their collections and thereby largely rejecting claims for the return of cultural objects.[47] In general, the dominant, state-driven, framing of heritage, which Laurajane Smith coined as the 'authorised heritage discourse',[48] is being increasingly challenged by communities, which seek to take their seats at the heritage governance table. While the ICOM Code of Ethics encourages museums to work in cooperation with relevant communities, the social role of museums has now even become part of the new definition of museum adopted by ICOM in 2022, placing it firmly 'in the service of society' more widely.[49]

[43] MONDIACULT Declaration, para 17.

[44] ICOM Code of Ethics (adopted 1986 and revised 2004). Note that at the time of writing, the Code of Ethics is being revised by the ICOM Ethics Committee; ICOM Code of Ethics, 6.2.

[45] ibid, VI.

[46] For a discussion of the declaration, see NGW Curtis, '"A Continuous Process of Reinterpretation": The Challenge of the Universal and Rational Museum' (2005) 4 *Public Archaeology* 50; and the reply by N MacGregor and J Williams, 'The Encyclopaedic Museum: Enlightenment Ideals, Contemporary Realities' (2005) 4 *Public Archaeology* 57.

[47] According to George O Abungu, former Director-General of the National Museums of Kenya, the conceptualisation of the 'universal museum' was also a reaction to the discussions around 'the illicit traffic in cultural heritage, and the emergence of museums as major players in the dialogue of culture, the question of ownership and repatriation'. See GO Abungu, '"Universal Museums": New Contestations, New Controversies' in M Gabriel and J Dahl (eds), *UTIMUT: Past Heritage – Future Partnerships* (Copenhagen, IWGIA/NKA, 2008) 32.

[48] L Smith, *Uses of Heritage* (New York, Routledge, 2006).

[49] According to this new definition, a museum is 'a not-for-profit, permanent institution in the service of society that researches, collects, conserves, interprets and exhibits tangible and intangible heritage. Open to the public, accessible and inclusive, museums foster diversity and sustainability.

In addition, the ICOM Code of Ethics hints at the link between provenance research and possible returns as it defines provenance research as 'the full history and ownership of an item from the time of its discovery or creation to the present day, through which authenticity and ownership are determined'.[50]

In addition to the general principles adopted by ICOM, which apply to museum objects originating from any context, ethical principles have also been elaborated specifically to address the issue of Nazi loot. As those principles are already well developed and widely implemented, they are worth considering with regard to objects taken in other contexts of duress. In particular, the 1998 Washington Principles on Nazi-Confiscated Art call not only for the identification of confiscated art through provenance research but also for making their records 'open and accessible' so that the original owners or their heirs can submit claims.[51] Calls for transparency in the case of colonial loot at the domestic level have indeed already been made.[52] Finally, beyond legal and ethical norms specifically applicable to cultural objects, human rights and a reparative approach to justice can further support the resolution of disputes over the return of cultural objects.

C. Adopting a Human Rights and Reparative Justice Approach

In principle, a claim for an object held in a European institution can be brought before a domestic court and eventually before the European Court of Human Rights (ECtHR) by any person, non-governmental organisation or group of individuals claiming to be the victim of a human rights violation by a state party.[53] This could possibly include a violation resulting from the continued retention of a cultural object. However, such actions are particularly challenging to bring, starting with the establishment of legal standing.[54] That said, beyond offering possible judicial routes, human rights standards can also inform alternative means of dispute resolution, in line with the paradigm shift towards the 'humanisation' of restitution as observed by legal scholar Evelien Campfens.[55] Indeed, applying a human rights lens to the question of the return of cultural objects can guide responses to return claims based on ethical grounds. In particular, it can support the identification

They operate and communicate ethically, professionally and with the participation of communities, offering varied experiences for education, enjoyment, reflection and knowledge sharing'. See ICOM, 'ICOM Approves a New Museum Definition', 24 August 2022, www.icom.museum/en/news/icom-approves-a-new-museum-definition.

[50] ICOM Code of Ethics, Glossary.

[51] Washington Conference Principles on Nazi-Confiscated Art (3 December 1998) principle 2.

[52] See ch 6 in this book.

[53] European Convention on Human Rights (1950), art 34.

[54] See, for example, the case of *Syllogos Ton Athinaion v United Kingdom* App No 48259/15 (ECtHR, 31 May 2016), which noted legal hurdles, both *ratione temporis* and *ratione materiae*.

[55] E Campfens, 'Cross-Border Claims to Looted Art', European Parliament's Policy Department for Citizens' Rights and Constitutional Affairs, October 2023, https://www.europarl.europa.eu/thinktank/en/document/IPOL_STU(2023)754126, 36–38.

of the cultural heritage rights holders within a particular context, which can in turn be crucial in the balancing of interests which is central to these responses. As underlined by the Special Rapporteur in the Field of Cultural Rights: 'Varying degrees of access and enjoyment may be recognized, taking into consideration the diverse interests of individuals and groups according to their relationship with specific cultural heritages.'[56] Accordingly, when considering a possible return, all of the existing meanings and uses associated with the object(s) should be taken into consideration.[57]

The holistic human rights understanding of cultural heritage, which includes both intangible and tangible elements, is also relevant, in particular for those rights holders which may place an emphasis on the intangible values of an object over its aesthetic quality, for example. Indeed, cultural objects, even when they have been removed from their contexts for decades, may still be regarded as sacred or necessary for the practice of certain traditions, which have been recognised as part of the exercise of cultural rights. In particular, the affirmation of the human rights of minority groups to their cultural practices has resulted in traditional ways of life being considered when assessing cultural rights' claims,[58] a consideration which may be similarly applicable to alternative means of dispute resolution. This is further supported by the near-universal ratification of the 2003 UNESCO Convention for the Safeguarding of Intangible Cultural Heritage, which has led to a global shift towards the integration of intangible elements in all heritage matters. When considering the return of cultural objects, their role in the safeguarding of intangible cultural practices should therefore also be systematically considered.

In this regard, specific provisions applicable to returns have already been adopted within Indigenous human rights law, which may also serve as a model in other contexts. Adopted in 2007, the UN Declaration on the Rights of Indigenous Peoples provides that: 'States shall seek to enable the access and/or repatriation of ceremonial objects and human remains in their possession through fair, transparent and effective mechanisms developed in conjunction with indigenous peoples concerned.'[59] Recognising that 'Indigenous peoples have the right to practise and revitalize their cultural traditions and customs', it affirms that:

> States shall provide redress through effective mechanisms, which may include restitution, developed in conjunction with indigenous peoples, with respect to their cultural, intellectual, religious and spiritual property taken without their free, prior and informed consent or in violation of their laws, traditions and customs.[60]

[56] Human Rights Council Report of the independent expert in the field of cultural rights, Farida Shaheed (21 March 2011) UN Doc A/HRC/17, para 62.

[57] On the European level, see the Council of Europe Framework Convention on the Value of Cultural Heritage for Society (Faro Convention) (27.X.2005) CETS 199.

[58] International Covenant on Civil and Political Rights (adopted 16 December 1966, entered into force 23 March 1976) 999 UNTS 171, art 27.

[59] UNGA, United Nations Declaration on the Rights of Indigenous Peoples (13 September 2007) UN Doc A/RES/61/295, art 12(2).

[60] ibid art 11.

The 2022 MONDIACULT Declaration appears to have already found some inspiration from these provisions, as it called 'for an open and inclusive international dialogue for the return and restitution of cultural property', while also committing to 'expanding efforts to promote the protection, return and restitution of cultural property, including in consultation with the populations concerned and with their free, prior and informed consent'.[61] In accordance with this commitment to integrate community level stakeholders in restitution efforts, a return process should not take place exclusively at the interstate level when the object being returned is of special interest to a community. As demonstrated in this book, the interstate approach has often been favoured, even in cases where there were obvious individuals or communities holding an interest in the object(s) being returned.[62]

Finally, a human rights approach may inform the restorative and possibly transformative aspect of returns of cultural objects. The obligation to repair the harm caused by a wrongful act is an established principle of justice.[63] However, as already mentioned, with regard to historic claims, it is rare that the taking of a cultural object amounted to a 'wrongful act' under the law recognised at the time. Still, with regard to objects taken in the colonial context, Kwame Opoku underlines that: 'Once you consider colonialism as a crime against humanity, it becomes difficult to justify the continuing illegal holding of colonial loot, which was only possible within the structure and conditions created by colonialism.'[64] While statutes of limitation, which bar claims due to the passage of time, should not apply in cases where the taking of a cultural object may have been part of widespread or systematic international crimes, in practice, they often do. Reparative justice initiatives have allowed to redress past mass human rights violations and to overcome the legal barriers identified above. The return of cultural objects could thus be part of sets of measures to redress past injustices, which may also include truth-seeking and truth-telling initiatives and memory efforts.[65] In some of the case studies selected for this book, reparative justice efforts were considered in parallel to the returns of cultural objects and, to some extent, informed those processes.[66]

Over the course of our research and as already mentioned, many of those involved in the return processes affirmed that an object was returned because it

[61] MONDIACULT Declaration, paras 10 and 17.

[62] See in particular chs 3, 6, and 7 in this book.

[63] See, for example, art 35 of the Articles on the Responsibility of States for Internationally Wrongful Acts (ARSIWA) (2001), according to which '[a] State responsible for an internationally wrongful act is under an obligation to make restitution, that is, to re-establish the situation which existed before the wrongful act was committed, provided and to the extent that restitution: (a) is not materially impossible; (b) does not involve a burden out of all proportion to the benefit deriving from restitution instead of compensation'. See also the Basic Principles and Guidelines on the Right to a Remedy and Reparation for Victims of Gross Violations of International Human Rights Law and Serious Violations of International Humanitarian Law (UNGA Res 60/147, 15 December 2005) (Basic Principles 2005), according to which reparations may also include rehabilitation and guarantees of non-repetition.

[64] See Opoku (n 6).

[65] When possible, restitution remains the primary means for redressing an internationally wrongful act: see ARSIWA, art 35; and Basic Principles 2005 (n 63).

[66] See chs 6 and 7 in this book.

was 'the right thing to do'. Although such statement may appear to emerge in a legal vacuum, legal standards remain very relevant, in particular if one considers a human rights approach to cultural heritage. Nevertheless, as this book looks 'beyond restitution' in the strict legal sense, it privileges the term 'return', which is apposite to encompass various processes than 'restitution' or even 'repatriation' (or 'rematriation'),[67] unless the context dictates otherwise.[68]

III. Research Methodology and Contents

While this book is not the first contribution to cross-border returns of cultural objects, other publications have generally focused on the return process and their legal and/or ethical frameworks, without considering their aftermaths. Nevertheless, several of those publications were extremely valuable to the background research conducted for this book, including the case selection.[69]

A. Case Studies and Research Methods

This book comprises a detailed analysis of seven case studies, allowing a rebalancing of the restitution debate through the consideration of both sides engaged in return processes and the inclusion of the voices of those who have directly participated in those processes. The selection of case studies was based on two factors: a set of four common criteria and a representative sampling. The following criteria determined the selection of comparable case studies: (1) return from a European museum (or other collection in Europe), (2) of an ethnographic or archaeological

[67] J Greenfield, *The Return of Cultural Treasures* (New York, Cambridge University Press, 1989) 368.

[68] In such instances, the term 'repatriation', referring to the return to one's own country or nation, may be more adequate as it underlines the status of a community within a state.

[69] These publications include E Barkan, *The Guilt of Nations: Restitution and Negotiating Historical Injustices* (New York, WW Norton & Company, 2000); Bories et al (n 9); E Campfens, *Cross-Border Claims to Cultural Objects* (Leiden, EM Meijers Instituut voor Rechtswetenschappelijk Onderzoek, 2021); A Chechi, *The Settlement of International Cultural Heritage Disputes* (Oxford, Oxford University Press, 2014); Gabriel and Dahl (n 47); Greenfield (n 67); A Herman, *Restitution: The Return of Cultural Artifacts* (London, Lund Humphries, 2021); J Nafziger et al (eds), *Cultural Law, International Comparative and Indigenous* (Cambridge, Cambridge University Press, 2010); R Peters, *Complementary and Alternative Mechanisms beyond Restitution: An Interest-Oriented Approach to Resolving International Cultural Heritage Disputes* (Fiesole, European University Institute, 2011); LV Prott (ed), *Witnesses to History: A Compendium of Documents and Writings on the Return of Cultural Objects* (Paris, UNESCO, 2009); Scott (n 30); L Tythacott and K Arvanitis (eds), *Museums and Restitution, New Practices, New Approaches* (Abingdon, Routledge, 2014); J van Beurden, *Treasures in Trusted Hands. Negotiating the Future of Colonial Cultural Objects, Interdisciplinary Studies in Culture, History and Heritage* (Leiden, Sidestone Press, 2017); AF Vrdoljak, *International Law, Museums and the Return of Cultural Objects* (Cambridge, Cambridge University Press, 2008). See also the ArThemis database, led by M-A Renold at the University of Geneva, which was also an invaluable source of information: https://plone.unige.ch/art-adr.

object (to the exclusion of human remains), (3) to its state or community of origin located overseas, and (4) which took place after the start of the decolonisation process.

On the basis of a long-list of cases responding to the above criteria, the final selection was aimed at a representative sampling of different types of cases and return processes that were: (1) reactive (that is, following a request) and proactive (on the returning's party own accord); (2) permanent and temporary (such as through a renewable loan); (3) unconditional and conditional (such as with the requirement to increase conservation or security capacities); (4) government-led, institutionally-led and community-led processes; and (5) covering different regions and different European countries.

The research for this book combined a thorough analysis of the historical, legal and political context with empirical work, which includes first-hand and often never before collected stories and views on the return processes. The qualitative research combined the observation of objects in their context (in museums or in communities) with semi-structured interviews of relevant stakeholders, with their informed consent. The selection of interviewees was based on their participation in the return processes, and their past or present connection with the object(s). Doctrinal and archival documents, as well as media sources from the time of the restitution, were all used in our analysis, in addition to the empirical material collected. Because COVID-19 imposed travel restrictions during the first year and a half of this research, local consultants partially carried out interviews for three of the case studies, as indicated in each respective chapter.[70]

The project addressed the following questions:

(1) What legal context or alternative solution made a return possible?
(2) What happened to the object(s) once returned?
(3) What has been the (longer-term) result of the return on the parties involved, if any?
(4) How do the different processes (proactive/reactive, conditional/unconditional, government-led or other, etc) affect the end result of the return?

By addressing these questions, this research sought to expand the understanding of the return of cultural objects by not only considering return processes in detail but also by exploring an understudied dimension of those processes, ie, the role these objects play for the source communities and/or source countries and for the returning institutions and/or returning countries after their return.

[70] See chs 4, 6, and 7 in this book. While this was not part of the initial plan, in hindsight, it has allowed for very rich data thanks to their familiarity with their own context and the absence of language barriers. At the same time, the authors are aware that respondents may respond differently to local researchers as opposed to international or European ones. Note that for all other chapters, interviews were conducted by either (or both) authors.

B. Overview of the Chapters

Each of the following seven chapters presents one case study, focused on one return process. Each case is briefly summarised below.

Chapter 2 considers the return in 2006 of the G'psgolox totem pole from the Museum of Ethnography in Sweden to the Haisla First Nation in Canada. While the museum first requested that the pole be housed in a purpose-built facility, the pole, once returned, was eventually placed back in nature. This chapter explains the meaning of the return of the pole to the community, as well as the decision-making process for the pole to be eventually returned to nature. In addition, it also considers the replicas which were made by community members as part of this process, including the one that now stands outside the Museum of Ethnography in Stockholm. Finally, it reflects on the role of the return of the pole in the development of the national guidance for managing the return of cultural objects.

Chapter 3 considers the return in 2000 of a stolen idol to Nepal. When the first objects were returned to Nepal, like the one on which this case focuses, the country followed a relatively standard approach, placing them in the care of major museums. Lately, however, a shift in approach has significantly impacted the 'after-life' of these objects. In this chapter, consideration is given to the unique approach of Nepal, which returns idols to their communities of origin rather than keeping them in museums. As Nepal prioritises the safeguarding of living culture, the chapter considers the future of an idol that was returned from Germany and the steps that may need to be taken for it to be returned to the community.

Chapter 4 focuses on the return of church bells from Wales to Chile in 2010 and 2013. Despite the bells having gained popularity and become the object of several cultural initiatives around Swansea, their return was facilitated by the multiple connections felt by the Welsh community and the Church of Wales towards Chile. This case study further denotes that the return of those bells, while welcomed in Chile, was not necessarily straightforward in Santiago, with the bells being first attached to a temporary structure which was later replaced and with the bells being dispersed to benefit different stakeholders.

Chapter 5 looks at the return of the head of a Harihara statute to Cambodia in 2016. It focuses on a return that took the form of 'crossed deposits' (known in French as '*dépôts croisés*'), an exchange of pieces of sculptures between the National Museum of Cambodia and the Guimet Museum in Paris. The head of a Harihara statue was returned to Cambodia to be reunited with the rest of its body, while a foot piece of a Koh Ker statue was lent to the Guimet Museum to be reunited with the rest of the statue that remains in Paris. It showcases how both museums, through a long-standing cooperation, found a way to exchange pieces of statues, on the basis of tacitly renewed loans, despite a restrictive legal context.

Chapter 6 examines the 2019 return by Germany of a Bible and a whip that belonged to national hero Hendrik Witbooi in Namibia. Over the past few years, significant strides have been made by Germany in terms of acknowledging the genocide in Namibia and reaching an agreement on reparations. By comparing this process with an earlier return in 1996 of a series of Witbooi letters, this chapter looks into the evolving approaches adopted by these respective returns in relation to the broader political context. By doing so, it delves into the wider framework of colonial reparations and how the return of these objects fits therein.

Chapter 7 concerns the return by the Netherlands in 2020 of a ceremonial dagger (*keris*) having belonged to Indonesian national hero Diponegoro. When Indonesia gained independence, it reached an agreement with the Netherlands to return major objects and collections taken under colonial rule. One of the priorities within this agreement was objects having belonged to Diponegoro. At the time, this dagger could not be located, and thus it was only many decades later that it was finally returned. The chapter looks at the ensuing provenance research, the engagement of Indonesian experts in the process, as well as at the political and local meanings of this belated return.

Chapter 8 presents the return in 2010 of a Makonde mask from a private Swiss collection to Tanzania. It considers the role played by the ICPRCP, as well as Switzerland, in the return process. It also looks at the limitation of the legal framework applicable to the case, despite the object having left Tanzania rather recently, as well as the requirements attached to the return, including regarding the status of the return itself (as a gift rather than a restitution) and the security conditions at the National Museum in Dar es Salaam, the entity from which the mask had been stolen and where it is now housed again, in a strong room, away from public view.

Finally, Chapter 9 concludes with some lessons learnt, offering a cross-analysis of the case studies presented in the previous chapters, with some key findings interspersed with recommendations. It thus suggests a number of ways forward, informing the global debate concerned with the return of cultural objects, as well as the laws and policies being developed to address it. In light of the longer-term view adopted by this volume, the lessons learnt go beyond the return of objects to consider their re-integration in their places of origin, the changing roles of the relevant stakeholders and of the wider context in which claims for the return of cultural objects occur.

2

From Stockholm Back to Haisla Ancestral Territory

A Totem Pole Returns Home

I. Introduction

This chapter tells the story of the return of the G'psgolox totem pole, which had been removed from the Kitlope Valley, in the traditional territory of the Haisla First Nation, along the coast of British Columbia in Western Canada. Carved and raised in 1872, it stood by the village of Misk'usa, at the mouth of the Kitlope River. The pole had been commissioned by Chief G'psgolox, the leader of the Eagle clan of the Xenaksiala people who would later become part of the Haisla First Nation.[1] Having lost all his children and many members of his clan to an epidemic of smallpox which had been introduced by Europeans, he spent time grieving his loss in the forest where his people were buried. There, he had a spiritual experience: he met a mythical being, Tsooda, who gave him a rock crystal, telling him that if he bit down on it while wishing for his family's return, his prayers would be answered.[2] Following his guidance, Chief G'psgolox entered into contact with the spirits of his relatives, which allowed him to heal. Thereafter, he commissioned a mortuary pole to commemorate his relatives, as well as his spiritual encounter, with Tsooda being placed at its top.

In 1929, the pole was cut down to be taken away, on the erroneous basis that it had been abandoned. Olof Hanson, the royal Swedish council stationed in Prince Rupert, had it exported to be gifted to the people of Sweden. It was thus shipped to Stockholm, where it entered the collections of the Etnografiska Museet (Museum of Ethnography), which is now part of the Museums of World Culture, along with three other museums.[3] Among the Haisla, the pole was never forgotten and,

[1] See Haisla Nation, 'Haisla & Our History', https://haisla.ca/community/haisla-our-history; see also JR Baird, A Solanki and M Askren (eds), *Returning the Past: Repatriation of First Nations Cultural Property* (Vancouver, UBC Museum of Anthropology, 2008) 25, according to whom the Haisla Nation formed in 1948 when the Xenaksiala people joined the Kitamaat Band.

[2] The story is told by Louisa Smith, descendant of Chief G'psgolox in G Cardinal, 'Totem: The Return of the G'psgolox Pole', 2003, www.nfb.ca/film/totem_the_return_of_the_gpsgolox_pole, at 06:45–09:15.

[3] The Världskultu museerna (Museums of World Culture) also include the Museum of Mediterranean and Near Eastern Antiquities, and the Museum of Far Eastern Antiquities, both also in Stockholm, and the Museum of World Culture, in Gothenburg; see www.varldskulturmuseerna.se/en.

when they located and identified it in 1991, it immediately became the object of a repatriation request.[4] What followed was a long-winded process for its return, including the offering of a replica by the First Nation to the Swedish Museum of Ethnography, as well as an agreement by the Haisla that the pole would be preserved in a museum-like facility. However, once returned, traditions prevailed and the pole was eventually returned to nature. Indeed, according to Indigenous custom, poles are meant to be left to decay and return to dust, in accordance with their life cycle.

The G'psgolox pole, like other totem poles of the Pacific Northwest, tells stories associated with a Nation, a family or an individual, acting not only as a link with the past but also as a vital expression of contemporary Indigenous identity. Requesting its return was thus also part of reclaiming a cultural identity, the expression of which had been curtailed by the Indian Act, a piece of Canadian legislation which prohibited certain cultural practices associated with the erection of totem poles until this ban was lifted in 1951,[5] as well as by the Indian Residential School system which removed Indigenous children from their families and cultures.[6] To recover from these assimilation attempts, efforts have been undertaken by Indigenous peoples to regain the culture that had been taken away from them, including through reclaiming totem poles. This chapter is thus focused on the return of an object with strong sentiments attached to it, as a sacred object and as a symbol of the mistreatment of First Nations people in Canada. Furthermore, it also reflects on issues that may be raised in any return processes: the making of replicas to replace a returned object and the imposition of conservation standards before allowing the return of an object.

II. From Kitamaat to Sweden: Becoming a National 'Museum Object'

A. A Removal and Export Authorised by the Government

Established in 1900, the Swedish Museum of Ethnography was looking to grow its collections with a Northwest Coast totem pole, a status symbol at the time for

[4] Note that the location of the pole was known by ethnographers such as Marius Barbeau. It had also been the object of publications; see, for example, G Lindblom, 'A Kwakiutl Totem Pole in Stockholm' (1936) 1(6) *Ethnos* 137, although he described the pole as having a Kwakiutl (Kwakwa̱ka̱ʼwakw) origin rather than Xenaksiala or Haisla (but correctly named its geographical origin as Kitlope).

[5] Potlaches (gift-giving ceremonies) taking place to mark important events, such as the raising of totem poles, were outlawed between 1884 and 1951. See An Act to Further Amend the Indian Act, 1880 SC 1884, c 27 (47 Vict) s 3.

[6] For more information on the history of the Canadian residential schools system, see the National Center for Truth and Reconciliation, 'Residential School History', www.nctr.ca/education/teaching-resources/residential-school-history.

ethnographic museums seeking to establish themselves.[7] Olof Hanson, a businessman who had become the Swedish Council in Northern British Columbia, was tasked with identifying a pole for the museum.[8] Through Iver Fougner, a local 'Indian agent' of Norwegian origin,[9] a couple of poles were identified as possible candidates for the Swedish museum. In 1927, a few pictures were sent to the museum director who selected the G'psgolox pole, which appeared to be of a suitable size.[10] Any hurdles to cutting and exporting the pole were easily lowered: while it was generally prohibited to acquire or remove totem poles,[11] it was nevertheless possible to do so with the consent of the Superintendent General of Indian Affairs.[12] In this case, governmental authorisation was given to remove and export the pole because 'the Indian reserve is uninhabited and very isolated … and provided that the Indian owners are willing to dispose of it'.[13] It appears that Iver Fougner misrepresented the location of the pole as being very isolated, given that it was standing on a gravesite that was still in use, and which was close to Kemano, where the tribe had established itself following landslides, a site that remains a popular spot for traditional oolichan fishing for the Haisla to this day.[14] Furthermore, Fougner had reported that the pole was about to fall down and thus be destroyed. Indeed, according to a picture taken shortly before it was removed, the pole, which had by then been standing for about 55 years, was leaning and thus likely close to falling over.[15] This may have been another argument in favour of its removal, demonstrating adherence to the Western conservation approach that seeks to preserve objects and for which the leaning pole would have appeared in need of preservation.

Yet, the removal disrespected Haisla Nuyem, which refers to the Haisla First Nation's way of life and its customary norms, according to which a totem pole

[7] See, for example, A Björklund, 'The Case of Chief G'psgolox's Totem Pole: "Rescuing", Keeping, and Returning' (2018) 11 *Baltic Worlds* 72; see also A Björklund, *Hövdingens totempåle: Om konsten att utbyta gåvor* (Stockholm, Carlsson, 2016) 43.

[8] For further details, see ibid.

[9] Between the 1830s and the 1960s, Indian agents represented the government on First Nations reserves and enforcing the Indian Act; see R Irwin, 'Indian Agents in Canada', *Canadian Encyclopedia*, 25 October 2018, www.thecanadianencyclopedia.ca/en/article/indian-agents-in-canada.

[10] Björklund, *Hövdingens totempåle* (n 7) 55.

[11] Some of them were even the object of an in situ preservation project, see, for example, D Darling and D Cole, 'Totem Pole Restoration on the Skeena, 1925–30: An Early Exercise in Heritage Conservation' (1980) 47 *BC Studies* 29.

[12] Amendment to Indian Act in 1926 with section 106A; see S Jessiman, 'The Repatriation of the G'psgolox Totem Pole: A Study of its Context, Process, and Outcome' (2011) 18 *International Journal of Cultural Property* 365.

[13] Fougner wrote in 1927 to the Department of Indian Affairs that the pole was 'standing on Kitlope Indian Reserve No 2', which was 'uninhabited and very isolated', asking for permission to purchase it 'provided the Indian owners are willing to sell it'. Letter of I Fougner, dated 16 December 1927 and addressed to the Secretary, Department of Indian Affairs in Ottawa, who responded positively on 11 January 1928; see Library and Archives Canada, RG10, volume number: 4087, microfilm reel number: C-10186, file number: 507787-2B.

[14] Cardinal (n 2) at 05:40–06:45.

[15] See Björklund, *Hövdingens totempåle* (n 7) 22, 168.

should be left to decay and not interfered with once it has fallen to the ground.[16] Furthermore, the cutting of the pole appears to have been opposed by at least one individual, likely a relative of Chief G'psgolox, while others (possibly members of another tribe) may have been interested in exchanging it for money or other goods.[17] However, no record of a sale has ever been found, despite extensive research.[18] While the conditions under which the pole was gifted to Sweden remain somewhat unclear, it is now widely considered that the pole was taken against the will of the community, even if it may have been exchanged for money. This was affirmed by Louisa Smith, a descendant of Chief G'psgolox:

> [T]he pole was taken against their will … in order for our ancestors to rest peacefully, everything must be in place and since the pole was a mortuary pole you can … feel what the Henaksiala and the Haisla people felt with the pole being missing.[19]

At the end of the nineteenth century and the beginning of the twentieth century, the removal of Indigenous cultural objects from their traditional lands was common practice.[20] This was not only driven by European museums seeking to make their collections as universal as possible, but also fitted with the Canadian policy of assimilation of First Nations. Liana Smith, Haisla language and culture teacher, underlined the importance of the wider context in which cultural objects were taken away: 'our people were told they were bad. People were lied to and told to burn them'.[21]

B. Becoming a Foreign State's Property: A Hurdle for its Return

As soon as it arrived in Stockholm, the pole entered the collections of the Museum of Ethnography and became part of Sweden's national heritage. After having been erected for a few months outside, it was put in storage for several decades for

[16] Nuyem is also referred to as Nuuyum; see J Green, R Green and M Green, 'Haisla Nuuyum: Cultural Conservation and Regulation Methods within Traditional Fishing and Hunting' (2013) 2 *Decolonization: Indigeneity, Education & Society* 57. It should be noted that, while under Haisla Nuyem it seems clear that the pole was stolen, it remains unlikely that an Indigenous legal system would be considered by a foreign entity in its application of foreign public laws, which is generally limited to the law enacted by the foreign state.

[17] See Björklund, *Hövdingens totempåle* (n 7) 172–73; see also Per Kaks, former Director of the Museum of Ethnography, in Cardinal (n 2) at 11:55–12:38; see also Jessiman (n 12) 370, who points to an interview given by Hanson at the time when he affirmed that younger members of the tribe were easily convinced to sell it, unlike older members of the tribe.

[18] Interview with Anders Björklund, former Director of the Museum of Ethnography, Stockholm, 4 May 2023.

[19] Cardinal (n 2) at 06:45–07:03; This was further affirmed by Gerald Amos, then Chief Councillor or the Haisla Nation, who stated that 'it was in fact stolen'; see at 14:40–14:50.

[20] See, in general, D Cole, *Captured Heritage: The Scramble for Northwest Coast Artifacts* (Vancouver, UBC Press, 1995).

[21] Interview with Liana Smith, Haisla language and culture teacher, Kitamaat Village, 1 June 2023.

better conservation.[22] In 1980, the pole would become the centrepiece of a new museum building that included a purpose-built exhibition hall, high enough to house the 9-metre-tall pole.[23]

In the meantime, the Haisla had remained on the lookout for their lost pole, even asking for help pinpointing its whereabouts.[24] In 1991, members of the Haisla Nation became aware of its location and initiated their claim for its return with a visit to the museum, with Gerald Amos, then Chief Councillor of the Haisla Nation, seeing it as 'one of the symbols that if we could repatriate it could heal the community'.[25] A 15-year-long process followed, with a Haisla delegation led by Amos and Louisa Smith visiting Stockholm on several occasions to complete the process. Anders Björklund, former Director of the Museum of Ethnography, recalls skilful negotiators, who made strong, convincing and heartfelt arguments. Yet, despite eloquent reasoning, various interests had to be weighed up, including against the Museum of Ethnography's policy, especially in light of the lack of any document proving the ownership of the Haisla over the pole. Indeed, the Haisla Nation, like all First Nations, relies on oral history, which means it had no written evidence to prove the pole was their possession. Thus, the museum had to go beyond legal considerations and anchor its decision-making on ethical concerns and questions such as: who has the better use of the pole? For whom is it more meaningful? According to Peter Kaks, the Director of the Museum of Ethnography at the time, the Swedish side also had to accept the Indigenous way of reasoning.[26] In particular, they had to acknowledge that a pole is more than an object. As Liana Smith explains, 'totem poles tell a story. Everything has meaning. That is our way, our spirituality. This is what is scared to our people'.[27]

In 1992, Per Kaks travelled to Canada to meet the Haisla for further discussions and to better understand their point of view. Eventually, the museum decided that the pole meant more for the Haisla Nation than for the museum, that the former would also make 'better use' of it and that, on that basis, it should be returned. However, by entering the collection of the Museum of Ethnography, a national museum, the pole had become state property under Swedish law.[28]

[22] For more details regarding this period, see Björklund, 'The Case of Chief G'psgolox's Totem Pole' (n 7) 73.

[23] See Jessiman (n 12) 370, who notes that while in storage, the pole suffered from dry rot and had to have conservation work done.

[24] See Baird, Solanki and Askren (n 1) 26; see also Jessiman (n 12) 370 and 371, who notes that Cecil Paul had sought assistance to locate the pole in the early 1980s, with the question being eventually raised by the Canadian Museum of Civilisation at the 1989 annual meeting of the International Council of Museums (ICOM).

[25] See Gerald Amos in Cardinal (n 2) at 14:10–14:30; see also Louisa Smith at 13:10–14:08, who recalls her emotional first sighting of the pole in December 1991.

[26] Per Kaks (Sweden, museum director at the time) in Cardinal (n 2) at 15:52–16:26.

[27] Interview with Liana Smith, Haisla language and culture teacher, Kitamaat Village, 1 June 2023.

[28] See, for example, National Museums of World Culture, *Policy for Return of Objects* (2021), which notes that claims from other countries are not covered by Regulation (1996:1191) on the transfer of state-owned movable property and thus requires separate approval from the government, following a

Therefore, although the museum had come to the conclusion that the pole should be returned, it had to seek and obtain the approval of the Swedish government.[29] As the process had appeared to stall, the Haisla Nation offered to make a replica of the original pole for the Museum of Ethnography, in order to move things forward and avoid leaving a vacant space which would have been 'doing the same as they did to our people'.[30] Eventually, in 1993, the Museum of Ethnography recommended to the Swedish government to authorise the return of the pole.[31] In the same year, the governments of Canada and British Columbia, which never actively participated in the process, sent a joint letter to support the return request.[32]

C. A Conditional 'Gift' and the Issue with Replicas

In February 1994, less than three years after the request was made, the Swedish Minister of Culture allowed the pole to be returned as a 'gift' to the Haisla Nation, adding that the pole must continue to be preserved upon its return.[33] The use of the term 'gift' was not welcomed by the Haisla, who considered that the pole had been stolen and could thus not be gifted.[34] Furthermore, they deemed that no condition should be attached to a gift.[35] Therefore, the Haisla sought to continue discussing the terms of the return, which would take another 12 years due to ongoing negotiations and arrangements regarding the pole's conservation, as well as logistical and financial hurdles associated with the shipment of the pole and its replica.

Alongside continued discussions about the return of the original pole, arrangements for the replica to be sent to Sweden also had to be made. This required finding an adequate log of red cedar, which was donated by a forestry company. It also required for the Museum to send drawings of the pole to guide the Haisla

request by the Authority of the National Museums. It should be noted that, in accordance with Budget Act Ch 8 Sec 6 (2011:203), the government can 'transfer ownership of movable property … if the property is no longer needed for central government activities or has become unusable': www.varldskulturmuseerna.se/siteassets/pdf/aterlamnande/final-policy-for-return-of-objects_eng.pdf. See also National Museums of World Culture, 'Routine Description for Handling External Incoming Claims for Return', 2021, www.varldskulturmuseerna.se/siteassets/pdf/aterlamnande/final-routine-description-external-claims_eng.pdf.

[29] Per Kaks (Sweden, museum director at the time) in Cardinal (n 2) at 15:20–15:47.

[30] As mentioned by Gerald Amos in Cardinal (n 2) at 21:42–21:58, even if some Haisla people, like Louise Barbetti disagreed.

[31] See Jessiman (n 12) 372. For the return process, see National Museums of World Culture (n 28), according to which the Museum can make a recommendation to the government through a request.

[32] See Jessiman (n 12) 373, who notes that the joint letter was sent to the Swedish Minister of Culture by British Columbia's Premier Mike Harcourt and the Minister of Aboriginal Affairs John Cashore.

[33] For more details on this period of negotiations, see Jessiman (n 12) 373–75.

[34] See Louise Barbett in Cardinal (n 2) at 19:24–19:35.

[35] See Björklund, *Hövdingens totempåle* (n 7) 129.

carvers in charge of making the replica.[36] In addition to the replica that was made for the Museum of Ethnography, the community decided to have another replica made to honour the old pole and to raise it close to where the original once stood.[37] According to custom, the spirit of this pole was awakened by circling around it and breathing life into it before putting it on a barge to Misk'usa on 29 August 2000. The raising of the replica on the ancestral land of the Haisla was attended by Swedish representatives, including Sámi people, the Indigenous minority of Sweden, as well as the daughter of Olof Hanson.

At the same time, the other replica arrived in Stockholm. It had not been completed in Canada, as it was planned that the Haisla carvers would spend about a month in Stockholm concluding their work at the Museum of Ethnography in front of its visitors. This turned out to be an extremely popular event, with many people including schoolchildren coming to learn about the pole and Haisla culture. The carvers noted that this process meant that their people were finally 'recognised as people, not objects of archaeology, not objects of anthropology'.[38] Once finished, they also breathed into this pole to wake up its spirit, officially gifting it to the people of Sweden on 1 October 2000. But while the Canadian Embassy in Sweden offered a reception to mark the presentation of the replica, the Haisla declined to take part, underlining they would only celebrate when the original was returned.

Afterwards, Andres Björklund, who had by then become the Director of the museum, asked the Haisla delegation whether the pole could be put outside of the museum, where it would be clearly visible to those approaching its entrance. In stark contrast to Sweden's offer to return the old pole on certain conditions, the replica was offered without any condition attached, in line with the gift-giving tradition of Northwest Coast First Nations. This meant that the museum could place the pole wherever it wished. However, in order to place the pole outside against Western museum-conservation practice, it could not formally enter the museum's collection. Otherwise, it would become state property which would require it to be preserved. Thus, to this day, the replica does not have a collection number. Nevertheless, a compromise between museum-conservation practice and the First Nations' understanding of the lifecycle of totem poles appears to have been struck: while the replica was erected outside, its top end was covered with a metal sheet to avoid the wood being damaged by the elements too rapidly.

[36] This part of the story is detailed in Cardinal's documentary; see Cardinal (n 2) at 19:50–21:30. It was Henry Robertson, a Haisla master carver and grandson of the carver of the original pole, who was in charge of making the replica, along with his nephews Derek and Barry Wilson and his granddaughter Trisha Robertson. Henry Robertson had been forced to attend residential school, where he had not been allowed to carve.

[37] See Drago Grabovak and Gerald Amos in Cardinal (n 2) at 38:28–39:52. The pole had to be reinforced with steel as it could not be raised in the traditional manner; indeed, the replica was an exact replica of the one that had been cut off, meaning that the bottom part of it was missing.

[38] See Derek Wilson in Cardinal (n 2) at 1:04:00–1:04:48.

Figure 2.1 The replica of the G'psgolox pole. Photo: Tony Sandin, 2015
Source: Museum of Ethnography/National Museums of World Culture, Sweden.

While the museum never asked for a replica, its offering was an incentive for it to recommend the return of the pole to the Swedish government, and for the latter to follow the recommendation. The making of two replicas also led to the transmission of a traditional skill, providing an opportunity for the younger generations to hone their carving knowledge. Yet, the production of replicas can be contested, as, according to traditional belief, a totem pole is a unique object which should not be copied. However, in this case, the carving of the other replica which had been erected on Haisla territory in 2000, to 'honour the old pole', was not frowned upon. The issue with the replica in this case derived from the Haisla delegation having likely felt obliged to produce it in order to obtain the original pole back. Some called the gifting of a replica a 'gesture of forgiveness',[39] but for many it seemed to be a 'hidden' requirement for the old pole to be returned. Even decades later, Shelley Bolton, Haisla Community Cultural Coordinator, mentioned that 'I would not have done it. I would not have given anything. It just had to return to the rightful owner.'[40] Liana Smith remembered when they were carving the replica, adding 'I still don't understand why we had to replace it. It was something that was part of us. So why we have to recreate something that was ours? These items are ours, they are part of our history which we are regaining.'[41]

[39] See L Barbetti in Cardinal (n 2) at 1:02:30–1:02:38.
[40] Interview with Shelley Bolton, Community Cultural Coordinator, Kitimat, 1 June 2023.
[41] Interview with Liana Smith, Haisla language and culture teacher, Kitamaat Village, 1 June 2023.

Thus, while appreciated in Sweden, among part of the Haisla community, the making of the replica appears to be a regretted aspect of the return process.

D. Lack of Financial Resources: A Major Obstacle to Enforcing the Agreement

The gifting of the replica did not lead to the immediate return of the old pole due to the costs associated with its shipping. This was difficult for the Haisla to understand and made the museum staff, who had agreed to its return, feel uneasy.[42] Eventually, the necessary resources were secured, largely by the Haisla Nation itself.[43] As neither the Swedish nor the Canadian governments offered financial or in-kind support, the process ended up being partially funded by Ecotrust Canada, a private foundation, and through in-kind support by Lufthansa.[44] Fundraising efforts to provide financial support were also undertaken by the Friends' Association of the Museum of Ethnography.[45] Jessiman underlined that, while there were many hurdles, the most problematic was likely the financial resources needed to make the return possible.[46] Overall, while it appears that in Canada there has been an acknowledgement of the past atrocities committed against First Nations and the need for reparation, the financial means to repair the harm suffered due to the loss of their cultural objects has not yet been put behind those words. As Rob Parker, Principal of the Haisla community school, mentioned, 'saying you're sorry is great but you are not really changing anything'.[47] And of course, a similar criticism can be emitted towards the foreign states which have entered those objects into their public collections, such as Sweden in this case.

As legal scholars Bell and Paterson noted, this reveals 'the significant problem of inadequate financial resources on the part of First Nations to assuage conservation and other concerns of foreign institutions responding to requests for the return of objects in their collections'.[48] Museum professionals recognise this as well, despite their own needs for funding provenance research and repatriation

[42] Interview with Anders Björklund, former Director of the Museum of Ethnography, Stockholm, 4 May 2023.

[43] According to Louise Barbetti, the Swedish side should not have waited for them to finance the return of the pole, which cost CA$300,000; see Louise Barbetti in Cardinal (n 2) at 1:02:40–1:02:58.

[44] Ecotrust Canada provided support in their role helping the Haisla preserve the Kitlope Valley, along with the Na'Na'Kila Institute, and Lufthansa cargo cooperated with Louisa Smith for the shipment of the replica pole to Sweden; see Cardinal (n 2) at 30:15–32:12 and 40:38–41:56.

[45] Interview with Anders Björklund, former Director of the Museum of Ethnography, Stockholm, 4 May 2023; see also Björklund, *Hövdingens totempåle* (n 7) 121.

[46] See Jessiman (n 12) 379.

[47] Interview with Rob Parker, Principal of the Haisla community school, Kitamaat Village, 31 May 2023, who added that many of the struggles faced by Indigenous peoples in Canada are ongoing. It should be noted that a financial settlement was reached with the survivors of residential schools.

[48] CE Bell and RK Paterson, 'International Movement of First Nations Cultural Heritage in Canadian Law' in CE Bell and RK Paterson (eds), *International Movement of First Nations Cultural Heritage in Canadian Law* (Vancouver, UBC Press, 2009) 97.

processes. According to Dr Susan Rowley, the Director of the University of British Columbia (UBC) Museum of Anthropology in Vancouver, while it would be good for museums to have more funding to do repatriation work, communities must be prioritised for any funding as 'every community would say this is important work but they have many needs and do not have funds to allocate for repatriation'.[49]

III. The Return and its Impact

A. A Burdensome Condition and a Difficult Decision

In 2006, after 15 years of negotiations and 77 years in Sweden, the pole finally returned to the Canadian Northwest Coast. It was the first time a totem pole had been returned to a First Nation from overseas.[50] To prepare it for its long journey back, the staff at the Museum of Ethnography had specifically designed a crate with the perfect climate conditions inside to ensure its preservation. This special storage box could thus act as a temporary repository, until an adequate facility would be built in Kitamaat Village to house the pole. Indeed, the museum had let the pole return on one condition, which had been imposed by the Swedish government: it had to be preserved for future generations, just like the Swedish Museum had preserved it.[51] The Haisla were thus made to adopt a Western conservation approach and commit to building a climate-controlled facility to conserve the pole for posterity.

The Haisla Nation commissioned plans for the building of a suitable facility but, as it would take years to complete, the pole was eventually sent back prior to the establishment of a permanent housing solution. Before returning to Haisla traditional territory, the pole transited via Vancouver, where it was exhibited at the UBC Museum of Anthropology for two months.[52] The arrival of the pole back in Canada attracted a lot of attention, underlining its importance not only for the

[49] Interview with Dr Susan Rowley, Director of the UBC Museum of Anthropology, Vancouver, 26 May 2023, who added that, with regard to museums, a lot of work remains to be done in terms of decolonisation (and transparency) and that it is a matter of prioritising within an existing budget, which means that other work may have to be deprioritised in order for proactive repatriation processes to be possible when external funding cannot be secured for it. She also added that, even in cases where provenance may appear solid, additional checks with object knowledge holders, such as Indigenous families to whom the object may have belonged, may provide differing provenance information than the one the museum has.

[50] This paved the way for the return of another pole – a pole which was returned from Scotland to the Nisga'a First Nation in British Columbia in 2023. See *CBC News*, 'Stolen Totem Pole Formally Welcomed Home to Nisga'a Territory after Nearly a Century in Scottish Museum', 28 September 2023, www.cbc.ca/news/canada/british-columbia/memorial-totem-pole-returned-1.6981891.

[51] See Björklund, *Hövdingens totempåle* (n 7) 128–29; see also Per Kaks in Cardinal (n 2) at 18:20–19:22, who mentioned that the pole should be seen by both parties as 'the property of mankind'.

[52] This museum already had close ties with the Haisla Nation: Haisla artist Lyle Wilson had been an artist in residence at the UBC Museum of Anthropology and several community members had worked there as interns.

Haisla but also for repatriation more in general.[53] Two months later, on 1 July 2006, the pole arrived back North.

During interviews conducted in Kitamaat Village in May and June 2023, only one Haisla member suggested that the totem should not have been returned at all because it was a bad omen, a symbol of 'everything bad that happened to the Haisla people since it was taken away'.[54] According to this minority view, the way in which the pole had been taken – that is stolen – desecrated it. But the large majority of Haisla people interviewed were pleased it had returned and hoped it would contribute to the beginning of a healing process for the community after all of their cultural expressions, including their language, had been outlawed. Liana Smith remembered a 'huge sense of pride' and 'an overwhelming emotional feeling'.[55] Shelley Bolton recalled that the return of the pole was 'uplifting and gave us the feeling that we can get part of our history back, it gave us hope'. Vicki Grant, the granddaughter of Dan Paul Sr, the last man to bear the hereditary chief title of G'psgolox, remembered crying when the pole returned.[56] The celebrations that occurred in Kitamaat Village felt important 'not only for Haisla Henaksiala people, but for Indigenous people all over'.[57]

While the pole had returned to its Ancestral land, the Haisla Nation was not free to handle its return as it saw fit. As already mentioned, the Swedish Minister of Culture authorised the return on the condition that the pole be preserved in a climate-controlled facility. In reaction, Cecil Paul, a member of the Haisla Nation, had noted that poles are meant to go back to the womb of Mother Earth and that, by agreeing to put the pole in such a facility in accordance with the wish of the 'white man', he felt like he had 'broken something'.[58] Louise Barbetti, a Haisla community leader, had added that it would be painful to erect a pole in a museum, which could be compared to the way Indigenous children had been treated in residential schools.[59] The Indian Residential Schools system was part of Canada's forced assimilation programme through which Indigenous children were sent to be educated away from their roots and prohibited to speak their native language, a programme for which the government has since apologised. The pole was thus described as a symbol of the imprisonment of the spirit of the Haisla children in the residential school system. Indeed, the pole had to have metal wires to stand

[53] As Gerald Amos mentioned, he wanted the story of the pole not to be forgotten and contribute to ongoing discussions about reconciliation; see G Cardinal, 'Totem: Return and Renewal', 2007, www.nfb.ca/film/totem_return_and_renewal, at 08:40–09:00. In addition, exhibiting the pole in Vancouver allowed the many Haisla people living in Vancouver to see it before it returned to Haisla territory.

[54] Interview with Haisla community member (anonymous), Kitamaat Village, 1 June 2023.

[55] Interview with Liana Smith, Haisla language and culture teacher, Kitamaat Village, 1 June 2023.

[56] Interview with Vicki Grant, granddaughter of Dan Paul Sr, Kitamaat Village, 1 June 2023.

[57] See Teresa Windsor in C Rayment, 'Haisla Celebrate 14th Annual G'psgolox Day', *Northern Sentinel*, 7 July 2020, www.northernsentinel.com/news/haisla-celebrate-14th-annual-gpsgolox-day, who stated that: 'It was well attended … pretty much the entire world came to Kitamaat Village on that day, that's what it felt like … The last Chief G'psgolox, he played a big part in the totem pole returning, because it was his grandmother who made her children aware of the missing pole and asked them to make it their life mission to locate it, to bring it back. It's a pretty significant piece of history.'

[58] See Cardinal (n 2) at 1:00:40–1:01:30.

[59] ibid at 1:00:30–1:00:47.

up in the Swedish museum since it had been cut down. These metal wires were compared to shackles: once they were removed, the pole was freed, just like the Haisla Nation.[60]

While the Haisla had no suitable facility to house the pole, it had detailed plans for establishing such a building in Kitamaat Village, the principal community of the First Nation and the seat of its government. Yet, as mentioned, this purpose-built facility would take time to complete so the Haisla Nation had to find another, temporary building to house the pole. Kitimat, the small town that lies above Kitamaat Village, has a museum, but it was too small to house the pole. The Haisla representatives thus discussed its possible temporary placement in an empty space within City Centre Mall, Kitimat's shopping centre, which was agreed with its owner.[61] There, lying down, the pole was sometimes used as a tool to teach Haisla children about their culture. In a documentary by Gil Cardinal, when children questioned whether the pole could be raised again, it was explained to them that, as it had been taken down, it should not be put back up.[62] But despite serving as a teaching tool, some members of the community felt sad at seeing the old pole in the mall, where it was usually kept covered for conservation purposes.[63]

B. Re-integrating the Pole According to Haisla Tradition

As the pole lingered in the mall, the project to build a cultural centre was stalling because of a lack of funding.[64] This led to the establishment of a 'Totem Pole Committee' consisting of Haisla members, including descendants of Chief G'psgolox and the current holder of the title, to decide on the next steps. One community member mentioned that this situation reflected the broader difficulties faced by the Haisla Nation in moving forward: adhering to Haisla Nuyem while adopting a contemporary lifestyle is a challenging balancing act, which also led to differing opinions among the community.[65]

Some Haisla members would have liked the pole to be conserved, to continue to educate the younger generations and serve as an inspiration for artists. This was the view of Louisa Smith, who said:

> I really wanted the old pole to be a teaching tool. It's an extension of our culture, it holds the invisible umbilical cord of our ancestors. If we were to take the old pole and put it in

[60] See Louisa Smith and Gerald Amos in Cardinal (n 53) at 05:21–05:58 and 19:33–21:56.

[61] Interview with Louise Avery, Director of the Kitimat Museum & Archives, Kitimat, 31 May 2023.

[62] See Louisa Smith in Cardinal (n 53) at 19:06–19:33. See also interview with Liana Smith, Haisla language and cultural teacher, Kitamaat Village, 1 June 2023, who explained that 'it is considered taboo or bad luck if it falls down and you move it'.

[63] Interview with Vicki Grant, granddaughter of Dan Paul Sr, Kitamaat Village, 1 June 2023.

[64] Interview with anonymous, Kitimat, 31 May 2023, who highlighted that some Haisla leaders were in favour of a mixed-use facility, serving both cultural and political activities, which was a deterrent to securing funding, which would have been easier for a cultural centre rather than for a facility that would also serve political functions.

[65] Interview with anonymous, Kitamaat Village, 1 June 2023.

> a museum our children could see and observe it first hand and understand the history of our people.[66]

This was echoed by Shelley Bolton, the Haisla cultural coordinator, who would have preferred to see it 'in a museum in Kitamaat Village where she could have taken children to see the first totem pole that was ever returned'.[67] Similarly, Lyle Wilson, a renowned Haisla artist and carver and the nephew of Dan Paul Sr, had hoped all the Haisla people would have been given a vote about its fate, as many like him had been deprived of their culture when growing up, given that so few older Haisla objects remain.[68] His view was also based on the disappearance of another tradition, the raising of a new pole once an old one has decayed, adding that when the old pole disintegrates, 'an irreplaceable part of Haisla heritage disappears'.[69]

Nevertheless, the prevailing view was that of the family which descended from the Chief who had commissioned the pole.[70] While the pole may be considered as an object that belonged to the community as a whole, within the Haisla Nation, its primary owner was Dan Paul Sr, who had inherited the G'psgolox title.[71] It was also to him that the ownership title had been transferred at the signing of the agreement with the Swedish museum in Vancouver in 2006.[72] The pole was thus eventually taken out of the shopping mall and placed outside of Dan Paul Sr's home. Having had the opportunity to spend time with the pole, he had felt that the spirit of the pole was upset because it had not been brought down naturally and that it should be brought back to Mother Earth.[73] As a particularly well-respected member of his family who was 'very kind and had carried the name of G'psgolox well',[74] Dan Paul Sr's view, which reflected the opinion of many members of the community, was instrumental in deciding on a final resting place for the pole. In 2012, six years after it had returned to Haisla territory, the pole was taken to lay down close to where it had originally been erected, a two-hour boat journey away from Kitamaat Village.

While the Museum of Ethnography had no realistic means to impose its condition regarding the preservation of the pole, it also came to understand that it was not meant to be a 'forever object'. The full life cycle of totem poles is now even explained within the First Nations' gallery of the museum, which indicates that the return process was also a learning process for the museum staff, with the

[66] See Louisa Smith in Cardinale' (n 2) at 59:42–1:00:20.

[67] Interview with Shelley Bolton, Community Cultural Coordinator, Kitimat, 1 June 2023.

[68] L Wilson on the G'psgolox pole, a letter written shortly after the pole's return, copy with the author.

[69] L Wilson, 'G'PSGOLOX GLA-GLA-GWILL-SALA', 20 May 2018, 3–4, an essay shared with the author, written when he was carving his own tribute to his uncle G'psgolox.

[70] For example, Vicki, his granddaughter, also believes that it was right to return the pole to the graveyard, see Interview with Vicki Grant, granddaughter of Dan Paul Sr, Kitamaat Village, 1 June 2023.

[71] Dan Paul Sr passed away in 2014 and is buried in Kemano, next to the original pole. Vicki Grant, his granddaughter, explained that Dan Paul Sr was the last one to carry the name G'psgolox as the hereditary title has not been passed down for various reasons, interview 1 June 2023.

[72] See Björklund, *Hövdingens totempåle* (n 7) 149.

[73] Interview with anonymous, Kitimat, 31 May 2023.

[74] Interview with Shelley Bolton, Community Cultural Coordinator, Kitimat, 1 June 2023.

traditional knowledge gained now being shared with the visitors. A decade after the pole was returned to nature, Anders Björklund explained that the process:

> [A]lso raised existential questions about museums. The Haisla value the totem as an object by taking it back to nature where it is gradually falling into pieces. This is very different from the Western museum perspective where efforts are made to preserve objects for eternity. It is a very different perspective on how you should deal with an object. On both sides, we are satisfied with the result: as a museum we learnt that it is ok to let an object go back to where it comes from, in this case the earth of the valley … perhaps it is us who are crazy to want to preserve everything in museums; perhaps we should think of their views in parallel to our saying 'from dust to dust'. In the end, our basic world views are perhaps not that dissimilar, but First Nations have retained that closer connection to nature, which we have in many ways lost.[75]

The totem pole can now be considered to play an educational role in the forest by pursuing its cycle according to tradition. Yet, according to Haisla master carver Sammy Robinson, the return of the pole may not have really changed anything with regard to the younger generations, which he deemed not very interested in learning the art of carving.[76] However, that view is not necessarily shared by those within the community who engage regularly with its younger members, including Shelley Bolton, who coordinates cultural programmes for the younger Haisla generation, which she believes is finding its voice and taking growing pride in its culture, including by taking up traditional drumming and singing classes.[77] Liana Smith, who teaches Haisla culture at the village primary school, also sees young people wanting to learn in carving and other traditional skills: 'we have a lot of young kids who are interested. I can feel that there are more interested in their ways so that is the direction we are going in'.[78]

C. The Longer-Term Impact of the Return of the Pole on the Haisla Nation

To retain the renewed sense of power and pride generated by the return of the pole, there have been attempts at celebrating the day it had first returned to

[75] Interview with Anders Björklund, former Director of the Museum of Ethnography, Stockholm, 4 May 2023.

[76] Interview with Sammy Robinson, Haisla master carver, Kitamaat Village, 31 May 2023.

[77] Interview with Shelley Bolton, Community Cultural Coordinator, Kitimat, 1 June 2023, who mentioned the story of the Haisla teenager who showed up at his Kitimat secondary school picture day wearing his regalia, which prompted his teacher to mock him and, thereafter, other pupils to react in strong support, all showing up in their regalia the following day. See also W Szeto, 'Haisla Nation, School District Investigate after BC Teacher Allegedly Mocks Student for Traditional Regalia', *CBC News*, 5 November 2021, www.cbc.ca/news/canada/british-columbia/haisla-nation-regalia-racism-1.6237893. Shelley Bolton also mentioned other youths, many of whom show an interest in learning Haisla skills, including her own son, who is learning to carve.

[78] Interview with Liana Smith, Haisla language and culture teacher, Kitamaat Village, 1 June 2023.

Haisla traditional territory, 1 July (which also happens to be Canada's national day), as G'psgolox Day.[79] While there was some initial hope this might become an annual celebration, this has not yet happened.[80] Nearly two decades on, the story of the return of the pole does not appear to be talked about as much as when it was in the mall, perhaps because the pole is now decaying in a remote location that is not often visited by members of the community or perhaps because of changing priorities. Nevertheless, the story of the G'psgolox pole, which has become part of Haisla history, is always mentioned when the repatriation of other cultural objects is envisaged or during cultural awareness training, a short course which is regularly offered to newcomers to the region.[81] The community also remains committed to establishing its own cultural centre, with sufficient space for holding feasts, as well as for carving, drumming and singing.[82] In addition, the Haisla Nation, the Kitimat Museum & Archives, and the District of Kitimat are currently exploring a possible shared museum facility noting that: 'The Haisla Nation is in the process of identifying cultural belongings in collections around the world, to eventually bring them home to Haisla Territory. A place will be needed for storage and display.'[83] The plan mentions that the '[d]esign parameters for exhibition space must take potential repatriation and loaned artifacts into account, including the length of canoes (the MOA [UBC Museum of Anthropology] Canoe is 18 feet long) and the height of totem poles (allow 35 feet)'.[84] But while the plan mentions the return of the G'psgolox pole once in passing, it does not (yet) provide for a specific space to tell its story.

The mention of repatriated objects in the feasibility study for the shared facility highlights the hope that more objects could be returned to the Nation.[85] For now, the lack of an adequate facility appears to be an obstacle for seeking the return of other artifacts, and so is the identification of Haisla heritage in museum collections. Nevertheless, the return of cultural objects has been referred to as an essential matter because 'the Haisla is a small nation which has already lost and forgotten

[79] See Rayment (n 57).

[80] Interview with Shelley Bolton, Community Cultural Coordinator, and Cassidi Bolton, Haisla Culture Camp Administrator, Kitimat, 1 June 2023.

[81] Interview with Shelley Bolton, Community Cultural Coordinator, Kitimat, 1 June 2023, who leads this training, which has become mandatory for the workers of some companies operating in the region.

[82] ibid.

[83] For more on the shared facility, see www.kitimatmuseum.ca/shared-facility. In addition, Louise Avery, Director of the Kitimat Museum, noted that for the municipal district of Kitimat and the Haisla Nation, talking about a new shared museum facility also represents a platform to discuss other possible opportunities to work more closely together, such as in the areas of employment and tourism. See interview with Louise Avery, Kitimat, 31 May 2023.

[84] See Donald Luxton & Associates Inc, D Jensen & Associates Ltd and Kinexus Consulting Inc, 'Shared Museum Cultural Facility Feasibility Study. Prepared for Kitimat Museum & Archives Haisla Nation Council District of Kitimat', July 2023, www.kitimatmuseum.ca/wp-content/uploads/2023/07/SHARED-FACILITY-Final-2023-07-05.pdf, 22.

[85] Shelley Bolton recalls that letters had been sent to many museums asking whether they possessed Haisla objects, but none responded positively: interview with Shelley Bolton, Community Cultural Coordinator, Kitimat, 1 June 2023.

a lot'.[86] This cultural loss is largely due to the governmental prohibition to conduct cultural practices, as well as the residential school system, an extremely traumatic period for First Nations peoples, from which they have yet to heal. When asked about the importance of returning cultural objects, Liana Smith further underlined that knowledge associated with those objects continues to disappear, along the passing of Haisla elders,[87] the knowledge holders, which renders the return of those objects not only important but also urgent:

> For our people to relearn and head in a direction of revitalising everything about us, it is a huge part. …. It would be nice to get these items in museums back so that I can learn about them and teach about them … These items are a huge part of who we are in our spirituality as Indigenous peoples. They all tell stories. They all have our history and I feel … a huge sense of urgency for [them] to be returned so that our history can be passed on from our elders and the stories behind these items, especially the ways we utilise these items. A lot of people don't understand that there were certain times to use these items. The children I teach deserve to know our history so that they get a sense of belonging, a sense of who we are.[88]

The oppressive system which was imposed on First Nations for decades has strongly impacted knowledge transmission. This has clearly emerged in the interviews conducted for this case study, with the topic of residential schools surfacing in nearly all of them. Cultural revitalisation is an effective means to regain lost practices while also providing healing from past trauma, including that inflicted by residential schools. While the repatriation of cultural objects can be part of cultural revitalisation initiatives, so can the commissioning of new ones. Such contemporary artwork, including a totem pole, can already be admired in front of the new Haisla Health Centre, and the local community school has also recently commissioned a pole for its memorial garden for the victims of the residential school system.[89] The commissioning of new poles is a practice that has also been adopted in Europe and which may perhaps develop further: instead of replicas, museums could more systematically consider purchasing newly created artwork, which can in turn support the revival of cultural practices.[90]

[86] Interview with Rob Parker, Principal of the Haisla Community School, Kitamaat Village, 31 May 2023. The local school counts 52 pupils, who are not all Indigenous. They have a daily Haisla culture class of 30 minutes with Haisla teacher Liana Smith.

[87] In this case, the holder of the G'psgolox title was still alive when the pole returned, which allowed him to guide it towards its final resting place. The situation could have been very different if the pole had been returned only a few years later, after the passing of Dan Paul Sr, especially since the honorary title of G'psgolox has not yet been transferred to another member of the clan.

[88] Interview with Liana Smith, Haisla language and culture teacher, Kitamaat Village, 1 June 2023.

[89] Kitimat *Northern Sentinel* Staff, 'PROGRESS 2023: Elders Bless and Unveil Artwork at New Haisla Health Centre Building' *Northern Sentinel*, 6 April 2023, www.northernsentinel.com/news/progress-2023-elders-bless-and-unveil-artwork-at-new-haisla-health-centre-building-6195659. The pole at the school is being carved by Gene Stewart, who has selected two youngsters to help him carve the pole as his apprentices; hence, the carving of the pole is an opportunity to transfer Haisla carving skills. The Haisla Health Centre has also commissioned a number of posts for its new building.

[90] See, for example, the commissioning of a pole by the Museem Volkenkunde in Leiden, the first and only totem pole in the Netherlands: 'Kwakwaka'wakw Pole Becomes Dutch Centrepiece',

IV. Repatriation in Sweden and Canada Beyond the G'psgolox Pole

A. A Point of Reference in Sweden

In Sweden, the return of the G'psgolox pole has undeniably had a major impact. As curator Maria Dahlström, who only joined the museum after the pole was returned, mentioned:

> [T]he story of the totem pole and of the Haisla people is still very much alive at the museum here and our museum teachers, some of whom were part of the process, still share that story with visitors and visitors still ask about it so it is a well-known case in Sweden. A lot of museum people are interested in how the museum dealt with this case. So, it is still a case we live with as staff and everyone learn about it, including good cooperation and dialogue with people.[91]

Dialogue is the first term that is mentioned when the Museum of Ethnography now considers a claim, as she added that:

> [W]hen we get a request we want to open a dialogue and get to know the other people and learn from the claimant and know if they are the only claimants and what is their argument about this object, what is it that they know that we don't know and what is the reason for the return. Previously, returns were based on legal terms such as if there had been a violation of a Convention but we have noticed that these Conventions aren't enough and museums have now moved toward more ethical reasoning. That is the problem with Swedish legislation as they don't really come together so we have to really think how we argue for return based on ethical reasons when it is almost against Swedish legislation … Sweden only ratified the 1970 UNESCO Convention in 2003, so there is almost no legal obligation to return anything but we want to be open, we don't want to keep things that should not be here. The objects that we keep in our collections are objects that should be here, and that people want to be there.[92]

Thus, despite the lack of legal obligation to return cultural objects, it is clear that the return of the pole has brought a fundamental shift in the way in which return claims are now considered in Sweden, a shift that has been put on paper with the adoption of a 'Guidance for Managing the Return of Cultural Objects', which was adopted by the Swedish National Heritage Board in 2020. This Guidance was part of a governmental proposal to address cultural heritage, which started with the enactment of Sweden's first museum law in 2017.[93] Developing this Guidance

North Island Gazette, 18 April 2013, www.northislandgazette.com/community/kwakwakawakw-pole-becomes-dutch-centrepiece-1367407.

[91] Interview with Maria Dahlström, Curator at the National Museums of World Culture, Stockholm, 4 May 2023.

[92] ibid.

[93] Swedish National Heritage Board, 'Good Collections Management: Guidance for Managing the Return of Cultural Objects', 2020, www.raa.diva-portal.org/smash/get/diva2:1433378/FULLTEXT01.

was complex for a governmental agency from which museums function independently: there was a risk of preparing a guidance that would be overly general and thus unhelpful. Hence, it was developed in consultation with museums, including the Museum of World Cultures and university museums that had already handled return processes. The process also included museums with Sámi collections, which may be the object of returns domestically, as well as some foreign institutions, such as the Museum of World Cultures in the Netherlands.[94] According to Gabriella Ericson of the Swedish National Heritage Board,[95] the Guidance was the product of participation and, after its publication, several museums adopted their own return policies, as suggested by the Guidance.[96]

Importantly, this Guidance calls on museums to adopt a 'proactive approach' to provenance research by not only 'observing due diligence and checking provenance in connection with processes such as purchases, loans and returns', but also by looking at their existing collections.[97] But while laudable, such recommendation may be difficult to implement fully, given that so far there has not been any specific funding allocated to allow museums to adopt a fully proactive approach. To fill this gap, some museums have applied for research grants to assess their collections, while others have sought to prioritise this matter within their existing budget.[98]

Neither the new law nor the Guidance has amended the requirement for national museums to obtain an authorisation from the government to dispose of an object: such a request is discussed within the Cabinet Office and, possibly, in the Parliament if the object in question was purchased with governmental funding.[99] So far, the government appears to have followed the view of the museums, which are considered independent knowledge institutions.[100]

Interestingly, the Guidance offers alternatives to returns, including the making of a copy, for the claimant or the museum.[101] And once an object has been returned, the Guidance suggests 'to implement a follow-up and evaluation of the return case so that lessons can be learned ahead of future return cases', considering 'What worked well/less well?'.[102] But overall, the process to return objects remains largely the same

pdf; Note that this governmental initiative also led to a study on the implementation of the Washington Principles in Sweden, as well as guidance on the care of human remains in museums and another on the return of Sami cultural heritage.

[94] Interview with Gabriella Ericson, Swedish National Heritage Board, online, 12 May 2023.

[95] ibid.

[96] See Swedish National Heritage Board (n 93) 17.

[97] ibid 15.

[98] Interview with Gabriella Ericson, Swedish National Heritage Board, online, 12 May 2023, who added that with regard to the recent study on the Washington Principles, one recommendation that emerged related to the need to release funding to ensure adequate implementation.

[99] This requirement is only waived in the event that a national museum transfers an object to another national museum.

[100] The Museum Act recognises a museum's high level of expertise and its role in knowledge building; see Museilag (2007:563), ss 4 and 8.

[101] See Swedish National Heritage Board (n 93) 17.

[102] ibid 21.

as it was at the time of the return of the G'psgolox pole.[103] When responding to a return request, the Swedish Museum of Ethnography still needs to seek governmental approval to de-accession any object within its collections, even when it has already assessed that the claimant has a greater interest in the object than itself.[104]

Finally, it is worth considering whether the relationship between the Haisla Nation and the Museum of Ethnography stood the test of time. Return processes lead to intense and, at times, very emotional discussions. In this case, it led to the creation of 'meaningful bonds', with those involved even talking of friendship.[105] However, more than a decade after the return of the pole, this friendship seems to have waned. While the return of the pole has served to educate the Swedish government, its museum community and its visitors, it has not strengthened the relationship with the Haisla Nation in the long run. As Jessiman mentioned, it is unrealistic to see the process as entirely win-win, even if it had benefits to both parties,[106] a point which appears even more accurate with the passing of time. When reflecting on the close relationships that developed over the course of the negotiations, Anders Björklund noted that the heartfelt discussions between the parties were instrumental in revealing that ethical grounds can be stronger than legal ones for affirming a claim over the pole. In this case, while the pole was a museum object for one party, it was:

> [S]trongly filled with religious and other values that museum cannot compete with. The result was that the Haisla arguments were stronger than any legal or other argument that the museum could put on the table and that was also the base for the government decision.[107]

This opened the door to an increased consideration of ethical arguments for the return of other objects. He also added that:

> [T]here is so much to be learnt from repatriation; it is probably the most rewarding work that museums can do. But this idea that repatriation brings people together and that relations could expand has not happened with the Haisla. They appear to be satisfied with their totem in the woods and we have had no contact.[108]

[103] One recent process appears to have been handled slightly differently: the return of a sacred deer head (Maaso Kova) to the Yaqui Peoples which was negotiated with the intervention of the Expert Mechanism on the Rights of Indigenous Peoples. For more on this, see K Prażmowska-Marcinowska, 'Repatriation of Indigenous Peoples' Cultural Property: Could Alternative Dispute Resolution Be a Solution? Lessons Learned from the G'psgolox Totem Pole and the Maaso Kova Case' (2022) 8 *Santander Art and Culture Law Review* 135, 152, where she explains that the Expert Mechanism clarified that although the object had been purchased, it had been done so in a context of duress, thus adding weight in favour of a return based on ethical rather than legal reasons.

[104] While restitution processes have generally not caused any issues, two recent cases have taken more time, with the government requesting additional information from the museum before making its decision, which may have been due to the change in government. According to Maria Dahlström, Curator at the National Museums of World Culture, Interview, Stockholm, 4 May 2023, the government has so far taken about one year to respond, sometimes asking for additional arguments.

[105] See Jessiman (n 12) 380–81, who cites an interview with Anders Björklund of April 2011.

[106] ibid.

[107] Interview with Anders Björklund, former Director of the Museum of Ethnography, Stockholm, 4 May 2023.

[108] ibid.

B. Reaching the Limits of the Ethical Framework?

While the return of the G'psgolox pole had a clear impact on the strengthening of the ethical approach to returns in Sweden, this development should also be considered in light of the Canadian context, where the pole was returned. In Canada, the question of repatriation has long been tied to the relationships that museums have with First Nations, with many museums being located on traditional Indigenous land. The need to review these relationships first emerged in 1988, when protests erupted against the Glenbow Museum, which had agreed to Shell sponsoring 'The Spirit Sings' exhibition, even though the oil company was then drilling on the land of the Lubicon Lake First Nation without its consent. This led to the creation of a Task Force on Museums and First Peoples and the publication of 'Turning the Page: Forging New Partnerships between Museums and First Peoples', a 1994 report jointly sponsored by the Assembly of First Nations and the Canadian Museums Association that sought to provide Indigenous peoples with a voice in Canadian museums.[109] While 'Turning the Page' already offered a useful ethical framework, it neither imposed an obligation on museums to conduct repatriation work nor provided them with funding for this type of work. This means that, as in the case of the G'psogolox, returns at the domestic level have so far largely happened only due to the efforts and resilience of First Nations.

The adoption of the UN Declaration on the Rights of Indigenous Peoples (UNDRIP) in 2007 and the creation of the Truth and Reconciliation Commission of Canada (TRC) in 2008 to address the consequences of the Indian Residential Schools system provided another opportunity to consider the relationships between museums and First Nations. In 2015, the TRC called for the release of governmental funding to ensure that Canadian museums comply with UNDRIP, thus also acknowledging the role of museums in addressing past injustices and reconciliation.[110] This eventually led the Canadian Museum Association (CMA) to publish a report and repatriation toolkit in 2022.[111] The CMA publications note that the period of duress often considered by museums, which covers the

[109] Task Force on Museums and First Peoples, 'Turning the Page: Forging New Partnerships between Museums and First Peoples', 3rd edn (Ottawa, 1994), https://museums.in1touch.org/uploaded/web/docs/Task_Force_Report_1994.pdf.

[110] Truth and Reconciliation Commission of Canada, 'Truth and Reconciliation Commission of Canada: Calls to Action', 2015, www.ehprnh2mwo3.exactdn.com/wp-content/uploads/2021/01/Calls_to_Action_English2.pdf, number 67. For more on the Declaration, see ch 1 in this book. It should be noted that Canada had originally voted against UNDRIP before eventually adhering to it and turning it into federal law in 2021 with the United Nations Declaration on the Rights of Indigenous Peoples Act; see Government of Canada, 'Backgrounder: United Nations Declaration on the Rights of Indigenous Peoples Act', www.justice.gc.ca/eng/declaration/about-apropos.html.

[111] Canadian Museums Association, 'Moved to Action: Activating UNDRIP in Canadian Museums. A Response to the Truth and Reconciliation Commission's Call to Action #67', 2022, www.museums.ca/uploaded/web/TRC_2022/Report-CMA-MovedToAction.pdf; Canadian Museums Association, 'More Than Giving Back: Repatriation Toolkit. A Toolkit in Support of Moved to Action: Activating UNDRIP in Canadian Museums', 2022, www.museums.ca/uploaded/web/TRC_2022/More-than-giving-back.pdf.

timespan of application of the strict laws under the Indian Act (1876–1951) when spiritual practices were made illegal, is not sufficient as 'in many cases the period of duress begins with contact and continues today'.[112] They also adopt a broad conceptualisation of what has been collected unethically and should be returned. Sharon Fortney, who is in charge of repatriation at the Museum of Vancouver, mentioned that duress is generally assumed and not the sticking point of a return process:

> We are looking at what laws were in effect when objects left their communities and consider potlach bans, residential schools and Indian agents controlling life on reserves. Even if someone received compensation, it does not necessarily mean there was no duress: the whole situation was duress. With anything that is older, we lean towards it not having been an ethical acquisition, so the main question becomes: is that Nation or family or individual the right entity to take custody of it?[113]

In many cases, the need for cultural revitalisation can be another argument in favour of repatriation, which museums consider.[114] This is tied to the way in which they see their role as preserving culture rather than objects, with their priority being 'on relationships rather than being the custodians of other peoples' belongings'.[115] Their work thus also often supports the transfer of knowledge and skills, through the commission of objects, the purchase of contemporary objects or the organisation of workshops focused on traditional skills.[116] Indeed, the Canadian museum professionals interviewed appeared unafraid to give things back 'as people will make new ones',[117] and the stories will remain.[118]

However, despite the need to do repatriation work now being widely acknowledged in the Canadian context, the applicable framework has perhaps not sufficiently changed since the publication of 'Turning the Page'. While there have been an attempt at legislating repatriation at the federal level and turning the ethical framework into a legal one, this has so far failed.[119] As noted by Rowley, the

[112] See Canadian Museums Association, 'Moved to Action' (n 111) 33.

[113] Interview with Dr Sharon Fortney, Curator of First Nations Collections and Engagement at the Museum of Vancouver, Vancouver, 28 May 2023. It should be noted that the Museum of Vancouver showcases its stance at its front door, with a sticker stating clearly that the museum supports reparation, and that Vancouver has created a task force to implement UNDRIP in the city, which thus also includes the Museum of Vancouver.

[114] ibid. Fortney added that 'we also consider whether it is an object that is needed for cultural renewal and if there is anything for young people to look at. That is a strong argument for something to go back'.

[115] ibid.

[116] ibid. Fortney, for example, runs a 'Knowledge Repatriation' project, which consists of workshop on traditional skills.

[117] ibid. Fortney notes that communities are also often gifting objects to the museum.

[118] Interview with Dr Susan Rowley (n 49).

[119] Private Member's Bill C-391 An Act respecting a national strategy for the repatriation of Indigenous human remains and cultural property, 42nd Parliament, 1st session, 3 December 2015–11 September 2019. See also K Brown, 'People across the Globe Want Their Cultural Heritage Back. Canada May Offer a Blueprint for How to Get There', *Artnet*, 24 June 2018, www.news.artnet.com/art-world/canada-restitution-indigenous-culture-1307060.

impetus that a law would provide is missing.[120] Crucially, she adds that, as a priority, funding should be provided to First Nations, which continue to do repatriation work without earmarked funding. Such funding should also cover their efforts to repatriate objects from abroad, as Canada often allowed (or even facilitated) their export, an issue that is exemplified by the case of the G'psgolox pole.

V. Conclusion

Repatriation to a First Nation community – like all return processes – may be very complex and lead to difficult conversations, not only between the parties involved in negotiating the return but also among the community in question. Unlike what is sometimes assumed, a community rarely shares one single view on what should happen to a returned object. Members of a community may value the same object for different reasons, including cultural, historical, artistic and personal ones. Indeed, in this instance, the pole was not only tied to a community but also, more specifically, to a family. Thus, while efforts at a proactive approach should be encouraged, given the urgency resulting from the ongoing loss of knowledge, such efforts should not impose processes on communities that have yet to heal from historical trauma and which may have other priorities.

Within the Haisla community, the return of the pole stirred a profound mix of emotions: community members remember it as a very special event that brought people together. However, since then, the pole returned to nature and its story is not often told. On occasion, it is mentioned, such as during short courses on Haisla history. Although the return of the pole brought some healing to the community, it was insufficient to mend the wounds inflicted by decades of systemic oppression. While the return was highly symbolic and a significant step for the Haisla in reclaiming their identity, it needs to be accompanied by broader reparative efforts, including additional returns of cultural objects, to further revitalise their culture. The wider context, including in particular painful history of the residential school system and the decades of prohibition of traditional cultural practices, cannot be dissociated from the removal (and return) of the G'psgolox pole. The approach to returning cultural objects should thus be holistic and contextualise the taking of an object within the wider historical background.

Another contentious aspect of the return of the G'psgolox pole was the creation of a replica. While the replica facilitated the release of the old pole and allowed the Swedish public to engage with Haisla culture during its carving at the museum, it left a sense of vexation among the Haisla community, with several members

[120] Interview with Dr Susan Rowley (n 49), during which she cited the Native American Graves Protection and Repatriation Act (NAGPRA), a US federal law enacted in 1990 that provides federally funded institutions with both an obligation to return Ancestral remains in their collections and the funding to do so.

noting that a replica should not have been necessary to reclaim something that was stolen from them. Yet, the main issue seems to have been the lengthy period of 15 years between the 1991 formal request to return the pole by the Haisla delegation and its actual return in 2006, and the fact that this was mostly delayed because of financial reasons. The lack of earmarked public funding for the repatriation of cultural objects is an ongoing challenge.

Despite these hurdles, the return of the pole has been hailed as a pivotal learning experience for the broader discourse on the return of cultural objects in Sweden. While at first, the museum focused on the long-term conservation of the pole, it eventually embraced the Indigenous perspective on the life cycles of totem poles, integrating this understanding into its exhibition gallery. Anders Björklund credited the length of the process for the knowledge gained:

> It's good that these processes take time, don't hurry with repatriation because there is so much to be learnt from them: who are the agents involved, what are the interests? A museum needs to know all this to make a good decision.[121]

While the length of the process was overall a source of frustration for the Haisla community, it allowed the museum to come to terms with the return of the pole and accept that it would not be preserved for posterity. Similarly, the carving of the replica remains a point of contention among the Haisla community, but in Sweden, it stands as a memorable event, with the replica now greeting visitors outside the museum. It has become an ambassador for First Nations in Scandinavia, showcasing not only their rich culture but also their spirit of generosity. By extension, the return of the G'psgolox pole has emerged as a critical reference point for the wider Swedish museum community and government, guiding future practices in the repatriation of cultural objects. To this day, it serves as a significant touchstone in various discussions surrounding the return of cultural objects.

[121] Interview with Anders Björklund, former Director of the Museum of Ethnography, Stockholm, 4 May 2023.

3

A Two-Step Process Towards Community Return

*The Return of a Stolen Idol to Nepal**

Where will the statues go when they come back? The idea would be that a statue that comes back, goes back to its original place, because that is logic. You don't want to bring something back from a western museum just to go to a Nepali museum. If we claim that Nepal is a living culture, then the God deserves to go back to that culture.[1]

Figure 3.1 Uma-Maheshwor statue at the Patan Museum. © Elke Selter (2022)

* Some initial findings of this fieldwork were discussed in E Selter, 'Returning the Gods to the People: Heritage Restitution in Nepal' (2022) 2 *Santander Art and Culture Law Review* 95. This chapter provides further details, more in-depth reflections and additional fieldwork carried out later on in the project.

[1] Interviews with Kanak Man Dixit, Vice-Chairman Nepal Heritage Recovery Campaign, Patan, April–May 2022.

I. Introduction

Nepal's Kathmandu Valley has often been described as an open-air museum. When that 'museum' opened up to foreign tourism following the fall of the Rana dynasty in 1951,[2] the uncountable number of artworks that were spread across towns – many freestanding in public spaces or semi-attached to temples and shrines – became vulnerable to looting. Today, more and more of these stolen objects are returning to Nepal, raising a crucial question: where should they go once back in the country?

In 1982, during the height of this trafficking spree, an Uma-Maheshwor (or Uma-Maheshvara) statue was stolen in the Wotol (or Wo Tole), an area in the village of Dhulikhel. This twelfth-century limestone idol represents Shiva with his consort Parvati at Mount Kailash, a typical iconography,[3] which is said to be very popular among art collectors.[4] The stele (or bas-relief) is a typical sculpture form in the Kathmandu Valley. The sculpted stones, with a non-sculpted backside, tend to be integrated into temples, small shrines or waterspouts (*hiti*). They can also be freestanding in public spaces. Until it was stolen, the Uma-Maheshwor was part of such a *hiti*.

When the idol was recognised in the Museum of Indian Art in Berlin nearly two decades later, the German museum cooperated in returning it to its country of origin. It was given a prime spot among the exhibition gallery in the Patan Museum, where it remains today. Yet, the icon may finally be leaving the museum. Since late 2021, the Nepalese government and its museums have started to actively implement a specific clause in its Ancient Monuments Preservation Act (AMPA),[5] according to which communities can ask for their heritage to be returned to the original location. Inspired by the return of a statue in late 2021, active (social) media attention and supported by a group of local activists, an unseen momentum has been created for community restitution in Nepal.

This chapter focuses on the Uma-Maheshwor, one of the first ever returns of cultural heritage to Nepal. Its fate in the Patan Museum is juxtaposed to more recent returns, which triggered a 'return to the temples' and a significant shift in

[2] The Rana dynasty had kept Nepal's borders closed to foreign visitors, until a revolution in 1951 ended the reign of the Rana kings and brought back the Shah dynasty. A few scientists had been allowed into the country in the late 1940s, but only after the fall of the Rana regime could foreign tourists enter. In 1953, the first road was opened and in 1955, the first group of tourists came in via the airport in Kathmandu. For more information on this, see A Michaels, *Nepal: A History from the Earliest Times to the Present* (Oxford, Oxford University Press, 2024).

[3] The Uma-Maheshwor iconography represents Shiva with his consort Parvati at Mount Kailash, surrounded by other deities. Shiva sits cross-legged with Parvati leaning against him. Underneath the Gods are dancers. Usually, such reliefs have a statue of Nanda (a bull) in front of them. The two elements form one whole. Also in this case, there is a Nanda, the original which remained in place after the Uma-Maheshwor was stolen. The Uma-Maheshwor iconography is both sensual and detailed, making it attractive for traffickers (and for the art market). Consequently, there are not many Uma-Maheshwor left in the Kathmandu Valley.

[4] KM Dixit, 'Gods in Exile', *Himāl Southasian*, 30 September 1999, www.himalmag.com/cover/gods-in-exile.

[5] Ancient Monument Preservation Act, 2013 (1956 AD) (AMPA).

government policy with regard to returns. Looking more closely at the case of Nepal makes it possible to highlight an approach that considers the living nature of heritage which is unique.

II. The Uma-Maheshwor in Context

A. Nepal's Living Idols

In the Kathmandu Valley, religious and historic statues, part of the Newari culture that adheres to both Buddhism and Hinduism, are not simply sculptures or objects of worship. It is believed that, after certain religious ceremonies (*puja*) are completed, the Gods they represent live in those statues. In other words, the stones are considered to be 'alive'. In this unique situation, the statues are much more than objects and even more than spiritual objects; they are seen as living Gods.[6]

As a result, the Gods are worshipped daily. Worshippers pass by to apply vermillion powder, place garlands of marigolds around the neck of the idol and bestow flower leaves upon them. Rice grains are provided to feed the Gods. Likewise, the Gods tend to be touched, mostly on the legs and face, during worship. When stolen, it is often the case that the remains of the idol or the place where it used to be continue to be worshipped.

Though these practices changed over time, it has remained crucial to acknowledge this living heritage status when the Gods return home, even after having been stolen and moved abroad. In this case, 'living heritage' has the double meaning of the idols being considered as living beings as well as the more common interpretation of living heritage as heritage that is still the object of active practice, implying a continuous link between the past, present and future of communities through their heritage.[7] These living statues also mean that the discrepancy between their life in the community and their fate in a museum is particularly striking:

> The Uma-Maheshwor was being worshipped by hundreds of Dhulikhel devotees when it was stolen in 1982. In Berlin it was just a piece of sculpture admired by connoisseurs for its artistic finesse. And if it is tucked away in a glass case in Patan Museum, Uma and Maheswor will be safe, but there won't be much difference between being in Berlin and being in Patan.[8]

[6] Nepalese worshippers do not consider these as statues or idols, and instead refer to them by the name of the God that is represented or by the name of the iconography. Only heritage or museum professionals will refer to 'statue' or 'idol'. In Nepali, the term *murti* is used, which translates as idol. In this chapter, and in order to respect their local tradition, we refer as much as possible to Gods or use their name, unless for reasons of clarity more technical terms like 'statue' or 'idol' are required.

[7] G Wijesuriya, 'Living Heritage' in A Heritage and J Copithorne (eds), *Sharing Conservation Decisions: Current Issues and Future Strategies* (Rome, International Centre for the Study of the Preservation and Restoration of Cultural Property (ICCROM), 2018) 43–56.

[8] S Tuladhar, 'Return of the Gods', *Nepali Times*, August 2000, www.archive.nepalitimes.com/news.php?id=11342#.YkqqerjRZpQ.

Following the theft, residents of Wotol continued to place flowers and offerings on the rounded rock in the empty neighbourhood shrine where the statue had been, praying for the Uma-Maheshwor's return:[9]

> In Dhulikhel's Wotol, elderly ladies crowd around a copy of Lain Singh Bangdel's Stolen Images of Nepal, which shows clearly the image of their Uma-Maheshwar as it was originally in the neighbourhood shrine. They find it hard to believe that the statue has been located years after it disappeared, at the Berlin Museum. 'Do everything you can to bring it back, please!' says 75-year-old Nanimaya … as she studies Bangdel's book. She then agitatedly points to the spot where a rounded rock receives the flowers and tikas meant for the Uma-Maheshwar. The nandi bull is still there in attendance of Shiva and Parvati, even though the godly couple are some thousands of miles away.[10]

B. Art Trafficking in the Kathmandu Valley

Because of the living nature of this heritage, Nepal's idols remained safe from looting, until the country opened to tourism in 1951: 'Here, it's a continuum of two millennia of worshipping and statues that were never anchored because nobody ever thought they would be stolen. The stone statues large and small all had a peg at the bottom, which was slipped into the rock platform.'[11] Since opening up to tourism, illicit art trafficking became a major issue, especially in the historic towns and villages of the wider Kathmandu area, where stone sculptures as well as wooden and metal sculptures or sculpted elements of buildings are often easy to reach in public spaces, making them vulnerable targets for looters. These objects were thus suddenly exposed to the interests of an international art market.[12]

The 1970s and 1980s were particularly active in terms of trafficking. It is during this period that two art historians had been working on inventories of the art that can be found throughout the Kathmandu Valley: Jurgen Shick published his work in *The Gods are Leaving the Country* and Lain Singh Bangdel in *Stolen Images of Nepal*.[13] Dixit described how since the 1960s, thousands of objects have been trafficked,[14] and Schick estimated that 50–60 per cent of all art in the Valley has been stolen.[15] Though trafficking has reduced today, Gods continue to be stolen.[16]

[9] Dixit (n 4).
[10] ibid.
[11] Interview with Kanak Man Dixit, Vice-Chairman of the Nepal Heritage Recovery Campaign, Patan, April–May 2022.
[12] J Schick, *The Gods are Leaving the Country: Art Theft from Nepal* (Bangkok, Orchid Press, 1997).
[13] ibid; LS Bangdel, *Stolen Images of Nepal* (Kathmandu, Royal Nepal Academy, 1989).
[14] Dixit (n 4).
[15] Schick (n 12).
[16] It was not the purpose of this research to look into ongoing trafficking in Nepal. Nevertheless, while conducting fieldwork, contacts mentioned that objects were still being stolen. For instance, on 7 December 2021, Roshan Mishra, founding member of the Nepal Heritage Recovery Campaign (NHRC), tweeted about the disappearance of a Bhairab statue from Kathmandu the night before: www.twitter.com/r0shanmishra/status/1468050279174078465?ref_src=twsrc%5Etfw%7Ctwca

Their careful documentation even allowed the Nepali in some cases, to keep track of the exact dates when objects disappeared, which has created a unique source of records that, today, is very useful when Nepal seeks to claim its idols back. Hence, while this was not their initial objective, these publications would soon become major resources in the quest for restitution.

III. The First Negotiated Return between a Public Institution and Nepal

The Uma-Maheshwor from Dhulikhel was also stolen during this period, but, prior to the theft, had been documented by Schick. Little is known about the whereabouts of the idol in the first years after it left Dhulikhel until the Museum of Indian Art, a museum in Berlin (now integrated into the Humboldt Forum), bought it from an art dealer in Wiesbaden in 1985 for about 100,000 Deutsch Mark (approximately €51,130).[17] The Museum of Indian Art was unaware that the Uma-Maheshwor had been stolen from its original location. According to Marianne Yaldiz, former director of the Museum of Indian Art, some due diligence was conducted at the time of such acquisitions:

> Generally, when the Museum of Indian Art Berlin – Prussian Cultural Foundation (Stiftung Preußischer Kulturbesitz) wanted to buy an art object in art collections in Europe, the United States or elsewhere originating from Nepal, India etc., we sent a letter to the Museums and Archaeological Surveys in the countries of origin, asking if they know whether this image left the country illegally. Normally we never got a reply.[18]

Sometime after this purchase, it came to the attention of Nepalese art specialist Lain Singh Bangdel and Götz Hagmüller, a Nepal-based Austrian architect who at the time was working on the restoration of the Patan Museum, that the Uma-Maheshwor was in Berlin. In terms of the applicable legal framework, Nepal was already a state party to the 1970 UNESCO Convention, which it had ratified in 1976. However, this treaty could not play a role in the return of the Uma-Maheshwor as Germany only ratified it in 2007. This is reflected in Germany's Cultural Property Protection Act, which considers imports from state

mp%5Etweetembed%7Ctwterm%5E1468050279174078465%7Ctwgr%5E%7Ctwcon%5Es1_&ref_url=https%3A%2F%2Fglobalvoices.org%2F2021%2F12%2F15%2Flost-and-found-repatriation-of-laxmi-narayans-statue-to-kathmandu-valleys-patan%2F. See also A Dhakal, 'The Enigma of Arrival of Nepal's Gods', *Nepali Times*, 2 December 2021, www.nepalitimes.com/banner/the-enigma-of-arrival-of-nepals-gods, who refers to a statue being stolen in Godavari in the week during which the article was beingb written.

[17] M Spice, 'Piece by Piece, Pillaged Art is Sent Home to Nepal', *The Guardian*, 6 September 2000, www.theguardian.com/world/2000/sep/06/nepal; Tuladhar (n 8).

[18] Correspondence with Marianne Yaldiz, former director of the Museum of Indian Art, March–May 2023.

parties to the 1970 Convention unlawful only after 26 April 2007 – that is, when the Convention became binding for Germany.[19]

Nevertheless, it was clear that the Uma-Maheshwor had been exported from Nepal illegally as the AMPA, which had already been adopted in 1956, prohibits the export of 'archaeological objects' – that is, objects that are more than 100 years old.[20] Having acquired in good faith the object 15 years before it was identified as stolen, the museum had acquired ownership of the object in accordance with the German Civil Code (acquisition by prescription).[21] However, as there is no principle of inalienability of public collections (as in France), museums are not legally prohibited to return objects to a country or community of origin if they deem it appropriate.[22] As Peters explains, 'once the governing body of a museum, cultural institution, or university collection has taken the decision that a certain object or group of objects should be returned and, thus, deaccessioned from the respective collection, no further legal restrictions exist under German law'.[23]

Therefore, it was possible for the German Museum of Indian Art to respond positively to Nepal's request. According to Marianne Yaldiz:

> We immediately decided to return it to the Nepal Government, and we informed the dealer who sold it to the museum about the fact that the image was stolen from Nepal and that he had to reimburse the State Museums Berlin, what he did. I, at that time director of the MIK [Museum of Indian Art], informed at once the Director-General of the State Museums Berlin and the Cultural Secretary of State who gave me the approval that I was allowed to return the sculpture. Then I contacted the colleagues in Nepal, and we decided at what time the image should be handed over by me personally to the Nepal Government in Kathmandu. The return was easy, the collaboration between the Berlin and the Patan Museum was very good. Unfortunately we seldom received an answer.[24]

The Uma-Maheshwor was formally returned to Nepal on 28 August 2000 by Marianne Yaldiz and was brought directly to the Patan Museum, where it has remained ever since. Several reasons explain the choice for the Patan Museum instead of the National Museum. First, the Patan Museum opened in 1997 and was at the time brand new, and the most modern museum in the country. Moreover, its

[19] Cultural Property Protection Act of 31 July 2016, s 32.

[20] AMPA, art 13.

[21] According to s 935(1) of the German Civil Code, there is no good faith acquisition of title for stolen art in principle. However, if a person acquires a stolen work of art in good faith and has it in their possession for at least 10 years – always in good faith – the person acquires ownership; see s 937 of the German Civil Code (of 2 January 2002) et seq. For more on this, see SKW Schwarz, 'Art Law in Germany', www.lexology.com/library/detail.aspx?g=9311edd6-803d-44a9-9814-111f7248c550.

[22] R Peters, 'Dealing with Collections from Colonial Contexts: Current Developments in Germany' (2022) 8 *Santander Art and Culture Law Review* 374.

[23] ibid 374–75, where Peters adds that, in practice, the returning institution should inform regional and federal (including in particular the Federal Foreign Office) authorities in advance to ensure a smooth process.

[24] Correspondence with Marianne Yaldiz, former director of the Museum of Indian Art, March–May 2023.

renovation had been undertaken with German and Austrian support, and designed by Austrian architect Götz Hagmüller, who happened to have also identified the Uma-Maheshwor in the museum in Berlin. Hence, it was a logical choice both for the Nepalese and German governments. While the formal decision to move the Uma-Maheshwor to the Patan Museum was taken by the Nepalese Ministry of Culture, Tourism, and Civil Aviation, it is likely that this was done on the request of (or at least in coordination with) Germany.

The return of the Uma-Maheshwor was the first ever bilaterally negotiated restitution case in which a public institution returned a stolen object to Nepal. It was only pre-dated, in 1999, by the return of four statues from a private collection in the US.[25] At the time, there was not yet a formal procedure in place for such returns.[26] Nowadays, the process, which has not been formalised, involves objects arriving first at the Ministry of Culture, Tourism, and Civil Aviation and its Department of Archaeology, before being handed over to the National Museum. The National Museum then has the discretion to further distribute the objects, for instance, to municipal museums or back to the source communities.[27] This process is also followed when an object has been claimed back directly by a community. It would not be directly handed back to the community. In 2000, before that process was in place, the Uma-Maheshwor was transferred directly to the Patan Museum, without transiting via the National Museum, albeit in the presence of the national authorities.

The documentation available at the Patan Museum does not reveal any further details about the return process or the reception of the Uma-Maheshwor idol in Nepal.[28] Interviews in Nepal spoke of celebrations or a ceremony having been organised upon its arrival in Patan, while according to Marianne Yaldiz, there was only an official press conference.[29] The limited memory of the events, including among museum staff, likely indicates that celebrations were rather limited to some more formal events, such as a handing-over ceremony at the Patan Museum.

The return of the Uma-Maheshwor in 2000 followed a typical conservation approach in which the Gods were treated as 'statues', art objects, and were brought to a museum where their material nature could be adequately safeguarded. The process was not mindful of the living nature of the heritage that was being returned. The Gods were placed in the guarded environs of a museum, where people could

[25] This first return concerned a Saraswati head from Parphing, a ninth-century Buddha from Patan, a fourteenth-century Surya from Panauti, and a tenth-century Garudasana Vishnu from Kathmandu. All these were brought to the National Museum in Chauni, where they have remained; M Spice, 'The Valley Where the Gods Have Vanished (Book Review of "The Gods are Leaving the Country: Art Theft from Nepal" by J Schick)', *South China Morning Post*, 3 September 2000.

[26] Interview with Jayaram Shrestha, Director of the National Museum, Kathmandu, April 2022.

[27] ibid.

[28] Fieldwork in Nepal, April–May 2022.

[29] Correspondence with Marianne Yaldiz, former director of the Museum of Indian Art, March–May 2023.

see them (but not worship them) and where conservators could preserve them. Even at the time, questions were raised about the relevance of this conservation approach to the return process, but the process that was followed in the case of Uma-Maheshwor remained in place until recently.

There are likely numerous reasons why the Uma-Maheshwor was not returned to Dhulikhel, its place of origin, in 2000. Today, the main reason cited relates to security concerns, as several stolen, recovered and re-installed sculptures were stolen again shortly after their return.[30] Kanak Man Dixit, a journalist who is currently part of the Nepal Heritage Recovery Campaign (NHRC), recalls the return of the Uma-Maheshwor on which he reported at the time:

> I went to Dhulikhel, talked to the locals. And one elderly lady told me, we want our God back. Another gentleman said, we will go to the airport, and we'll have a band and music and we'll bring it back. But none of that happened. I even tried to talk to the locals to take it back, but they were reluctant. And I think mainly for a reason that if it gets stolen again, we will be blamed. So, it came to the Patan Museum.[31]

One community member interviewed in Dhulikhel in 2022 said that he had seen the Uma-Maheshwor at the Patan Museum over a decade ago and that, since then, it has always been his dream to bring it back to the village. At the time, he added, it did not seem possible, but now he was hopeful that things had changed.[32]

IV. The Return of the Laxmi-Narayan as a Pivotal Point

Indeed, since 2021, Nepal's approach to returns changed, and the returned Gods are increasingly finding their way back to their original home in the community. A pivotal moment triggering this new development was the return of a Laxmi-Narayan idol from the Dallas Art Museum in the US, first to the Patan Museum and then to its original shrine at Pathko Tole in Patan.[33] When the Laxmi-Narayan was returned to Nepal in March 2021, it first followed the standard governmental procedure. Since it originated in Patan, it was handed over by the government to the Patan Museum, where it was exhibited as part of a stone sculpture exhibition.[34] By the end of the year, it was moved out of the museum

[30] Tuladhar (n 8).

[31] Interview with Kanak Man Dixit, Vice-Chairman of the Nepal Heritage Recovery Campaign, Patan, April–May 2022.

[32] Discussions with the community in Dhulikhel, May 2022.

[33] In a blog post for the NHRC, Sijapati narrates how the pending return of the Laxmi-Narayan already in early 2021 triggered increased interest in various communities throughout the country, including among the residents of Dhulikhel; see A Sijapati, 'Nepal's Gods Return from Exile', *NHRC*, 28 January 2021, www.nepalheritagerecoverycampaign.org/news/nepals-gods-return-from-exile.

[34] Interview with Suresh Lakhe, Director of the Patan Museum, Patan, May 2023.

and back to its original location in a shrine nearby.[35] The return of the God was cause for major celebrations. The *Nepali Times* local newspaper quoted a 70-year-old resident of the area saying that 'Laxmi-Narayan travelled to America, but he missed being home', emphasising the living nature of the Laxmi-Narayan by referring to feelings.[36] Local sources also documented how Bimal Lal Shrestha and his family, whose ancestors had built the shrine, were joined by a priest to perform a special ceremony on its return, and how the family had in its possession copper 'clothing' for the Laxmi-Narayan.[37] For some four decades, the family had kept the clothes, hoping that one day they could be fitted to the idol.

The return of the Laxmi-Narayan to its original location received significant media and social media attention, which was an important stimulant for community returns. It made people throughout the Kathmandu Valley aware of the possibility to request such a return.[38] Another example is the return of a Buddha figure by the National Museum to Bhinche Bahal, in Patan, in early 2022. Like many other Gods, the idol had been at the National Museum for several years. The celebrations around the return of the Laxmi-Narayan inspired the community of Bhinche Bahal to also request for their idol to be returned, a request that was fulfilled a few months later.

This new momentum is supported by a group of citizen activists, who form the NHRC.[39] Where official capacities to follow up on large numbers of cases are sometimes limited, the NHRC helps to identify Nepalese art in foreign collections, prepares documentation, pushes the authorities to submit formal claims, sustains media attention and assists with many other aspects of the return process.[40] The aims of the NHRC and those of the authorities are largely aligned, allowing them to jointly make significant progress.[41] This is not only driven by the need for stolen idols to return to Nepal, but also by a strong belief that these Gods belong in their communities, where they can be worshipped.[42] On the occasion of the

[35] See NHRC, 'Laxmi-Narayan's Return to Patko Tole, Patan', press release, 4 December 2021, www.nepalheritagerecoverycampaign.org/news/press-release-laxmi-narayans-return-to-patko-tole-patan. Media coverage of the return to the shrine, including pictures of the celebrations, is given in A Dhakal, 'Laxmi-Narayan is home', *Nepali Times*, 4 December 2021, www.nepalitimes.com/banner/laxmi-narayan-is-home.

[36] Dhakal (n 35).

[37] ibid; EL Thompson, 'Returned to Nepal by the FBI, a Sculpture Becomes a God Again', 17 December 2021, www.hyperallergic.com/700760/returned-to-nepal-by-the-fbi-a-sculpture-becomes-a-god-again. Both sources also include pictures of the copper clothing applied to the Gods.

[38] Various interviews with community members, experts, and museum professionals in Nepal, April–May 2022 and 2023.

[39] Z Small, 'Citizen Activists Lead the Hunt for Antiquities Looted from Nepal', *New York Times*, 29 October 2021, www.nytimes.com/2021/10/29/arts/nepal-looted-antiquities-citizens.html.

[40] Interview with Kanak Man Dixit, Vice-Chairman of the Nepal Heritage Recovery Campaign, Patan, April–May 2022.

[41] For instance, on 24 May 2022, the Department of Archaeology announced the arrival of five more pieces from the US (announced on social media by the Department of Archaeology; press release issued by the Nepalese Embassy in Washington DC on 18 May 2022, on file with the authors).

[42] Interviews with various members of the NHRC, April–May 2022.

Laxmi-Narayan's return, Riddhi Baba Pradhan, Chair of the NHRC and former Director of the Department of Archaeology, said that:

> The return and restoration of stolen statues to their original temples and plinths is important because they are the centre of focus of communities, besides being a part of our culture and history. Tangible heritage as represented by the statuary is vital in keeping Nepal's intangible heritage intact and vibrant, through associated rituals, processions and festivals. We, in the Campaign, hope that the return of Laxmi-Narayan to Patko Tole and the security features introduced will encourage other communities to work for the return of their stolen gods and goddesses.[43]

The efforts of the NHRC and the government are further aided by social media activism, such as the anonymous Facebook group Lost Arts of Nepal that works to identify Nepalese objects in foreign collections. This stimulates requests for return by the Nepalese authorities. Of course, the numbers of Nepalese Gods abroad remain very high, and the returns are few in comparison, but the change in pace since early 2022 is notable. With the increased numbers of returned idols, the public attention remains high, which in turn stimulates requests from communities. Another important factor to note is that most of these returns are from the US, whose ambassador to Nepal is highly supportive on the matter. Moreover, the returning institutions from the US seem to understand Nepal's intent to bring the idols back to the communities. At least for the recent cases, the returning institutions did not impose demands on the Nepalese authorities in terms of where the idols would be kept. It is an approach that gives the Nepalese government full discretion over what it does with its heritage, and the government clearly decided to support a return to the communities. Moreover, according to Kanak Man Dixit, the living nature of Nepal's heritage can be of help: 'When you confront museum curators and others with the reality of theft from a living culture, in the beginning they will try to waffle, but in the end, there is no way. They have to consider returning it.'[44]

Thus, the Laxmi-Narayan case not only created a momentum in terms of the number of returns to Nepal (from the US), but also led the way to those idols being returned to their original locations, which is the real novelty of the Nepalese approach.

V. An Enabling Legal Framework

The pressure from communities to receive their Gods back was accompanied by increased efforts by various governmental institutions to make this happen. Interestingly, government officials as well as experts, who made clear that the

[43] See NHRC (n 35).

[44] Interview with Kanak Man Dixit, Vice-Chairman of the Nepal Heritage Recovery Campaign, Patan, April–May 2022.

intention is to bring as many retrieved objects back to their communities as possible, added that this was in line with the AMPA.[45] The Act adopts a very standard approach to heritage that does not seem to take into account Nepal's unique, living heritage dimension, which is not surprising considering that the AMPA was adopted in the 1950s at a time when the heritage conservation field did not consider matters of intangible or living heritage much.[46]

Although Nepal was never colonised, the original format of the Act, including its title, adopts a common law approach as it is modelled on the one adopted under British rule in India in 1904. For movable heritage, Article 2 of the AMPA distinguishes between 'archaeological objects', and 'curios' defined as 'modern handicrafts not exceeding Hundred years of age'.[47] As already mentioned, according to the Act, archaeological objects cannot be moved outside of Nepal, nor can they be moved within the country.[48] As the AMPA was adopted only five years after the country opened up to foreign visitors and prohibited the export of archaeological objects, Nepalese objects more than 100 years old that can be found abroad were likely illegally exported.

The AMPA also has provisions for the government to place objects under its protection, even in the case of private property – for instance, if there is a risk that they may be damaged.[49] In 1986, a third amendment to the Act added Article 20A, which allows for those objects under government protection to be returned:

> To reinstate or put it to its usual place: If the ancient monument or the archaeological object received at the Department of Archaeology pursuant to paragraph (a) of the Proviso to Section 20, is requested by the concerned owner or the trusties to be given back to them for reinstalling or for keeping it to its usual place, with a recommendation from the Local Office Chief and the concerned Village Development Committee or Municipality the Department of Archaeology may, if deemed proper, give back the said object to the concerned owner or the trustee by causing them to enter into a deed as necessary.

At the time, this was mainly added because Nepali police and customs were confiscating objects that were stolen but had not yet left the country. The AMPA before

[45] Fieldnotes, visit to Nepal, April–May 2022; interviews with Department of Archaeology, National Museum, Patan Museum, and four experts from the NHRC, conducted in Nepal in April–May 2022.

[46] The 1950s were the early days of UNESCO's existence (it was created in 1945). This was a time when the International Council on Monuments and Sites (ICOMOS) was internationally setting the standards for heritage conservation through the Athens Charter (1931), which was replaced in 1964 by the Venice Charter. Both documents are very much focused on material conservation and the importance of archaeology. While Europe and North America were the strongholds of this early conservation movement, their influence spread internationally, including in Asia. Attention to the non-material heritage in the professional heritage field only really occurred in the late 1990s and early 2000s – for instance, through the adoption of the UNESCO Convention for the Safeguarding of the Intangible Cultural Heritage (2003) or ICCROM's Living Heritage Sites Programme (2003).

[47] AMPA, art 2(b) and (c).

[48] ibid art 13.

[49] ibid arts 7 and 14.

the fifth amendment made those objects the property of the Ministry of Culture and did not allow the return to the village from where they had just been stolen.

This amendment, although already added in 1986, is at the centre of the recent development within Nepal, where objects are increasingly returned to their communities of origin. The article includes a provision that the original owner(s) of an object – which can also mean 'the community' – can ask for the return of an object in the care of the Department of Archaeology (and thus also of the public museums that fall under the responsibility of the Department) provided that it returns the object to its original location. Therefore, Article 20A, like some others in the AMPA, recognises private ownership and the role of communities for heritage preservation. However, it remains focused on the material aspects of heritage, without explicitly acknowledging the dimension of living heritage. Thus, while the Nepalese are well aware of the living status of their heritage, and the current approach to restitution fully acknowledges that, this is not much reflected in their main heritage legislation, and the first (and principal) heritage law in Nepal remains the AMPA.

VI. Community-Centred Approaches to Provenance Research and Conservation

These community returns are supported not only by the authorities but also by the museum community in Nepal. Globally, the restitution debate pays a lot of attention to the museum infrastructure in source countries. Having the 'adequate' infrastructure and conditions for preservation is often an important part of the negotiations. Where these infrastructures do not exist, projects are often mounted to improve or even build the necessary environments for the artworks that are to be returned.[50] In Nepal, too, the National Museum, like the Patan Museum, houses returned objects and is the first place of storage for returned Gods. However, most (if not all) of Nepal's conservators are fully in favour of 'emptying' their museums and bringing the returned Gods back to the communities. The National Museum, for instance, has a room specifically dedicated to returned Gods and invites Nepalese people and heritage experts to help identify their provenance if that is not yet known.

The Patan Museum also has experience with this approach. Its director, Suresh Lakhe, recounts the story of how the community of Lele, a village on the outskirts of Patan, had lost a Saraswathi idol. Because too many years had gone by, few people in the village recalled what the original had looked like, and assumed it was similar

[50] An example is the new museum for returned art that it was recently announced would be built in Senegal; see A Villa, 'Albers Foundation to Launch New Museum in Senegal Aimed at Housing Restituted Artifacts', *ARTnews*, 16 May 2022, www.artnews.com/art-news/news/albers-foundation-launch-new-museum-senegal-restitution-1234628808.

to a famous Saraswathi idol in Parphing (a sitting image of the Goddess Saraswati). The Patan Museum received a confiscated idol from the police of which the provenance was unknown. The Lele community brought an 80-year-old villager along to the museum. The museum staff met with the man, who – prior to visiting the museum – described what he remembered of the Lele Saraswati: it was a standing idol, with four hands and some damage on the right chest. The description led the museum staff to the idol that had been received from the police, which could then easily be identified by the man as having come from his village. They then worked with the villagers to compile all required documentation, and once all documentation work was completed, it was returned to the village.[51] The case demonstrates the importance of local knowledge in this process of community returns, something that will become increasingly difficult over time as the number of people who still remember the idols before they were stolen is decreasing. Facing similar problems, the National Museum in Chauni also decided to put up an exhibition of returned objects, not only to show them to the visitors but also to seek information on their provenance.[52]

Although Nepal's museum professionals are concerned about security and material conservation, they also believe that in the case of Nepal's Gods, the living traditions should prevail and that the Gods belong with the people:

> I think, like last time we visited the Lakshmi Narayan … it was covered with red vermillion … It can cause damage, and there's no way we can stop that. When we talk about a living culture, we have to touch it, we have to feel it, we have to put the tikka, touch the forehead, … that is a part of our culture. And I keep on saying, that is what I call "letting the god die with dignity". If they are at the original place, and if they are worshipped in that way, that's the dignified way of letting that object go … We have seen in so many temples, after putting all these tikka and fruits in their face, the contour of the sculpture is disappearing. They will eventually turn into a stone, and that is a dignified way of letting them go. And the other generation can create something.[53]

That such an approach is possible in Nepal may at least in part be linked to the fact that the country was never colonised and did not inherit museums as colonial institutions with a Western-inspired conservation tradition.[54] Those that were established are striving to find a balance between their conservation role and the living culture that surrounds them:

> One reason might be because Nepal did not face colonisation, so while we have a living culture and everything is a 'living museum', the formal museum establishments are not strong. Whereas in a colonised country, even if it's Ghana or Sierra Leone or India, the colonials left behind strong institutions, which is a good thing when it comes time to

[51] Interview with Suresh Lakhe, Director of the Patan Museum, Patan, April–May 2023.

[52] Interview with Jaya Ram Shrestha, Director of the National Museum, Kathmandu, April–May 2022.

[53] Interview with Roshan Mishra, founding member of the NHRC, Bauddhanath, April–May 2022.

[54] Based on interviews with Roshan Mishra, founding member of the NHRC, and Swosti Kayastha, Nepal Arts Council, in Nepal, April–May 2022.

> reclaim heritage. These include the Department of Archaeology, the National Museum or other institutions that have a lot of clout.[55]

Hence, Nepal appears to have decided to adopt a model which aims for an increasing number of returned idols to leave its museums and return to the people. The Director of the Patan Museum was quoted as saying that: 'The priority is always full restitution … To install them in situ is our priority. The deities become stale and stagnant in museums. Restored to their shrines, the gods can be worshipped again.'[56]

Jaya Ram Shrestha, the Director of Nepal's National Museum, agrees:

> Our artefacts definitely are very important. It is very valuable. It cannot buy with any value thing. But our ancestors created [them] for what? To make alive … People, they should go to temple morning, evening … it makes not only to conserve our culture. The people also making good health. You understand?[57]

He also referred to Article 20A of the AMPA, adding that accordingly communities have the right to ask their Gods back and that the museum is thus happy to cooperate when such requests are received. However, he added that the National Museum requires three conditions to be met: (1) the community must demonstrate that the object will be 'used' (that is, worshipped); (2) the community or local authority needs to demonstrate that it can guarantee the security of the object; and (3) basic preservation standards must be in place.[58] These provisions are not explicitly part of the AMPA and there is no additional policy that formally explains this, but they seem to nevertheless be demanded, and it is understood by the communities that are requesting returns. While these requirements are considerate of the living heritage status of the Gods, unlike the AMPA itself, which does not accord them any special status, they have not yet been formalised in any manner.[59]

Of utmost importance is the first condition, namely, that the Gods must be worshipped. This means, for instance, that the Gods should not move to a local museum. To some extent, Article 20A of the AMPA implies this by referring to 'reinstalling or for keeping it to its usual place'. This means that the God should return to the place where it was used to be worshipped, and the culture being very much alive, worshipping would logically follow. Thus, returns to the community first and foremost support living culture.

This prioritisation of living heritage comes combined with two provisions that take a more standard conservation approach. The community must ensure the security of the returned idol and commit to the proper material conservation. How

[55] Interview with Kanak Man Dixit, Vice-Chairman of the Nepal Heritage Recovery Campaign, Patan, April–May 2022.

[56] Dhakal (n 35).

[57] Interview with Jaya Ram Shrestha, Director of the National Museum, Kathmandu, April–May 2022.

[58] ibid.

[59] From informal discussions in 2022–23, it seems that the Department of Archaeology is looking into the development of guidelines or procedures to make these demands and the associated processes more formalised and clearer.

to secure the returned idols remains an important question because, in earlier decades, idols that had been confiscated and returned were later stolen again.[60] Today, people believe that the risk is lower because the general awareness about the looting risk is higher and there are tighter controls on illicit trade. In the case of idols that return to the communities, people and local authorities rely on a combination of police, increased awareness and technological tools like closed-circuit television (CCTV) and alarms. The latter systems in particular require reliable electricity supply and regular maintenance. There are also ways to better fix the idols to the shrine, temple or whichever context they are located. Of course, safeguarding the Gods in publicly accessible places will always entail a higher risk. At the same time, the current trend towards bringing the Gods back to the people may be jeopardised if one of the Gods is stolen again. For now, though, a pragmatic approach prevails to the application of the conditions for returns to the communities, while discussions on how to improve security continue.

The provision on material conservation leads to further complexities. Of course, preserving the intangible heritage – that is, the application of vermillion powder or the 'feeding' and touching of the Gods – impacts the preservation of the tangible heritage. At the Nepal Art Council, the message was clear that it is more important to ensure maintenance of the heritage and to not damage it on purpose, whereas 'preservation' should not imply that the heritage cannot be used.[61] Roshan Mishra, Founding Member of the NHRC, added that, while the tangible heritage should be protected as much as possible, the living nature of the traditions should prevail;[62] after all, the Gods were made to be part of intangible traditions, not for being preserved forever in sterile museum environments. Many, however, seem to struggle with balancing the preservation of tangible and intangible values, especially in those situations where both cannot be guaranteed at the same time. Yet, for the time being, practical approach has prevailed in which the Gods are returning to the people and worshipping takes place. A gradual deterioration of the tangible heritage aspects will automatically, albeit slowly, follow.[63]

VII. A Possible Return Home for the Uma-Maheshwor: Outstanding Challenges at the Community Level

Back in 2000, the Uma-Maheshwor was not returned to Dhulikhel for several reasons. One of them was that, at the time, it seemed to be standard practice to

[60] Tuladhar (n 8).
[61] Interview with Swosti Kayastha, Nepal Art Council, Kathmandu, May 2022.
[62] Interview with Roshan Mishra, founding member of the NHRC, Patan, May 2022.
[63] There are further reflections on the challenges of Western-style conservation approaches and the management of living heritage in Kathmandu Valley in E Selter and K Weise, 'Kathmandu Valley and the Management of Living Heritage Sites: A Shifting Approach', *BIICL Blog*, 30 May 2023, www.biicl.org/blog/61/kathmandu-valley-and-the-management-of-living-heritage-sites-a-shifting-approach.

transfer the idol to a museum, and this practice also addressed existing security and preservation concerns. Yet, worshippers in Dhulikhel would have preferred the Uma-Maheshwor to return home. For instance, interviews conducted in Dhulikhel by Kanak Man Dixit at the time reveal that:

> In Dhulikhel's Wotol, the locals have no doubt that they want the real thing. 'Do everything you can to bring it back, please', said 75-year-old Nanimaya … The mount where the Uma Maheswor stood is presently occupied by a piece of rock, but the vermilion and flower offerings on it show that even the spot is regarded as sacred by local people.[64]

A group of activists in Dhulikhel has been active at least since early 2021, asking the Patan Museum for the return of the Uma-Maheshwor. They have interviewed the museum director repeatedly for social media posts, are advocating with local politicians, and were at the time of the author's fieldwork very actively engaged in finding a workable solution in coordination with the Patan Museum.[65] Considering that this involves the first bilaterally negotiated return to Nepal and a prominent piece of the museum's collection, moving the Uma-Maheshwor out of the Patan Museum would be a major feat and a symbolically important step in implementing this new policy.[66]

In 2022, the Patan Museum was also actively engaged in moving the Dhulikhel case forward, in part inspired by the Laxmi-Narayan case and other ongoing community returns, and in part encouraged by the actions by the people in Dhulikhel. Suresh Lakhe, the director of the Patan Museum, even visited Dhulikhel in May 2022, indicating that a return of the Uma-Maheshwor may be forthcoming. His visit was followed by a visit by a group of residents from Dhulikhel to Patan to further advance the return of the Uma-Maheshwor.[67] Despite the apparent interest of both the Patan Museum and the Dhulikhel community, no agreement had been reached regarding the return of the Uma-Maheshwor to its place of origin at the time of writing.[68] There are a number of reasons for this.

First, as documented during the visit to Dhulikhel by the director of the Patan Museum, it became clear that the original *hiti*, of which the Uma-Maheshwor was originally a part, was surprisingly no longer there. Recent 'renovation' works of the main (pedestrian) road and its surroundings had led to the demolishing of the ancient brick *hiti*, which had been replaced with a stone and cement structure.

[64] Dixit (n 4).

[65] Sijapati (n 33) refers to the group being active in early 2021. During fieldwork in spring 2022, additional social media posts were being made, and a meeting was set with the group together with the Director of the Patan Museum in May 2022. Two days after the visit to Dhulikhel, the group also visited the Patan Museum to continue the discussion, which seemed to be in its advanced stages at the time of this research.

[66] Another return that is currently high on the agenda is that of the Saraswathi head from the village of Pharphing, which was the first ever return to Nepal in 1999 from a private US collection, and has since been housed in the National Museum; see fieldnotes, visit to Nepal, April–May 2022.

[67] At the time of the fieldwork, local elections were under way, which took place on 13 May 2022 and are one of the main reasons why no final decision had yet been taken.

[68] This was confirmed by a follow-up with the Patan Museum, particularly in correspondence with Suresh Lakhe, Director of the Patan Museum, throughout 2022 and 2023, and interview with Suresh Lakhe, Patan, May 2023, as well as with a second field trip in April–May 2023.

In addition, a replica of the Uma-Maheshwor had been built and added to the new *hiti*. Discussions with local bystanders revealed that the new *hiti* had been built sometime in 2021, with the replica Uma-Maheshwor having been installed earlier in 2022. The current state of the *hiti* is an important factor in the possible return of the Uma-Maheshwor. Leaving aside the aesthetic question, which is ultimately to be addressed locally, the concrete cement of the new *hiti* could pose conservation problems for the Uma-Maheshwor. The director of the Patan Museum made it clear that returning to a brick and natural mortar structure would be a precondition for the return of the Uma-Maheshwor, although such requirements are not part of the three preconditions set out (informally) by the National Museum.[69] At the same time, it could be a good example of putting into practice what was discussed by several interviewees: ensuring maintenance and avoiding purposeful damage of the heritage, whilst at the same time not preventing the daily worshipping and any material changes that this may cause.

Second, there is now also a 'new' Uma-Maheshwor installed, making it more complex to return the original one.

Figure 3.2 Copy of the Uma-Maheshwor statue in Dhulikhel © Elke Selter (2022)

[69] This also corresponds to the requirements listed by the National Museum, ie, that proper conservation conditions need to be in place; fieldnotes, visit of Dhulikhel with Suresh Lakhe, Director of the Patan Museum, May 2022.

There now seems to be agreement among the villagers that a copy was better than an empty space, but that the original would still be better than the copy. A community member who lives next door to the *hiti* mentioned that:

> [T]he old one was stolen a long time ago and it was found somewhere in Europe. It stays somewhere now in a museum, somewhere in Kathmandu. They advise us to bring back the statue and stand there, install it in there [points at the *hiti*]. But people are afraid that it would again be stolen.[70]

The shopkeeper across the street agreed: 'we want the old one, but we are afraid that again it would be stolen'.[71] Despite a certain fear of re-installing the idol back in its original place, it appeared that locals generally want the Uma-Maheshwor to return to its original location. Furthermore, many bystanders and people sitting near the local temple knew about the case and had explicit opinions about it. Thus, it appeared that the ongoing developments in which statues were being returned to the communities had been well spread through various (social) media channels, thereby also reaching a broad range of age groups in the village of Dhulikhel: during the field visit, elders as well as young adults and teenagers were met with, all lingering around the temples and the various shrines and *hiti* in the village.

Hence, perhaps the most important issue is to which location the original Uma-Maheshwor would be brought back. People had continued to worship the empty niche at the *hiti* and in 2022, a replica was made and installed where the original used to be. Normally, when a replica is installed, a ritual *puja* is performed to bring the idol to life. In this particular case, the corresponding *puja* had not yet been performed, precisely because discussions were ongoing about the possible return of the original.[72] Locally, not everyone agreed that the original Uma-Maheshwor should return to the *hiti*; some residents preferred to place it in a local museum and keep a copy at the *hiti*. In that case, worshipping of the original would not be possible, which would contravene the AMPA provisions and the requirements currently imposed by the government. While many wished for the Uma-Maheshwor to be returned to its original location where they could once again worship it, there is no unanimity or even agreement within the community. This demonstrates that such processes are not necessarily straightforward and that residents usually do not speak with one voice. On the other hand, that this disagreement exists openly and is not being dominated by a single stronger voice – for instance, the majority who wishes to see the Uma-Maheshwor in a local museum – speaks to the democratic nature of the ongoing process, which can ultimately only be beneficial to the case.

[70] Interview with Dhulikhel community member, Dhulikhel, May 2022.

[71] Discussions with the community in Dhulikhel, May 2022.

[72] Fieldnotes, visit to Dhulikhel with Suresh Lakhe, Director of the Patan Museum, May 2022. There was also no agreement (yet) as to what would happen to the replica in the event that the original Uma-Maheshwor returned to the *hiti*. Since it has not yet been brought to life, the situation would likely be less complex than in the case of the Laxmi-Narayan.

Third, the security of the Uma-Maheshwor has to be addressed. Clearly, returns to a *hiti* are riskier than to a temple or shrine, because the Gods are more exposed, and it is harder to protect them in an open *hiti* than in a space that can be closed off. The fears for the safety of the Uma-Maheshwor were confirmed when talking to various citizens in Dhulikhel.[73] Others did not agree and claimed that there were sufficient ways to ensure its safety. There are indeed many means of protection that are available today that were not available in the 1980s, or even at the time the Uma-Maheshwor returned from Germany. At the same time, the current process of returning heritage to the communities is unfolding and avoiding one of these Gods being stolen again should be a priority.

Provided that these issues can be adequately addressed, it seems likely that, two decades after its return to Nepal, the Uma-Maheshwor can one day return to its original location. That this is possible today, whereas it was not in 2000, is no coincidence, as it is part of a new policy to return as many Gods as possible to their original homes.

Nevertheless, upon the return of the Gods, the communities are faced with new questions, challenging their traditions in novel ways. In the case of the Laxmi-Narayan, its return to the community was delayed by several months, in part because security measures needed to be installed, but also because there were discussions within the community on the 'status' of the Gods.[74] The idols had left the shrine and even the country. Back when the whereabouts of the Gods were unknown, a replica had been installed in the shrine and the necessary rituals had been performed to bring the copy to life. Moreover, the original Laxmi-Narayan had succumbed to some damage. Traditionally, damaged statues tend to no longer be worshipped and are normally replaced by a replica.[75] What was to happen to idols that had left the country, had been replaced by a replica and were now returned?

According to Swosti Kayastha, a member of the Nepal Arts Council:

> Our culture is very different from the Western concept of conservation. Some texts … they mention that when the image of a deity is damaged or broken, it loses its impact as a spiritual object, so you replace it. We don't usually repair it. In the West, you repair it. I think this was more for the sustainability of the artisans who produced this. Because one statue will last for centuries. What will happen to the artists? So, I think this was because of that, whenever something was lost or broken – like after the earthquake, you can see at the Patan Museum – replicas take the place of the original. We call it replicas, but once it is consecrated it becomes the original. According to the living value, it is the

[73] Fieldnotes, visit to Dhulikhel with Suresh Lakhe, Director of the Patan Museum, May 2022.

[74] Thompson (n 37); fieldnotes, visit to Patan, discussions with community members and Patan Museum, April–May 2022.

[75] The idea of 'copy' refers here to the material form of the statue having been copied from the older one. According to local belief, of course, once the necessary rituals are performed, the 'copy' is the idol that is alive and could thus from that perspective be considered 'the original', or at least the main one. However, for ease of reference, in this chapter 'original' refers to the version of the idol that was trafficked and returned, while 'copy' is the one that was made after the theft.

> original. That is the difference that we should understand, because it is very different from Western philosophies.[76]

For the Laxmi-Narayan, the community decided that it wanted the original back, and that both the original and the replica could stay within the shrine. To that end, the replica was moved to the side. A *puja* was conducted to bring the original back to life, which in principle means that there are now two living statues side by side. This is something that traditionally would not have happened, since replicas were only made when the original needed to be disposed of.[77] In Swosti Kayastha's words, 'these are new ways of thinking. It was not traditionally like that, but these are new ways in which we should be able to understand, interpret it'.[78]

The cases of the Uma-Maheshwor and of the Laxmi-Narayan demonstrate that communities are not only faced with novel questions regarding their heritage, but they also come up with different solutions, depending on the case. After all, there are no fixed rules for these situations since the return of stolen idols poses an entirely new set of questions to a community. For the time being, communities seem to figure out on a case-by-case basis how they wish to address these new questions. As it goes with intangible heritage, it may be that with an increasing number of returns to communities, new traditions will take shape and will become more standardised than is currently the case.

VIII. Conclusion

The case of Nepal is not one of colonial looting; on the contrary, it is a case that is grounded in the country never having been colonised. This resulted in a late opening up to foreigners, followed by an immense looting spree. At the same time, it has also resulted in a country that, in terms of cultural institutions and the management of heritage, has experienced relatively little influence from the West. This is not to say that there has been no influence at all. The AMPA is a prime example of a Western-inspired act that to a large extent copies similar Anglo-Saxon (and Indian) models. Interestingly, a clause was added that allowed for community returns and has served as a legal basis for the government support to returning idols to their original 'homes'. However, this provision and the rest of the heritage legislation in force are limited. In addition to this unique legal basis, which was adopted in 1986, the National Museum, which has become an obligatory step in all returns to Nepal, imposes obligations which have yet to be formalised through guidelines or protocols. Beyond requiring a certain level of security in place for the

[76] Interview with Swosti Kayastha, Nepal Arts Council, Kathmandu, May 2022.

[77] If in the past copies were made – for instance, to replace a damaged statue – there were traditions in place to dispose of the damaged original; Selter and Weise (n 63).

[78] Interview with Swosti Kayastha, Nepal Arts Council, Kathmandu, May 2022.

object and basic preservation standards, the community must demonstrate that the object will be worshipped.

Furthermore, institutions like museums were also created based on the Western model, but they continue to struggle finding their place in Nepalese society. A major reason for that is that much of Nepal's material culture is living. Idols may have an artistic value when put on display in museums, but they are considered as living Gods and Goddesses, and accordingly they do not belong in a sterile museum environment.

It is this understanding of Nepal's heritage that has been at the basis of a recent development in which objects returned from foreign collections are increasingly finding their way out of Nepal's museums and back to their communities of origin where they can be worshipped. The case of the Uma-Maheshwor that returned from Germany to Nepal in 2000 is an example of how, more than two decades later, the new approach is being implemented. However, it is also revealing of the complexities of such an approach. While the Patan Museum is ready to move the idol back home, the inhabitants of Dhulikhel have trouble coming to an agreement on where the idol should go. A mixture of a fear of renewed looting, a desire to worship and a political interest to fill up a newly built village museum have led to a stalemate.

4

From Wales to Chile

*The Return of Church Bells**

I. Introduction

This chapter tells the story of Jesuit bells that had been installed in a Roman Catholic church in Santiago de Chile.[1] Following the destruction of the church in a fire, the bells were shipped to Wales, likely to be melted and repurposed but, given their good condition, they were donated to different local churches instead, where they remained for about 150 years. By chance, the Chilean government became aware of their existence, leading to a request for their return that resulted in three bells being shipped back in 2010 and another in 2013.

These bells represent the remnants of a shared history: the copper trade between Chile and Wales and, in particular, Swansea. The historical and cultural connections with Latin America, as a result of the copper trade, have shaped the south coast of Wales and its people. This link is exemplified by the bells, which tell a story anchored in *cynefin*, a Welsh term that can be defined as:

> [T]he place where we feel we belong, where the people and landscape around us are familiar, and the sights and sounds are reassuringly recognisable … not just a place in a physical sense or geographical sense: it is the historic, cultural and social place which has shaped and continues to shape the community which inhabits it.[2]

Thus, this chapter delves into the meaning of the bells not only for Chile but also for those who allowed their return, despite no legal obligation to do so. Indeed, while at some point the bells were no longer wanted in Chile, most of them had found a new, mostly active, 'life' within a Welsh community and, in contrast to other objects considered in this book, they had never entered a museum collection.

* Interviews in Chile were conducted in Spanish by Dino Schiappacasse, a Chilean lawyer and expert in cultural heritage law, who also translated them.

[1] According to the Historic Bells Association, the bells were cast in Huesca, Spain, from where they were then shipped by Jesuit missionaries to Chile in the early nineteenth century; see Rev Canon K Evans, *The Bells of Santiago* (Swansea, Parish of Oystermouth, 2013) 8.

[2] Sketty Primary School curriculum, Swansea, courtesy of Beverly Phillips, headteacher.

Beyond looking at how the location of the bells in Wales shaped their meaning and the sentiments of those around them, this chapter analyses the complex re-integration of the bells into the Chilean context, which not only led to the creation of several different memorials but also to the bells being displayed in separate locations. The chapter also considers the impact of the return on policy and legislative changes, including Chile's ratification of the 1970 UNESCO Convention. But first, it presents the context in which the bells were first shipped to Wales as the historical background is crucial to understanding why somewhat ordinary church bells were deemed worthy of a government-led return process and why the lawful owners of the bells agreed to let them go so rapidly.

II. From Santiago to Swansea

A. Cultural Objects as Remnants of a Tragedy

On 8 December 1863, in the centre of Santiago, the capital of Chile since its independence in 1818, the Church of San Miguel de la Compañía de Jesús was almost entirely destroyed by a fire.[3] The fire occurred during a celebration of the Immaculate Conception, killing over 2,000 parishioners,[4] mostly women and children,[5] who had remained trapped inside.[6] The enormous loss of lives amounted to about one per cent of the city's population at the time. To this day, it remains one of the world's deadliest fire disasters.

As a result of this tragedy, a fire brigade was established in Santiago a few days later, on 20 December 1863. Individuals from all walks of life, who had likely all lost a relative or friend in the fire, joined the newly formed brigade as volunteers.[7] This was the start of its highly respected volunteer fire and rescue service. On the site of the church, a memorial was erected in 1873 to remember the victims of the tragedy,[8] which became part of the gardens of the National Congress

[3] Note that some of its remnants are housed in the Cathedral of Santiago; others are kept in the Church of San Juan Evangelista in Santiago, including the altar and the doors of the church. See the interview with Fernando Montes Matte, member of the Jesuit Order, online, 16 March 2022.

[4] According to the history of the Santiago Fire Brigade, approximately 2,200 individuals perished; see Cuerpo de Bomberos de Santiago, 'Institución', www.cbs.cl/historia. Other sources note that 2,500 individuals may have died; see Evans (n 1) 16. See also 'Terrific Tragedy in Chili', *New York Times*, 18 January 1864, www.nytimes.com/1864/01/18/archives/terrific-tragedy-in-chili-two-thousand-five-hundred-persons-roasted.html, which reported 2,500 deaths.

[5] The Immaculate Conception was the focus of devotion of a newly formed sisterhood called the Daughters of Mary, which explains why the ceremony was mostly attended by women and girls.

[6] The tragedy was reported in details in *The Cambrian*, Swansea on 5 February 1864 (copy with the author, courtesy of Susan Rees, member of the parish of All Saints Church).

[7] See the history of the Santiago Fire Brigade: Cuerpo de Bomberos de Santiago, 'Historia', www.cbs.cl/Institucion/historia.

[8] This memorial was eventually moved to the General Cemetery.

(until its seat was moved to Valparaiso in 1973, following the coup d'état).[9] After the fire, the remains of the church included several bronze and copper bells,[10] each weighing between 300 and 400 kg and likely manufactured in Spain between 1753 and 1818.[11] The largest bell, which was badly damaged, was reportedly recovered by the Jesuits and melted down to make the two smaller bells that were subsequently installed in the Church of San Ignacio de Loyola in Santiago.[12] The remaining bells were sold as scrap to a Welsh merchant, William Graham Vivian, whose family owned a copper refinery in Swansea with business connections in Chile.[13] In the nineteenth century, Swansea was known as 'Copperopolis' due to its copper works that smelted the ore with the coal available in the area. Chile was then the world's largest supplier of copper, with much of it being shipped via the Cape Horn to be refined in South Wales.

At the time, there were no laws in Chile restricting the transfer of cultural objects and, in any case, it is unlikely that any cultural value would have been associated with the bells, which would have likely been deemed worthless.[14] The bells thus arrived legally in Wales, where they were donated to local churches. Three of the bells arrived at the Anglican Church of All Saints in Oystermouth,[15] a village just outside Swansea, in 1865.[16] From 1865 to 1964, the bells were kept in the church tower. However, their heavy weight was damaging the tower and, by 1964, it could no longer support them. Thus, the bells were put on display on a metal frame on the church's porch, described by a plate as: 'The Bells of Santiago, Chile'.[17] Hence, although no longer in use after 1964, they remained at the heart of the parish. Another bell was donated to St Thomas in Neath, a town near Swansea, where it was on permanent display in

[9] Listed as a national monument in 1976, the former National Congress building still hosts some political activities and the Library of Congress of Chile; see 'Monumento Historico. Ex-Congreso Nacional y Sus Jardines (Actual Ministerio Relaciones Exteriores)', www.archive.ph/20130628081448/http://www.monumentos.cl/OpenSupport_Monumento/asp/PopUpFicha/ficha_publica.asp?monumento=835.

[10] It is unclear how many bells were in the belfry of the church, but it is likely that there were eight; see Evans (n 1) 7.

[11] Parish of Oystermouth, 'The Bells of Santiago', www.oystermouthparish.com/bells-of-santiago.

[12] Ministerio de las Culturas, las Artes y el Patrimonio, 'Ministra Valdés Participa en Reinstalación de las Campanas de la Ex Iglesia de la Compañía de Jesús', 15 March 2019, www.cultura.gob.cl/ministra/ministra-valdes-participa-en-reinstalacion-de-las-campanas-de-la-ex-iglesia-de-la-compania-de-jesus.

[13] It is likely that he was not himself in Chile, as he appears to have stated that 'he never heard from which Santiago they came from'; see GR Orrin and FG Cowley, *A History of All Saints Church Oystermouth* (Llandysul, Gomer Press, 1990) 75.

[14] Interview with Lina Nagel, former coordinator of the Counter Illicit Trafficking of Cultural Heritage (CITCH) Unit of the National Cultural Heritage Service, online, 2 February 2022.

[15] He may have also exchanged them for the old bells that were in the church; see Orrin and Cowley (n 13) 75.

[16] It has been reported that Graham's brother, Henry Hussey Vivian, a collector of antiquities, had convinced him to donate these bells to the church as the Vivian family had a pew there; see EFE, 'Las Campanas que volverán a Santiago', *El Mostrador*, 10 August 2019, www.campaners.com/php/textos.php?text=10467. Other sources believe that the bells were not donated, but were given in exchange of the church's medieval bells; see Parish of Oystermouth (n 11).

[17] See Orrin and Cowley (n 13) 77.

the back of the church but never used.[18] All of these four bells would eventually be returned to Chile.

In addition, there may yet be more of these 'Santiago bells' still in Wales. One of them appears to have been handed over to the parish of St Mary's in Swansea after having been 'shipped to Wales with a cargo of copper ore from mines in Chile owned by a Mrs Raby, of Llanelli'.[19] St Mary's made use of the bell in its 'new daughter church', St James, which was consecrated in 1867. In the absence of a steeple, this bell still hangs by the north wall of the church, although it is no longer rung.[20] Three more bells could have come from Santiago, including one that hangs in the clock tower at Clyne Castle, another in Christ Church Carmarthen, and a smaller bell that had originally been donated to St John's in Hafod and was later on moved to Oystermouth.[21] While the origin of these three bells is contested, it is possible that one or all of them once belonged to the church that had burnt down in Chile. In any case, these bells will not be considered further in this chapter as they were not part of the return processes.

B. Capturing Local Hearts and Souls

In contrast to all of the cultural objects at the heart of the other case studies, the bells did not become museum objects. By entering churches, they resumed their original function, permeating once again the spiritual lives of their local communities. The parishioners, deeply aware of the tragic circumstance that brought them to Wales, have made it a point to regularly hold memorial events to honour the memory of the victims of the fire. One such event is the special mass held at All Saints Church on 8 December, a tradition that has lasted for over a century. The parish has also regularly hoisted the Chilean flag, including on Chile's national day and in connection with other important events for that country, such as following the rescue of 33 miners in October 2010.

Being so well integrated within the community, the bells also captured the attention of local artists. As part of the Mumbles Open Air Theatre, a *son et lumière* production entitled 'The Bells of Santiago', written by Malcolm Phillips and with music by Terry Minty, was played annually for 10 years, between 1973 and 1983, in the gardens of Oystermouth Castle.[22] With hundreds of people in the miming cast and thousands of attendees each year, the popularity of the show meant that

[18] Interview with former vicar Canon Stephen Ryan, Neath, 28 March 2023.

[19] D Walker, *Saint James' Church Swansea 1867–1992*, revised and expanded edn (Cardiff, The Church in Wales, 1992) 6, 9.

[20] Interview with Margaret Lamb, St James' churchwarden, Swansea, 28 March 2023, who added that at some point, the bell was sent to Whitechapel to be restored.

[21] See Evans (n 1) 20–21, who had been informed of the other bells by the Historic Bells Association. See also G Davies, 'Clyne Chapel', *The Story of Mumbles*, 22 May 2024, www.storyofmumbles.org.uk/stories/memories/20th-century/clyne-chapel-4.

[22] See Evans (n 1) 25–27; see also Orrin and Cowley (n 13) 77.

the story of the bells became part of local folklore.[23] There is even a filmed version of the event that is still shown, on occasion, at All Saints Church.[24] According to Cristián León, former cultural attaché at the Embassy of Chile in the UK, who traveled to Oystermouth to assess the bells and discuss their possible return, 'it was so nice to have the bells in Wales, where they even did some theatre around them … The bells in Wales were fantastic as it was a way to spread our culture and history to remote parts'.[25] Indeed, the bells were certainly not meaningless in Oystermouth, even though they were no longer rung. Actually, the fact that they were no longer in use meant that their return could be rapidly agreed upon.

III. A Very Swift Return Process

A. A Unanimous Will to Donate Almost Halted by Legal Restrictions

For more than a century, the bells, which were believed to have been smelted, had been mostly forgotten in Chile until around 2005, when its government was made aware of their continued existence.[26] Mariano Fernández, Chile's former Minister of Foreign Affairs, recalled becoming aware of the bells while he was Ambassador to the UK: someone first approached him during a congress and, shortly thereafter, a Chilean national living in London wrote to him with the story of the Oystermouth bells.[27] Following these reports, the general view within the Chilean government was that the return of the bells should be the object of a formal request. Thus, Rafael Moreno, who had since become Chile's Ambassador to the UK, was instructed to negotiate their return. A letter was sent to the then vicar of All Saints, the Reverend Canon Keith Evans, at the end of October 2009, asking the

[23] See Evans (n 1) 27. The show even attracted many out-of-town visitors who would time their stay in the area to attend it.

[24] Interview with Canon Keith Evans along with members of the Oystermouth Parochial Church Council (PCC), Oystermouth, 30 March 2023, with Judge Stuart Batcup, the Vicar's Subwarden, noting that one of these showings took place as recently as February 2023.

[25] Interview with Cristian León, former cultural attaché at the Embassy of Chile in the UK, online, 2 May 2023.

[26] Some have also mentioned a BBC report of 2009 as a possible trigger for the request for return; see D Espinoza, 'Campanas perdidas hace 150 años tras histórico incendio vuelven a la vida', *LT Latercera*, 14 March 2019, www.latercera.com/cultura/noticia/campanas-perdidas-150-anos-tras-historico-incendio-vuelven-la-vida/570154.

[27] Interview with Mariano Fernández Amunátegui, former Chilean Ambassador to the UK and former Minister of Foreign Affairs, Santiago, 21 January 2022. It should be noted that he did not play a role in the return of the bells as he was about to leave his post in London when he was made aware of them, handing the affair over to his successor, Rafael Moreno. David Vasquez and Cazu Zegers, during their respective interviews, have both corroborated that the Chilean authorities became aware of the existence of the bells in 2006 following a letter sent by Augusta Correa Larraín Ugarte.

parish to consider gifting the bells to Chile for its bicentennial anniversary.[28] As Evans recalled, this was not the first time that the bells had been requested back: in the 1980s, his predecessor was asked by a Chilean businessman to consider returning the bells, a request which had been refused due to the lack of democracy in Chile at the time.

Requesting the return of the bells could not be based on any legal provision. The bells had been legally acquired and removed from Chile long before the adoption of heritage protection laws, such as Law No 17,288 of 1970 on National Monuments, which protects certain historical objects. Even if such a law would have been applicable at the time, it is unlikely that these bells would have fallen under its protection, given that there was a strong popular desire to see the church entirely demolished after the tragedy. And while Chile has signed a few bilateral agreements protecting and facilitating the return of cultural property (without having to bring a dispute before a foreign domestic court), such as with Peru,[29] it has not signed any with the UK.[30] Likewise, no multilateral treaty could apply to the return of this piece of heritage, including the 1970 UNESCO Convention, which only covers the return of stolen property and which is in any case non-retroactive; in any case, Chile had not yet become a party thereto, only ratifying it in 2014.[31]

As the ownership of the bells by the Welsh church could not be legally contested, the return could only proceed on the basis of goodwill, through negotiations.[32] In his letter to the vicar, the Chilean Ambassador underlined the bells' historic importance for Chile and the good relationship between both countries.[33] Adding weight to his demand, he further noted that the bells were no longer in use in Wales and that the intention was that they return 'for a memorial to the victims of the fire'.[34]

[28] Interview with Canon Keith Evans, Oystermouth, 30 March 2023. See also Ministerio de Relaciones Exteriores, 'Memoria del Ministerio de Relaciones Exteriores de Chile. Año 2009', *Archivo General Hisórico*, www.minrel.gob.cl/biblioarchivo/site/artic/20131015/asocfile/20131015154606/memoria_2009__rev_abril_2014_.pdf.

[29] The bilateral agreements with Peru were signed in 1978 and again in 2002, and with Mexico in 2013.

[30] It should be noted that Chile also signed a bilateral agreement on Preventing Theft, Clandestine Excavation and Illicit Import and Export of Cultural Property with the People's Republic of China (in 2008) and a Memorandum of Understanding with the Government of the United States of America concerning the Imposition of Restrictions on the Importation of Certain Categories of Archaeological Materials from Chile, through Decree No 124 of 15 September 2020 of the Ministry of Foreign Affairs.

[31] It is worth noting that the Organization of American States (OAS), which includes Chile, adopted a Convention on the Protection of the Archeological, Historical, and Artistic Heritage of the American Nations in 1972, aimed at strengthening the UNESCO 1970 Convention in Latin America. According to its Article 11, restitution must also be sought primarily through diplomatic channels. However, Chile has so far only signed and not ratified this treaty, which is in any case only applicable among its Member States; see Department of International Law OAS, 'Multilateral Treaties. Signatories and Ratifications', www.oas.org/juridico/english/sigs/c-16.html.

[32] See Ministerio de Relaciones Exteriores (n 28) 118–19.

[33] See Evans (n 1) 28.

[34] ibid 4, 28. See also 'Church Bells May Return to Chile', *BBC News*, 8 February 2010, www.news.bbc.co.uk/2/hi/uk_news/wales/south_west/8504057.stm.

The ambassadorial request was quickly put before the Oystermouth Parochial Church Council (PCC), which agreed to explore the possibility of their return at its meeting of 9 November 2009 , about ten days after the letter had been received by the vicar.

This was followed by a meeting between representatives of the Chilean Embassy, the parish, the diocese and the Church in Wales in January 2010, which Canon Evans recalled as 'very amicable and positive'.[35] The Chilean representatives not only found the three bells at Oystermouth, but also came across a fourth – namely the 'little bell' that had originally been placed at St John's in Hafod but moved to Oystermouth a few years earlier. However, given that this smaller bell had not been authenticated, the Chilean representatives decided to solely focus on the three bells that had been associated with Oystermouth for a longer time period.[36]

If the bells were to be back in time for Chile's bicentennial anniversary the following September as desired by the Chilean government, the process had to be quick. On 25 January 2010, the PCC agreed in principle on the return of the bells and started a four-week consultation with the parish, which generated great support for their return and not a single objection.[37] The unanimous local support likely stemmed from the strong connections of the community towards Chile, due in part to its many descendants from Cape Horners, and a sense of shared tragedy between the Chilean lives lost in the fire and the Welsh lives lost at sea. It is also believed that Christian values of empathy and compassion guided the decision of the parish council.[38] Thus, on 22 February 2010, the PCC unanimously agreed on the return of the bells. According to Evans, it was 'probably one of the most historic decisions' made by the parish, a decision which was supported by the British government,[39] as well as the then President of Chile, Sebastian Piñera, and the British Ambassador to Chile, Jon Benjamin, who were in favour of their return as a 'political gesture'.[40]

However despite the unanimous decision of the PCC, the consent of the community, and governmental approval, the church could not freely dispose of its assets for two reasons: (1) ecclesiastical property in Wales is 'vested' with the Representative Body of the Church in Wales;[41] and (2) the church is a registered charity and thus cannot give away its assets.[42] Therefore, the church had to apply for a special

[35] See Evans (n 1) 29.

[36] ibid 29. This was confirmed by Cristián León, former cultural attaché at the Embassy of Chile in the UK, interview, online, 2 May 2023, as there was doubt as to its authenticity.

[37] Interview with David Vásquez, historian at the Library of the National Congress, Santiago, 25 January 2022, who also believes that the Anglican community was well disposed towards the return, given that they knew the story of the bells and where they had come from.

[38] These three sources emerged clearly during discussions with the parish community conducted in March 2023.

[39] See Evans (n 1) 31. It should also be noted that the UK government support may have been due to Chile's support of the UK during the Falklands War.

[40] According to former Ambassador Fernando Schmidt, interview, online, 23 February 2022, former President Piñera was also fond of history and thus had a personal interest in the bells.

[41] Welsh Church Act 1914, s 4.

[42] Charities Act 2011, amended by Charities Act 2022, which consolidated the Charities Act 1993 and according to which a charity must act in accordance with its charitable purpose, with trustees protecting its assets; see also Charity Commission for England and Wales, Guidance, 'The Essential Trustee:

authorisation ('faculty') from the Diocesan Advisory Committee, a process that generally takes several months, as well as obtain the assent of both the Bishop of Swansea and Brecon and the Representative Body of the Church in Wales.[43] The advice given to the church at that time was that the charity status of the church meant that the disposal of the bells would have to be financially compensated by Chile in order for the church not to diminish its assets. But although the bells had then been estimated at £4,000–5,000, the local community remained keen to donate them as it did not deem acceptable to ask for money in exchange for their return.[44]

Eventually, a way forward was identified with the Bishop's intervention: as the bells were no longer housed in a ringing frame, they were no longer a fixture of the church, which meant that they could be gifted without a faculty if he authorised it.[45] Both the Charity Commission and the Church authority, further swayed by the tremendous earthquake that had just hit Chile on 27 February 2010,[46] agreed with the Bishop's view and allowed the bells to be donated without compensation, in the spirit of friendship. According to Evans, this was agreed because it was deemed beneficial to the parish in the long run as 'gifting them becomes part of the story'.[47]

B. From Oystermouth to Santiago: A National Celebration for their Return

On 23 April 2010, the bells left Oystermouth without a handover ceremony, which has since been described as 'perhaps the most fitting and respectful way for them to leave'.[48] The lack of formalities was due to time constraints: the bells could be transported back on a Royal Navy ship, but had to make their way to the naval port right away to embark on the five-month-long voyage to Chile, in order to arrive in time for the country's bicentenary.[49] Therefore, the return process was effectively

What You Need to Know, What You Need to Do', May 2018, www.gov.uk/government/publications/the-essential-trustee-what-you-need-to-know-cc3, ch 7.

[43] See Representative Body of the Church in Wales, 'The Church in Wales Faculty System, A Guidance Note', 29 August 2019, https://faculty.churchinwales.org.uk/Data/Sites/3/media/guidance-notes/faculty_faq_v2.pdf.

[44] See Evans (n 1) 32. Furthermore, according to Cristián León, former cultural attaché at the Embassy of Chile in the UK, interview, online, 2 May 2023, Chile was not ready to pay compensation to the Church of Wales to have the bells in return.

[45] Interview with Canon Keith Evans, Oystermouth, 30 March 2023, who underlined that the Bishop, the Rt Revd John Davies, 'saved the day' thanks to his legal understanding.

[46] Interview with former Ambassador Fernando Schmidt, online, 23 February 2022, who underlined the earthquake as a trigger for the return of the bells, adding that it was a particularly expedite process as a result.

[47] Interview with Canon Keith Evans, Oystermouth, 30 March 2023.

[48] See Evans (n 1) 33.

[49] ibid 5, 33, adding that a local removal company, which was going to the south of England, offered to transport them to the naval port free of charge. See also Óscar Acuña, lawyer, interview, Santiago, 27 January 2022, who recalled that the UK financed the transportation of the bells from the UK to the seaport of Valparaíso.

conducted in less than six months from the time that a formal request from the Chilean Ambassador was received to the moment they left Wales.[50]

Their return was not only a national affair for Chile but also for the UK, with both the then British Minister for Latin America, Jeremy Browne, and the then Chilean Minister of Foreign Affairs, Alfredo Moreno, formally announcing on 10 August 2010 that the three bells were being transported to Valparaíso on *HMS Portland*.[51] Mr Moreno expressed gratitude for the donation and the 'enormous generosity of the Oystermouth community in a gesture so significant for Chile'.[52] Mr Browne echoed his words, announcing that: 'The trio of bells, which rung out in the city 150 years ago, are on their way home. I cannot think of a more fitting memorial to those who lost their lives.'[53]

In Chile, the bells were handed over by the Anglican Bishop of Chile, who represented, for the occasion, the parish of Oystermouth and the Church in Wales at the concluding event of the bicentennial celebrations, taking place on 29 September 2010 in Santiago's central Plaza de la Constitución, in front of the presidential palace. It was a high-profile event with 500 guests, including then President Piñera of Chile.[54] A concert of bells, the performance of a university's choir and the ringing of firefighter sirens completed the celebrations.[55] Those who had been directly involved in the return process were not present, which Cristián León regretted because 'restitution processes are about people rather than institutions'.[56]

Nevertheless, Lina Nagel, former coordinator of Chile's Counter Illicit Trafficking of Cultural Heritage Unit (CITCH), recalled that 'it was a very emotional ceremony. The ringing of the bells, the firefighters' sirens, the choir. They did not just arrive to the ceremony to say, "thank you, let's take a picture" and stow

[50] Mariano Fernández, the then Chilean Ambassador to the UK, had hoped for speedy arrangements to ensure that the bells would arrive before the end of Michelle Bachelet's presidential term, but, in the end, they arrived during the subsequent government's term.

[51] See Foreign & Commonwealth Office and J Browne, 'From Swansea to Santiago: Historic Church Bells to Return Home', 10 August 2010, www.gov.uk/government/news/from-swansea-to-santiago-historic-church-bells-to-return-home, which noted that their return would be announced by Jeremy Browne, then Minister for Latin America.

[52] Ministerio de Relaciones Exteriores, 'Piezas Patrimoniales Retornan a Chile para el Bicentenario', 10 August 2010, www.chile.gob.cl/chile/blog/reino-unido/londres/piezas-patrimoniales-retornan-a-chile-para-el-bicentenario.

[53] See Foreign & Commonwealth Office and Browne (n 51).

[54] Other dignitaries included Alfredo Moreno, and former British Ambassador to Chile, Jon Benjamin; see Cámara de Diputados de Chile, 'Entrega de Campanas de la Iglesia de la Compañía de Jesús', 7 December 2010, www.youtube.com/watch?v=GWx04Egb-pc&t=380s. This video features comments from Jon Benjamin, as well as David Vásquez (historian at the library of the National Congress), Antonio Marquez (historian and journalist) and Tulio Guevara (director of the general cemetery, who talks about the mass grave).

[55] Gobierno de Chile, 'Ceremonia de Entrega de Campanas de Iglesia de la Compañía', 20 September 2010, www.youtube.com/watch?v=wJiAghNcdgY. It should be noted that Jesuit priest Fernando Montes Matte was also invited. At the time, he was the rector of the Universidad Alberto Hurtado, the choir of which sang at the ceremony.

[56] Interview with Cristián León, former cultural attaché of the Chilean Embassy to the UK, online, 2 May 2023.

them away. There was an emotional element, instead'.[57] Given the deadly earthquake that had struck Chile seven months earlier, the ceremony served not only to honour those who had perished in the nineteenth century fire, but also to mourn the victims of the recent tragedy. At the ceremony, a bell was first rung by Martina Maturana, the 12-year-old girl who saved several individuals from the tsunami that followed the February earthquake by striking a warning gong on Robinson Crusoe Island.[58] According to former Ambassador Fernando Schmidt, who was then Undersecretary of Foreign Affairs, the return of the bells became a 'political act' of domestic importance to Chile, symbolising hope in the face of tragedy, as well as underlining the importance of early warning in disaster management.[59] Thus, its meaning went far beyond the historic fire or even the bicentennial anniversary of the country.

While the Welsh side had not attached any conditions to the return of the bells, Chile had mentioned that the bells would become part of a memorial dedicated to the victims of the fire.[60] Thus, the Cultural Affairs Division of the Ministry of Foreign Affairs of Chile requested prominent Chilean architect Cazú Zégers to arrange a memorial.[61] Within less than two weeks and with limited financial support, Zégers designed a wooden memorial, with the help of sculptor Jessica Torres. The design was financed by the Ministry of Foreign Affairs, while the installation was funded by the Fire Brigade. The memorial was temporarily placed in front of the governmental palace for the handover ceremony.[62] Afterwards, a longer-term location was to be identified.

IV. A Complex Re-integration Process

A. A Competition for a New Memorial

As the church where the bells used to hang had burnt down, placing them back in their original context was not an option. Hence, the re-integration of the bells became a multi-stage process. As Cristián León recalled, 'everyone wanted to have

[57] Interview with Lina Nagel, former coordinator of the Counter Illicit Trafficking of Cultural Heritage (CITCH) Unit of the National Cultural Heritage Service, online, 2 February 2022.

[58] See Espinoza (n 26).

[59] Interview with former Ambassador Fernando Schmidt, online, 23 February 2022.

[60] Telex of January 2010 (when Mariano Fernández was the Minister of Foreign Affairs) explaining the conditions agreed for the restitution of the bells. These conditions consisted of the construction of a memorial in the place of the fire and respecting the procedures for approving the restitution.

[61] See the 'Coloquio sobre Rescate Patrimonial en el Congreso' organised by the Centro de Extensión del Senado, la Academia Parlamentaria de la Cámara de Diputados y la Biblioteca del Congreso Nacional at Biblioteca del Congreso Nacional de Chile, 24 May 2019, www.bcn.cl/portal/noticias?id=video-segundo-coloquio-rescate-patrimonial-congreso. During this seminar, Martín Holmes and Gonzalo Vergara also discussed their design of the memorial that won the competition in 2013.

[62] Consejo de Monumentos Nacionales de Chile, 'Las Campanas de la Iglesia de la Compañía Han Vuelto para Honrar a los Caídos', 29 September 2010, www.monumentos.gob.cl/prensa/noticias/campanas-iglesia-compania-han-vuelto-honrar-caidos.

the bells back but they did not know what to do with them at first … so everything happened organically'.[63] In the absence of any authority specifically tasked with handling the return of cultural objects,[64] the Council of National Monuments played an operational role in the re-integration of the bells and their installation, as well as an advisory role to the Cultural Affairs Division of the Ministry of Foreign Affairs.[65] Although it was not part of its functions, the Council had already dealt with return processes in the past, which made it the most obvious body to coordinate the re-integration of the bells.[66]

After the handover ceremony, the bells and their wooden memorial were relocated in the gardens of the former National Congress building, where the church had burnt down. At that time, it was also decided that one of the three bells would be relocated to the headquarters of the fire brigade that had been founded following the deadly fire. Before the bells had even returned to Chile, then British Ambassador Jon Benjamin had informed the 14th Fire Company (also known as the British and Commonwealth Fire & Rescue Company or Bomba Inglesa) about their existence as he believed they might be of interest to its members, all descendants of emigrant families from the Commonwealth and the British Isles in particular. Luis Alberto Ovalle, then General Intendent of the Santiago Fire Brigade, recalled that 'when we received news of the existence of the bells, there was such enthusiasm and revolution inside the Santiago Fire Brigade, it was almost as if they had injected us with airplane fuel'.[67] It was decided that one of the three bells would be moved to the headquarters of the Fire Brigade.[68] This happened a few months later, in December 2010, with a parade attended again by many dignitaries.[69]

According to David Vásquez, historian at the Library of the National Congress, the return of the bells 'meant an injection of identity energy to the building', which is likely why the National Congress decided to support the construction of a new,

[63] Interview with Cristián León, former cultural attaché at the Embassy of Chile in the UK, online, 2 May 2023.

[64] According to Óscar Acuña, lawyer, interview, Santiago, 27 January 2022, by the end of 2009, the then British Ambassador to Chile, Jon Benjamin, had already reached out to the Council of National Monuments to let them know about the possible return of the bells. It is worth noting that neither the Jesuit order (which had been expelled at the time of the fire) nor the Catholic Church was asked to play a role in the restitution processes; see interview with Fernando Montes Matte, member of the Jesuit Order, online, 16 March 2022.

[65] Interview with Óscar Acuña, lawyer, Santiago, 27 January 2022, who recalled that the Council of National Monuments convened a meeting with the Ministry of Foreign Affairs, which was already involved in the process, and its Cultural Affairs Division (DIRAC).

[66] Interview with Óscar Acuña, lawyer, Santiago, 27 January 2022, who mentioned that the Council had already dealt with the return of some objects and of human remains.

[67] Interview with Luis Alberto Ovalle, General Intendent of the Santiago Fire Brigade, Santiago, 10 February 2022.

[68] According to Óscar Acuña, lawyer, interview, Santiago, 27 January 2022, the decision to relocate one bell was facilitated by the fact that the Fire Brigade's headquarters had been listed as a national monument, which gave the Council some oversight over the relocation.

[69] One of the bells was transported by a military jeep from the former National Congress building to the headquarters of the Santiago Fire Brigade. For a video of the parade, see J Cannobbio, 'cerem 01', www.youtube.com/watch?v=V6iQuYZaaLU. For the ceremony at the headquarters, see J Cannobbio, 'cerem 02', www.youtube.com/watch?v=_yQAJChSHE0.

more permanent, memorial.[70] A public competition was organised, selecting the winning design in 2013.[71] This design, by architects Gonzalo Vergara and Martín Holmes, offered an innovative perspective on the bells: while bells are normally placed at height, it envisaged to hang them at ground level, above a dug out acoustic chamber.[72] Entitled 'Elegy', the memorial refers to a lament meant to materialise 'emptiness and loss'.[73] It uses the colour blue as an homage to Yves Klein while at the same time seeking to offer a reflection on the tragedies that marked the history of Santiago and of Chile beyond that of the fire of 1863.[74]

Figure 4.1 The bells at the former National Congress building, Santiago.
© Dino Schiappacasse (2022)

[70] Interview with David Vásquez, historian at the Library of the National Congress, Santiago, 25 January 2022.

[71] Televisión Nacional de Chile, 'Campanas de la Iglesia de la Compañía Tienen Nuevo Memorial', 2018, www.youtube.com/watch?v=NuPzeUfnYfU; No one from the Fire Brigade was invited to be part of the jury, with some members having considered making a complaint about it at the time.

[72] When the studies were conducted to install the bells below ground, evidence was found of life on site all the way back to pre-Columbian times, with pottery, arrowheads and bones being discovered; see interview with David Vásquez, historian at the Library of the National Congress, Santiago, 25 January 2022.

[73] See Espinoza (n 26.

[74] The memorial was built not only in remembrance of the victims of the fire, but also of those affected by the earthquake and tsunami of 2010; see Ministerio de las Culturas, las Artes y el Patrimonio (n 12).

Inaugurated in March 2019, the new memorial, financed by the National Congress and the Ministry of Public Works,[75] is not necessarily appreciated by all. For example, Fernando Montes Matte, a member of the Jesuit Order who had participated in the handover ceremony, is critical of the bells being 'hidden in the ground' rather than 'hung in a tower'. He believes that they are thus put at the margins of history rather than being a continued part of history: 'ideally, if these bells are a reminder of a historic event that took place in the city, they should be rung. After all, they are some of the few bells that have history. They don't have that history anymore, because they are hidden, stored away'.[76] Furthermore, as the National Congress moved to Valparaíso in 1990, the building is no longer central to political life, which means that its gardens are not generally accessible to the public, with only certain officials or those working in the building having access to them.[77] Yet, the bells became the object of a new tradition: since 11 March 2011, they have been rung at noon from Monday to Saturday.

Despite the construction of the new memorial, the temporary wooden structure has for now also remained in the gardens of the former National Congress building, acting as a testament to the different stages of the return process. The construction of several memorials dedicated to the bells also emphasise the importance of their return to Chile.[78]

B. The Third Bell and the Construction of a New Museum

As already mentioned, one of the three bells was relocated to the headquarters of the Santiago Fire Brigade. It was again Zégers who was entrusted with the design of a display for this bell in the courtyard of the brigade's headquarters. According to Ovalle, 'we didn't have time at all. We had to act and we put our hands inside our pockets to finance the project. We must be honest, we were so excited with the bells that we closed our eyes and said "let's do it"'.[79]

[75] ibid.

[76] Interview with Fernando Montes Matte, member of the Jesuit Order, online, 16 March 2022. See also Ministerio de Relaciones Exteriores, 'Memoria del Ministerio de Relaciones Exteriores de Chile. Año 2010', *Archivo General Histórico*, www.minrel.gob.cl/biblioarchivo/site/artic/20131015/asocfile/20131015154606/memoria_2010__rev_abril_2014_.pdf, 328 (listed under 'patrimonio'); Biblioteca del Congreso Nacional de Chile, 'Campanas del Congreso Nacional de Chile', 13 December 2010, www.bcn.cl/portal/noticias?id=campanas-congreso.

[77] Biblioteca del Congreso Nacional de Chile, 'Nueva Tradición en el Ex Congreso: Repique de las Campanas de la Compañía de Jesús', 11 March 2011, www.bcn.cl/portal/noticias?id=nueva-tradicion-repique-campanas-compania-de-jesus. This 'new tradition' ceased in part due to the COVID-19 pandemic.

[78] Interview with Lina Nagel, former coordinator of the Counter Illicit Trafficking of Cultural Heritage (CITCH) Unit of the National Cultural Heritage Service, online, 2 February 2022, who further described the new memorial as a dignified, thought-out structure with a meaning behind it.

[79] Interview with Luis Alberto Ovalle, General Intendent of the Santiago Fire Brigade, Santiago, 10 February 2022.

When this bell arrived at the brigade's headquarters, there was already a small, informal museum therein.[80] What Zégers designed there was a cenotaph composed of a metal structure and the stones that had fallen from the firefighter's mausoleum in the General Cemetery.[81] Following the 2010 earthquake which damaged the building of the Fire Brigade's headquarters, the museum reopened in its current guise in 2018 as the Firefighters' Museum of Santiago (Museo de Bomberos de Santiago, also known as MUBO) after a complete revamp. To make space for the new entrance, the memorial had to be altered and moved from the back to the centre of the courtyard, which means that it is now immediately visible to visitors.[82] In addition, the memorial is now publicly and freely accessible during the museum's opening hours, which was not the case previously.[83] María José Lira, the director of the museum, believes that the bell is 'essential' to the museum as it is 'the first image people get of the Firefighters' Museum'.[84]

Although this bell is never rung, it is deemed 'a very powerful symbol, both visually and for the history behind it'.[85] This is also where guided tours of the museum start, thus providing a visual cue for explaining the foundation of the Santiago Fire Brigade in 1863. According to Natalia Portugueis, who works at the museum, it allows visitors to directly connect with an 'important story of the city', with heritage being thus 'activated'.[86] This is deemed to be particularly important as the bells are the only remnants of a church that has long disappeared. As Marco Antonio Cumsille, Superintendent of the Santiago Fire Brigade, mentioned:

> [W]e used to build our history on the basis of myths or oral testimonies. We did not have any material evidence of the tragedy … the restitution provided a very strong mysticism. Especially, to the younger generations who can understand and see another dimension of the foundation of the Santiago Fire Brigade. One thing is when people tell you the story of the foundation of the Santiago Fire Brigade. Another thing, that is very different, is seeing with your own eyes a piece of history hanging in a courtyard. I think that is very powerful. It has helped us with the younger generations.[87]

[80] Interview with María José Lira, Director of the Firefighters' Museum of Santiago, Santiago, 17 February 2022. For a tour of the original exhibit in the headquarters, before the creation of MUBO, and the memorial for the bell as it was first set up, see CBS1863, 'Programa City Tour visita el Cuartel General de la Institución', 17 December 2012, www.youtube.com/watch?v=wy585GGk6YQ. See also the museum's history on its website www.mubo.cl/museo.

[81] Interview with Marco Antonio Cumsille, Superintendent of the Santiago Fire Brigade, online, 3 February 2022.

[82] ibid; interview with Luis Alberto Ovalle, General Intendent of the Santiago Fire Brigade, Santiago, 10 February 2022.

[83] The museum is located in the heart of Santiago, behind the Plaza de Armas, the city's main square; its courtyard is freely accessible during the museum opening hours, from Tuesday to Saturday (10 am–6 pm).

[84] Interview with María José Lira, Director of the Firefighters' Museum of Santiago, Santiago, 17 February 2022, who added that the previous memorial was not particularly known by the general public, given the limited access to the courtyard before the opening of the new museum.

[85] Interview with Julieta Rivera, education team professional at the Firefighters' Museum of Santiago, Santiago, 17 February 2022.

[86] Interview with Natalia Portugueis, Deputy Director of Education and Public Programs at the Firefighters' Museum of Santiago, Santiago, 23 January 2022.

[87] Interview with Marco Antonio Cumsille, Superintendent of the Santiago Fire Brigade, online, 3 February 2022.

Despite the significance of the bell, there is no plaque next to it detailing its origin. This means that a visitor will only find out the history of the bell once inside the museum, or through a guided tour. Earlier attempts at drafting such a plaque failed for several reasons, including the lack of an official history of the bells. Thus, although the story of the fire is explained inside the museum or by a museum guide to those taking a tour, the story of its sojourn in Wales and return therefrom is not immediately apparent. According to Chilean lawyer Dino Schiappacasse, the lack of an explanatory plaque gives the feeling that the bell is 'present but absent at the same time', a sentiment that may also apply to the two bells that have remained in the gardens of the former National Congress as they are not generally accessible to the public.

C. A Fourth Bell Returns

Following the return of the three bells, members of the 14th Fire Company, who happened to be in the UK for a meeting, travelled to Oystermouth in September 2010 to deliver a painting as a sign of gratefulness from the Santiago Fire Brigade. They took this opportunity to enquire about the presence of other bells, in the hope that another one could be returned and installed in the building of their own division. Evans suggested that the bell that been housed at St Thomas Church in Neath might be a suitable choice.[88] Kept in the back of the church, this bell had never been hung or rung, unlike the other remaining bells in Wales.[89]

Therefore, in 2012, the 14th Fire Company wrote to the then rector of St Thomas church, Reverend Canon Stephen Ryan, enquiring about this bell.[90] As was the case in Oystermouth, there was a willingness to donate the bell and its return was quickly arranged so that it would be back in Chile in time for the 150th anniversary of the tragedy and of the foundation of the Fire Brigade in 2013.[91] According to Canon Ryan, 'there was never a hesitation that we wouldn't give the bell back … we were very pleased that it went'.[92] Everyone was delighted that His

[88] See Evans (n 1) 36.

[89] 'St Thomas's Church, Neath, Returns Bell to Chile', *BBC News*, 24 September 2012, www.bbc.com/news/uk-wales-19678810. See also the intervention of Canon Stephen Ryan, Rector of Neath, who says that the bell was neglected as there was no clear information as to its origins: 'Bell Salvaged from Disaster Returns to Santiago, Chile', *BBC News*, 27 November 2013, www.bbc.com/news/av/uk-wales-25131577.

[90] According to a BBC report, historians from Chile discovered its whereabouts; see 'Bell Salvaged from Disaster Returns to Santiago' (n 89). Luis Alberto Ovalle, General Intendent of the Santiago Fire Brigade, interview, Santiago, 10 February 2022, also noted that the British and Commonwealth Fire & Rescue Company was the sole institution which intervened in the return of the fourth bell and the financing of its installation.

[91] C Evans, 'Bell at Neath's St Thomas's Church Returned to Chile', *BBC News Wales*, 24 September 2012, www.bbc.co.uk/news/uk-wales-19707617. See also Foreign & Commonwealth Office, 'Fourth Bell of Historic Jesuit Church Returns to Chile', 5 November 2013, www.gov.uk/government/news/fourth-bell-of-historic-jesuit-church-returns-to-chile.es-419.

[92] Interview with Canon Stephen Ryan, Neath, 28 March 2023.

Royal Highness the Duke of Edinburgh, then Earl of Wessex, Honorary Member of the 14th Fire Company – the British and Commonwealth Fire & Rescue Company, participated in the handover ceremony in Neath, as no royal visit had graced the church since medieval times.[93] The bell's send-off in Wales was therefore very different from the previous one, with a symbolic handover taking place during a special religious service in September 2012, attended by many dignitaries, including the Ambassador of Chile to the UK, the Archbishop of Wales, as well as children from the local primary school waving Chilean flags.[94] Ryan remembers that there were also many volunteers of the Santiago Fire Brigade: 'about 20 firemen came with their families and it was very emotional for them and the many other people who came from Chile'.[95]

When receiving the bell on behalf of the 14th Fire Company, Prince Edward thanked the community of Neath 'and in particular St Thomas Church, for looking after this bell and agreeing to part with it after all this time', adding that it was 'a token of friendship between our two countries' and that Welsh visitors would always be welcomed at the fire company where the bell was heading.[96] Making the link with the bells previously returned from All Saints Church, Ryan explained that:

> [W]e had always known it was from South America and had been given to the church by the Vivian family of Swansea … But we had no idea how significant it was until we found out about the other bells in Oystermouth. We are delighted now that it is to return to where it belongs and be part of a memorial to the brave volunteers who risk their lives fighting fires in Chile.[97]

Unlike the first three bells, the fourth bell was shipped to Valparaíso on board a private ship, paid for by the 14th Fire Company.[98] The official reception of the bell at the 14th Fire Company station took place in October 2013, with the participation of the Minister of Foreign Affairs, the Ambassador of the UK in Chile and the

[93] 'Historic Church Bell Returns to Chile', *Christian Today*, 22 September 2012, www.christianto-day.com/article/historic.church.bell.returns.to.chile/30686.htm. See also A Morrell, 'Press Release: Neath Church Returns Historic Bell to Earl of Wessex for Chilean Fire Service', *The Church of Wales*, 20 September 2012, www.archive.is/20121223203445/http://www.churchinwales.org.uk/press/display_press_release.php?prid=5462.

[94] See 'St Thomas's Church, Neath, Returns Bell to Chile' (n 89). In an interview with Brian Murtagh, member of the 14th Fire Company and Vice President of the British and Commonwealth Fire Foundation, online, 28 January 2022, he recalled an emotional ceremony with the local community displaying sentiments towards Chile through the flag waving and hoisting.

[95] Interview with Canon Stephen Ryan, 28 March 2023.

[96] M Duggan, 'Fire Bell', *Church Times*, 19 October 2012, www.churchtimes.co.uk/articles/2012/19-october/news/uk/fire-bell.

[97] See 'St Thomas's Church, Neath, Returns Bell to Chile' (n 89).

[98] One of the difficulties faced following the arrival in Chile was the paperwork required from the Chilean Customs Service. To satisfy the requirement, the Anglican Church of Wales issued an invoice consigning the bell to the 14th Fire Company's foundation: interview with Andrés Verdugo, Director of the 14th Fire Company – the British and Commonwealth Fire & Rescue Company, and Brian Murtagh, member of the 14th Fire Company – the British and Commonwealth Fire & Rescue Company – and Vice President of the British and Commonwealth Fire Foundation, online, 28 January 2022.

local mayor.[99] A memorial was also specifically designed to hang the returned bell, this time by Anglo-Chilean architect Enrique Brown. Dedicated to the victims of the fire of 1863 and the 150th anniversary of the foundation of the Santiago Fire Brigade, the memorial is also a tribute to the firefighters and the spirit of volunteerism.[100] Hanging over the pavement, the memorial can be seen from the street, with a plaque explaining its full history.[101] This makes it arguably the most visible bell among the four that have returned from Wales.[102]

For the 14th Fire Company, the presence of such as piece of history in their operational fire station is deemed as very important.[103] Therefore, this bell is now rung every day at noon, as well as to mark special occasions.[104] According to members of the company, the return of the bell has strengthened their relationship with the UK, while also giving them a sense of belonging, especially in light of their founders being British.[105]

V. The Wider and Longer-Term Impact of the Return of the Bells

A. The Impact of the Return of the Bells in Chile: A Work in Progress

It is clear that the return of the bells was extremely meaningful for the firefighting community of Santiago. Ovalle stated that the return of the bells strengthened the relationship between the volunteers and their roots and 'made us love our

[99] Ministerio de Relaciones Exteriores, 'Ministro (s) Recibe Cuarta Campana de la Iglesia de la Compañía de Jesús', 4 October 2013, www.minrel.gob.cl/ministro-s-recibe-cuarta-campana-de-la-iglesia-de-la-compania-de-jesus/minrel_old/2013-11-05/155924.html.

[100] Interview with Brian Murtagh, member of the 14th Fire Company – the British and Commonwealth Fire & Rescue Company – and Vice President of the British and Commonwealth Fire Foundation, online, 28 January 2022.

[101] The large plaque states that: in 1863, the fourth bell was recovered from the fire of the Church of the Jesuit Order, in 1870, the bell was received in St Thomas Church of Neath, Wales; and in 2013, the bell was given in custody by Prince Edward and repatriated to the present memorial in remembrance of the victims and in commemoration of the 150 years of the foundation of the Santiago Fire Brigade.

[102] However, it should be noted that this station is located in an upper-scale neighbourhood of the class-divided city of Santiago, which means it is mostly visible to an affluent demographic.

[103] Interview with Brian Murtagh, member of the 14th Fire Company – the British and Commonwealth Fire & Rescue Company – and Vice President of the British and Commonwealth Fire Foundation, online, 28 January 2022.

[104] Special occasions have included Prince Edward's 2016 visit and the funeral of Prince Philip in 2021; see the webpages of the British Commonwealth Fire and Rescue Company 'J.A.S. Jackson', 'Ceremonias', www.14.cl/multimedia/videos/ceremonias. See also British Commonwealth Fire & Rescue Company 'J.A.S. Jackson', 'Nuestra Compañía Rinde Honores en el Momento del Funeral del Príncipe Felipe', www.14.cl/nuestra-compania-rinde-honores-en-el-momento-del-funeral-del-principe-felipe.

[105] Interview with Andrés Verdugo, Director of the 14th Fire Company – the British and Commonwealth Fire & Rescue Company, online, 28 January 2022.

institution even more. It is so linked to the history of Chile. It goes hand in hand with everything that has happened in Chile'.[106] Yet, despite the official nature of the return of the bells, the participation of the highest level of government in the return ceremonies held in Santiago, and the press releases and reports issued at the time, their stories remain largely unknown by the population of Chile and even of Santiago. While at the time of their return, many members of the public became aware of the bells via the media, the fast nature of the news cycle means that any return ceremony, even a grandiose one, may not necessarily have a lasting impact on a population. However, as for many objects, their return is still of interest to a niche public like the Santiago firefighting community in this case.

Beyond the impact at the local level, the diplomatic involvement of the central Chilean government in the return of the bells raises the question of its impact on the relationship between the two countries involved. While their relationship was already good, Óscar Acuña, a lawyer who worked at the Council of National Monuments when the first bells were returned, noted that:

> [T]he bond with goods is not only of a material nature, but also of an intangibly emotional kind. The restitution of this kind of goods contributes to the development of a soft diplomacy in the context of international affairs. This soft diplomacy is deeper than the one that only concerns commercial issues. It adds value to a closer relationship. There was no money in between, but a remarkable contribution.[107]

At the national level, it is possible that Chile deemed the bells important because its colonial heritage is more extensive than its pre-Columbian heritage, unlike other Latin-American countries, such as Peru, Ecuador or Mexico.[108] Thus, Chile regained cultural objects of historical importance even if, at the time they were taken to Wales, their significance was not recognised. Moreover, their historical value likely increased because the Welsh decided to keep the bells and use them rather than smelt them, allowing Chile later on to reconnect with a lost part of its history. Indeed, '[the bells] had not been extracted surreptitiously, there was no illicit trafficking. This had implied the sale of things that at some point nobody valued and that now, looking back at history, one can wonder "how could this have been sold per kilogram?"'[109]

Although the bells had not been stolen or illicitly trafficked, their return was a catalyst for Chile's ratification of the 1970 UNESCO Convention in 2014.[110] When adhering to the treaty was being considered, the return of the bells was expressly

[106] Interview with Luis Alberto Ovalle, General Intendent of the Santiago Fire Brigade, Santiago, 10 February 2022.

[107] Interview with Óscar Acuña, lawyer, Santiago, 27 January 2022, who also noted that the Council of National Monuments built a relationship of trust with Jon Benjamin through the process, which led him to open his ambassadorial house on Cultural Heritage Day and personally guide the tour.

[108] Interview with Fernando Montes Matte, member of the Jesuit Order, online, 16 March 2022, who noted that the archives of 'Los Jesuitas de América' were even declared Memory of the World by the UNESCO in 2003.

[109] Interview with Óscar Acuña, lawyer, Santiago, 27 January 2022.

[110] Chile ratified the 1970 UNESCO Convention through Decree No 141.

mentioned because it demonstrated the lack of a national policy for the recovery of cultural objects more generally.[111] Thus, the return of the bells had an impact, even if only a marginal one, on Chile's ratification of the 1970 UNESCO Convention. Indeed, it may have helped to convince Congress, which appeared to have feared that ratifying the Convention would oblige Chile to return cultural objects that had been removed from foreign territory a long time ago, such as the spoils of the Pacific War of 1879–83, not realising that the treaty does not apply retroactively.[112]

However, while the ratification of the 1970 UNESCO Convention led to some institutional changes,[113] it is yet to lead to a national policy on the return of cultural objects. So far, the focus has been on combatting trafficking.[114] To this day, cultural objects are considered as falling either under the CITCH Unit concerned with illicit trafficking or under the Council of National Monuments. Thus, a similar return process would today likely be handled in the same manner as the bells. But according to Óscar Acuña, Chile's overall approach should be amended as 'our institutional framework from the 70s is obsolete. Let's think that the Council is concerned with objects called monuments whereas, in the rest of the world, we talk about cultural heritage. The concept heritage is broader than the term monument'. Although such a drastic change does not seem to be on the horizon, Lina Nagel, the former coordinator of the CITCH Unit of the National Cultural Heritage Service, noted that a protocol on the restitution or return of cultural property is being drafted to implement the 1970 UNESCO Convention, but that the Protocol will likely go beyond that Convention to apply to cases falling outside its scope as well.[115] If that is the case, it may at least

[111] The Chamber of Representatives requested the President of the Republic to ratify the 1970 UNESCO Convention and to submit such ratification to the Congress' approval; Cámara de Diputados de Chile, 'Proyecto de Acuerdo Nº 402-A. Adhesión del Estado de Chile contra tráfico ilícito de bienes culturales de UNESCO', 2011.

[112] However, it should be noted that Chile had previously not been against historical claims, since it had already returned cultural objects without any legal obligation to do so – for example, the return of nearly 4,000 books to Peru, which had been pillaged from the National Library of Lima during the Pacific War, as a 'gesture of peace' in 2007. Some of these books had been declared national monuments, so they had to be released from such legal status in order to be exported; see D Collyns, 'Chile Returns Looted Books to Peru', *BBC News*, 7 November 2007, http://news.bbc.co.uk/1/hi/world/americas/7082436.stm.

[113] A Board against the Illicit Trafficking of Cultural Heritage was created in 2013 by the DIBAM, now the National Service of Cultural Heritage, through Exempt Resolution No 582 of 5 May 2013. In 2019, the CITCH Unit of the National Cultural Heritage Service was established to complement the work of the Board; see Servicio Nacional del Patrimonio Cultural, 'Mesa de lucha contra el tráfico Ilícito de Bienes patrimoniales', www.sngp.gob.cl/sitio/Contenido/Institucional/76445:Traficoilicito. It should be noted that the CITCH Unit has been developing a collaborative online database to gather information about lost cultural property, including objects that have been missing for a long time; see Chile's National Report on the Implementation of the Convention on the Means of Prohibiting and Preventing the Illicit Import, Export and Transfer of Ownership of Cultural Property (2023) UNESCO C70/23/National-report/Chile.

[114] A Lopes Fabris, 'South-South Cooperation on the Return of Cultural Property: The Case of South America' (2017) 49 *Case Western Reserve Journal of International Law* 173, 177.

[115] Interview with Lina Nagel, former coordinator of the Counter Illicit Trafficking of Cultural Heritage (CITCH) Unit of the National Cultural Heritage Service, online, 2 February 2022, who also mentioned

broaden the framework facilitating the return of cultural objects and perhaps even amplify the role of the CITCH in that regard. While the return of the bells cannot be directly credited for these legal and institutional developments, it appears to have played a role, even if only a marginal one.

B. The Impact of the Return of the Bells in Wales: Out of Sight, Out of Mind?

While in Chile the return of the bells has been meaningful for at least some segments of the population, the absence of the bells in Wales, where they had remained for nearly 150 years and entered local folklore, could have had a reverse impact, leaving a gaping hole in the local cultural fabric. However, a little over a decade after the bells departed, this does not appear to be the case. There have been numerous signs that the people of Oystermouth remain attached to Santiago and their bells. For example, a few months after the bells were sent off, following the rescue of the 33 Chilean miners, the bells of All Saints Church were rung in celebration, with Canon Evans stating that 'there's a close link between the church and the copper community in Chile – all of us wished to share in their joy'.[116] On this occasion, the flag that had been sent to Oystermouth by the Chilean government following the return of the bells was hoisted for the first time and it is now raised every 18 September, which is Chile's National Day.[117] The mining accident also inspired a song, composed at a school in Conwy and performed by local pupils. It was then broadcasted on both the national radio in Chile and the BBC World Service.[118]

In March 2011, the year following the bells' return, the Chilean Ambassador visited Oystermouth to thank the local population. He also presented the Order of Bernardo O'Higgins, the highest honour that can be awarded to a foreign national by the State of Chile, to Canon Evans and to the Bishop of Swansea and Brecon, the Right Reverend John Davies, who accepted it on behalf of their parish and diocese, respectively.[119] During that ceremony, Ambassador Tomás Müller Sproat said he had 'been surprised to find out that there have been performances re-enacting the event and that a musical piece about the tragedy has been written by a local

that the Unit was not considered important when it was attached to the Ministry of Education. This changed when it became part of the Ministry of Culture, which was established in 2017.

[116] 'Church Bells Ring in Mumbles for Rescued Chilean Miners', *BBC News*, 14 October 2010, www.bbc.com/news/uk-wales-south-west-wales-11543578.

[117] Oystermouth Parish, 'Flag Flying Days', www.oystermouthparish.com/flag-flying-days.

[118] The song, called 'Seren Esperanza' (Esperanza's Star), was performed by Welsh primary school; see 'Church Bells Ring in Mumbles for Rescued Chilean Miners' (n 116).

[119] See, for example, 'Swansea Clergy in Chilean Honour for Bells of Santiago', *BBC News*, 2 March 2011, www.bbc.com/news/uk-wales-south-west-wales-12607117. For a video news item, see 'Visit of Chilean Ambassador to All Saints Church Oystermouth, Swansea', *ITV Wales Tonight*, 13 May 2011, www.youtube.com/watch?v=8P32pHJe924. For more information on the decorations, see Ministerio de Relaciones Exteriores, 'Condecoraciones', www.minrel.gob.cl/minrel/ministerio/ceremonial-y-protocolo/condecoraciones.

musician', acknowledging the impact that the bells have had on the local community and adding that 'for us the bells toll of Welsh friendship'.[120] This was echoed by Canon Evans, who recognised the friendship between the Chilean officials, the Santiago Fire Brigade, and the representatives of All Saints Church, who remained in regular communication for several years following the process.[121]

Beyond these principally symbolic gestures, the story of the bells also continued to inspire artists, who have somewhat replaced the loss of tangible cultural heritage with intangible cultural heritage.[122] While the tradition of an 8 December requiem service in remembrance of the victims of the fire had carried on at All Saints Church,[123] the 150th anniversary of the tragedy led to the creation of songs by Vernon Hopkins and recorded by the Swansea Philharmonic Choir, which were performed in both Wales and Chile on 8 December 2013.[124] In 2017, the bells were also at the centre of a play specifically put together by the Lighthouse Theatre for the Swansea's Theatre in Education Programme aimed at primary school pupils.[125] Actress Sonia Beck recalled that the topic of the bells was chosen because those approached to develop the play had recently travelled to Chile, where they had been taken to see the bell now hanging at the 14th Fire Company station after mentioning that they were travelling from Wales.[126] Entitled the 'Bells of Santiago' like the musical drama from the 1970s,[127] it re-enacted the fire tragedy, while also telling the wider story of the relationship between Wales and Chile, from the copper trade and the local Cape Horners to those who fled the Pinochet regime in the 1970s to settle in Swansea. According to Derek Cobley, the play's director, 'it was not just the bells that came to Swansea but refugees as well … Some went back but some decided to stay.'[128] Furthermore, according to headteacher Beverly Phillips:

> [C]hildren now understand better that some things don't belong to us, and we've acquired them through various reasons and that sometimes they have to be given back.

[120] See Evans (n 1) 40. The Ambassador was presented with a painting by Malcolm Phillips of the arrival of the bells at All Saints; see 'Chile Honours Clergymen', *Welsh Icons News*, 25 February 2011, www.welshicons.org/chile-honours-clergymen.

[121] Interview with Canon Keith Evans, Oystermouth, 30 March 2023, who also noted that communications had naturally waned about a decade after the return process.

[122] In addition to intangible forms of heritage, the bells have also continued to inspire visual artists, such as Swansea-based artist Jeff Phillips.

[123] This tradition continued at least until the COVID-19 pandemic, with plans for reviving it thereafter.

[124] R Turner, 'How Swansea and Chile are Linked by the Bells of Santiago', *WalesOnline*, 6 December 2013, www.walesonline.co.uk/lifestyle/nostalgia/swansea-chile-bells-santiago-6377327; 'Santiago Bells: Swansea Service to Mark Chilean Cathedral Fire', *BBC News*, 8 December 2013, www.bbc.com/news/uk-wales-south-west-wales-25279970.

[125] Interview with Beverly Phillips, Sketty Primary School, Sketty, 30 March 2023. Five schools with Year 6 children took part in this programme, which was accompanied by a substantial teachers' resource pack.

[126] Interview with Sonia Beck, actress, Oystermouth, 27 March 2023.

[127] Lighthouse Theatre Company, 'Bells of Santiago', www.lighthouse-theatre.co.uk/productions/bells-of-santiago.

[128] Interview with Derek Cobley, theatre director, author and consultant in the role of the arts in education, Oystermouth, 27 March 2023, who added that Swansea is officially recognised as a 'City of Sanctuary', a city where the many Chilean refugees who remained made a significant contribution thereto, thus garnering the goodwill of the South Wales mining communities.

> So, it is a good story to try to portray as this is not only true about the bells but about a lot of other things too.[129]

Integrating the story of the bells in several local primary schools ensured that it remains vivid in Welsh minds, while also offering an opportunity to tell a bigger and more complex narrative.

So far, the absence of the bells has not diminished the sentiments of the Oystermouth community towards Santiago. Of course, this may change over time and it appears that the COVID-19 pandemic already dampened some traditions, such as the holding of a requiem service on 8 December. However, the remaining Santiago bells in Wales as well as the new ways their story has been narrated and honoured since the return of the others may support the perseverance of those transatlantic ties. Furthermore, All Saints Church, where the bells were most revered, has not been left without a trace: the 'Little Bell' which was left behind is now exhibited within the Church's Lady Chapel with a plaque explaining its story and that of the other bells which have now returned to Chile.

Figure 4.2 The 'Little Bell' at All Saints Church, Oystermouth. © Kristin Hausler (2023)

[129] Interview with Beverly Phillips, headteacher, Sketty Primary School, Sketty, 30 March 2023.

The 'Little Bell' serves as a memorial to the 1863 disaster but also as a tangible reminder of the once-great copper industry in Swansea and its trading history with Chile. And beyond this tangible link, the sound of the returned bells can still be heard over the parish as they were digitalised, thus reminding the inhabitants of the parish that the story of the bells of Santiago is also their story.[130]

VI. Conclusion

The bells have been hailed a symbol of 'co-operation and sympathy',[131] which is largely due to the way their return was handled. While the fact that the bells were no longer in use certainly eased their return, allowing to bypass the rules hindering their donation, the swift reaction of the parish, along with a unanimous will to donate the bells, ensured a constructive process that provided satisfaction to both sides. While Chile regained a piece of its history and means to better disseminate the message of the firefighting community, the Welsh community was left not only with the feeling of having 'done the right thing' but also with a compelling story that continues to be told in different ways.

In Santiago, the presence of the bells and their meaning is not yet commonly known by the general population outside of specific groups like the firefighting community. This may partially be due to the locations where they were placed upon their return to Santiago, which may not be considered as highly visible, but it might just as well be the result of the bells being of particular importance to the firefighting community and less so to others. After all, while some of the chosen locations can be criticised, efforts were nevertheless made to create special memorials. For instance, awarding the design of one of memorials through an open competition made it possible to engage local artists in their narrative. And while some may have wished that the returned bells be hung together as a group, it can also be argued that, by disseminating them in four different locations, the Chilean government and the firefighting community increased their visibility. And while none of the bells was restored to its original function within a church, it is clear that they have all become tremendously symbolic for Santiago's body of volunteer firefighters.

In addition to not having been restored to their original function, it is also worth noting that neither the parishes in Wales nor the religious community in Chile had a say in the re-integration of the bells, despite the fact that they had always belonged to a church prior to their return, whether in Chile or in Wales. The entities which decided on the re-integration of the bells were limited to those who had initiated the return process. In the case of the first three bells, it was

[130] See Evans (n 1) 45. During the interview, Evans added that the sound of the bells is used for the Sunday call to worship.
[131] See Turner (n 124).

the Chilean government and, in the case of the fourth bell, it was the 14th Fire Company – the British and Commonwealth Fire & Rescue Company.

While the story of the bells remains for now better known around Swansea than it is in Santiago, the Welsh community members who closely associated with them believe that they are back where they belong, not just in a physical or geographical sense but also in a historical, cultural and social one, a sense of belonging, a sense of *cynefin*. In parallel, returning the bells may have also provided a sense of *cynefin* to the Welsh communities by connecting them to their own history and by leaving them with the feeling of having 'done the right thing'.

5

Museums in the Lead

*'Crossed Deposits' between France and Cambodia**

I. Introduction

In 2016, an exchange of two parts of statues originating from Cambodia took place between the Musée Guimet (Guimet Museum, also known as the National Museum of Asian Arts – Guimet) in Paris, France, and the National Museum of Cambodia in Phnom Penh. One was the head of a Harihara statue that originated from Phnom Da in Angkor Borei District, Cambodia, which had ended up in the collection of the Guimet Museum. The body of the statue was in Phnom Penh and, through the exchange, the head could be re-attached to its body. In return for the Harihara head, the Cambodian museum lent the pedestal of a dancing Uma statue from Koh Ker to the Guimet Museum,[1] so that it could in turn be itself reunited with the rest of its statue, which was in the Guimet's collection. The Phnom Penh Harihara, which is the focus of this chapter, represents a Hindu iconography that combines aspects of Vishnu and Shiva, the deities of creation and destruction.[2] This statue comes from the Phnom Da area in Takeo province, near Angkor Borei, south of Phnom Penh. The main Phnom Da temple was built in the sixth century on the tops and slopes of small hills with shrines established in caves carved into the rocky sides of the northern hill. Today, only pedestal elements remain on site.

Most Phnom Da statues date back to the sixth century, in line with their stylistic Indian influence. However, the Phnom Penh Harihara is a late Phnom Da type that was most likely sculpted in the seventh century.[3] Its initial place of worship is not

* Unless indicated otherwise, all translations in this chapter are the authors' own.

[1] This statue had been collected by Louis Delaporte, a French naval officer, who was authorised to conduct a mission in Cambodia in 1873, where he asked King Norodom for some cultural objects to be brought back to France. When the pieces arrived at the Louvre, they were not deemed suitable for being exhibited there as they were not made of marble, which is why they were then exhibited in a gallery at the Trocadero, before being transferred to the Guimet Museum in 1927.

[2] The statue that this case study focuses on is often referred to as the 'Phnom Penh Harihara' to distinguish it from the 'Paris Harihara' that remains in the collection of Guimet Museum. Both come from Phnom Da in Angkor Borei.

[3] SR Mace and B Porte, *Revealing Krishna. Essays on the History, Context, and Conservation of Krishna Lifting Mount Govardghan from Phnom Da* (Cleveland, D Giles Ltd, 2021) 40.

known with certainty. It is classified under a later style,[4] due to the hairstyle and costume of the Harihara. The statue's head is typical of the Harihara iconography.[5]

Figure 5.1 Harihara statue at the National Museum in Phnom Penh. © National Museum of Cambodia (2024)

According to Bertrand Porte, former head of the École Française d'Extrême Orient (EFEO) in Phnom Penh (which was part of a sculpture conservation workshop set up in partnership with the National Museum of Cambodia), it is difficult to know the exact, initial location of most Phnom Da statues and even to retrace how the

[4] It is classified under the later Phnom Da 'Style B'; see P Dupont, *La Statuaire Préangkorienne* (Ascona, Artibus Asiae Publishers, 1955) 42.

[5] See ibid for details on the iconography and style of the Phnom Penh Harihara.

statues, or pieces thereof, moved around over time. What is known is that Phnom Da experienced a revival in the twelfth century, when some of the sculptures appear to have been moved around and even altered.[6] Afterwards, pieces of the statues were found in different locations on the Phnom Da mount, which indicates a change in the use of the statues.[7] For the Phnom Penh Harihara, the two lower arms and hands were found separate from the body in 1923. Parts of the body were brought to Phnom Penh in 1944. Its head, which had made its way to France, was eventually returned to Cambodia, to be reunited with its body. This case is significant because it is the first 'return' that has happened thus far from the Guimet Museum, which houses the largest collection of Khmer art outside of Cambodia.

Despite animated debates about restitution in France since President Macron's 2017 call for the return of (African) heritage and Cambodia having already received back considerable numbers of stolen objects from American and private collections, such as those of Douglas Latchford or from the Metropolitan Museum of Art,[8] the extensive Cambodian collection of the Guimet Museum seems almost immune to the ongoing commotion. This chapter considers the reasons for this situation by analysing the exchange between both institutions. Thereby, it explains how returns can largely bypass a state-to-state process and restrictive legislation. In addition, the case also raises questions relating to the robust and continuing French influence pertaining to heritage matters in Cambodia, resulting in a conservation approach that, to a large extent, ignores the religious (spiritual) value of the idols. This has often been discussed in terms of built heritage conservation,[9] but it also appears to persist in the approach to moveable heritage.

II. French Indochina, Colonial Decrees and Heritage Management

Cambodia became a French protectorate in 1863 as part of the larger, French-controlled Indochina. From the early days of exploration and colonisation

[6] Interview with Bertrand Porte, former head of EFEO in Phnom Penh, Phnom Penh, August 2022.

[7] See also Mace and Porte (n 3) 133–38. Some statues were also gilded or painted much later (eg, the Paris Harihara has traces of gilding that Porte assumes are post-sixteenth century).

[8] There has been a lot of reporting on returns of art and artifacts to Cambodia. Some examples are the statement by the US Embassy in Cambodia, 'United States Welcomes Return of Khmer Artifacts to Cambodia', 17 March 2023, www.kh.usembassy.gov/unitedstateswelcomesreturnofkhmerartifacts tocambodia23, or reports on the return of parts of the Latchford collection; see A Villa, 'Cambodia Receives over 70 Rare Gold Artifacts in Deal with Estate of Disgraced Antiquities Dealer', *ARTnews*, 21 February 2023, www.artnews.com/art-news/news/cambodia-douglas-latchford-repatriation-1234658517. See also the July 2024 return of statues from the Metropolitan Museum of Art: Associated Press, 'Cambodia Welcomes the Met's Repatriation of Centuries-Old Statues Looted during Past Turmoil', *CNN Style*, 5 July 2024, www.edition.cnn.com/2024/07/05/style/cambodia-statue-repatriation-met-museum/index.html.

[9] M Falser, *Angkor Wat: A Transcultural History of Heritage (Volume 1 Angkor in France; Volume 2 Angkor in Cambodia)* (Berlin, De Gruyter, 2020).

of the area, the heritage of Cambodia played a central role in the French colonial interests in the region. The French authorities developed extensive heritage policies, involving for instance the establishment, in 1898, of the EFEO, which took control over all documentation and restoration work in Angkor and other heritage sites in Cambodia.[10] The French administration also created the first museums in Cambodia, including the current National Museum and the adjacent School of Cambodian Arts.[11] As a result, extensive and detailed documentation is available on the movement of heritage objects in Cambodia since the late nineteenth century. These initiatives also included moving large numbers of statues and parts of the carved exteriors of temples to museums in Cambodia and France.[12]

In relation to how statues were perceived and the role they played in daily life, 'the introduction of scientific colonial practices produced a big dichotomy with the traditional popular practices'.[13] Although several researchers reported Khmer culture as having been abandoned early on during the establishment of the French protectorate,[14] many monuments and statues continued to play an important role for the local communities.[15] Most research on Cambodian heritage practices focuses on the major site of Angkor, but, to a certain extent, the key characteristics of the approach can be extended to other heritage places too. It consisted of decades-long efforts led by France to treat Angkor and other temple areas in the country as *parcs archéologiques* (archaeological parks) rather than living heritage sites, with many local communities being displaced and ending up living away from the heritage sites.[16] In addition, targeted efforts by the Khmer Rouge

[10] Today, the EFEO continues to work in Cambodia, governed through a decree with the Cambodian authorities that was established in 1967: Accord du 16 mars 1967 entre le Gouvernement Royal du Cambodge et l'Ecole Française d'Extrême-Orient relatif à la reconduction des accords bilatéraux de 1956 sur la conservation d'Angkor et sur le régime des fouilles archéologiques (Agreement between the Royal Government of Cambodia and the Ecole française d'Extrême-Orient respecting the renewal of the 1956 bilateral agreements of the Angkor conservancy and on terms and conditions for archaeological excavations).

[11] The National Museum, alongside the Ecole des Arts Cambodgiens, was built by Georges Groslier for the EFEO in 1917. In 1920, it was officially opened and named the Musée Albert Sarraut. Groslier became the first curator, and for about three decades, the museum and school remained entirely in French hands. Yet, also since the transfer to Cambodia, the cooperation with France has remained very close (except for the period under the Khmer Rouge), and today, an office of the EFEO remains present inside the National Museum.

[12] G Abbe, '"Decadence and Revival" in Cambodian Arts and the Role of George Groslier (1887–1945)' in M Falser (ed), *Cultural Heritage as Civilizing Mission: From Decay to Recovery* (Cham, Springer, 2015) 123–47; Falser, *Angkor Wat: A Transcultural History of Heritage (Volume 1)* (n 9); J Paquette, *Museum-Making in Vietnam, Laos, and Cambodia: Cultural Institutions and Policies from Colonial to Post-colonial Times* (New York, Routledge, 2022).

[13] S Biard, 'Réflexions sur l'histoire de l'exposition et de la restauration des effigies de culte anciennes au Cambodge' (2017) 30 *Recherche en sciences humaines sur l'Asie du Sud-Est* 131.

[14] See Abbe (n 12).

[15] K Miura, 'From Property to Heritage: Different Notions, Rules of Ownership and Practices of New and Old Actors in the Angkor World Heritage Site' in B Hauser-Schäublin (ed), *World Heritage Angkor and Beyond: Circumstances and Implications of UNESCO Listing in Cambodia* (Göttingen, Universitätsverlag Göttingen, 2017) 97–119.

[16] Falser, *Angkor Wat: A Transcultural History of Heritage (Volume 2)* (n 9).

to eradicate religious worshipping in the preceding decades almost annihilated the number of local people who still venture into the temples to worship. Finally, the arrival of mass tourism since the 1990s further pushed the local population away from the most public temples.[17] However, none of this means that people have become less religious; worshipping continues, both in private and in more remote temples. This raises the question of where a once-venerated object should be returned.

Historian Aldrich described the French colonial heritage practice as follows:

> Meanwhile, the French came to see themselves, through their role of colonial masters, as guardians of the heritage of the countries they governed, exporting metropolitan notions of heritage, conservation, exhibition and the *mise en valeur* of cultural sites into the colonies. In doing so, the French arrogated to themselves godlike powers to create, preserve or destroy heritage in the countries they conquered, and colonialists marshalled military might, engineering and technological skill, scholarship, subventions, labour and every other means available to shape and reshape the *patrimoines* over which they acquired authority … French authorities compiled inventories of historic sites. They classified sites for conservation and preservation and passed laws that protected natural and built features of the landscape. They carried out archaeological digs and pioneered anthropological and ethnographical studies. The French set up learned societies and published countless academic works devoted to heritage, with such institutions as the EFEO … and they opened numerous museums … Heritage policy formed part of colonial policy, mirroring its ideas and ideologies.[18]

Moreover, many consider the removal of the statues, and their study and preservation in France under the Protectorate, to have been part of a rightful conservation practice. As Pierre Baptiste, Conservator for Southeast Asia at the Guimet Museum, mentioned:

> Legally, it [the Harihara head] arrived officially [in France] in 1889, in a colonial context, but [in a context of] heritage protection. She [the Harihara head] was published as such. It is not a pillaged object.[19]

This understanding that there is a fundamental difference between the numerous objects that were looted during the civil war and thereafter, which often found their way into private collections, and those present in French public collections resonated not only through interviews with staff at the Guimet Museum, but also at the EFEO. French experts also continue to play an important role in preserving Cambodian heritage. Moreover, they consider that there was a certain

[17] It should be noted that this balance had improved when visiting the site in 2022, right after the country re-opened to tourism following the COVID-19 pandemic.

[18] R Aldrich, 'France and the *Patrimoine* of the Empire: Heritage Policy under Colonial Rule' (2011) 4 *French History and Civilization* 202.

[19] Original quote: 'Légalement, c'est-à-dire qu'elle est arrivée officiellement en 1889, dans un contexte colonial, mais de protection patrimoniale. Elle était publiée comme telle. Ce n'est pas une œuvre pillée.' Interview with Pierre Baptiste, Conservator for South-East Asia, Guimet Museum, Paris, France, 28 April 2023.

scientific legitimacy in the way in which French Indochina dealt with heritage. And although they agree that colonialism was a historic wrong overall, this seems largely dissociated from what happened to heritage during the same period. The French engagement with Cambodia's heritage was generally seen as a positive outcome of colonialism, ensuring the preservation of Cambodian culture into the present. According to Baptiste:

> He sent these objects to France. Why? Because back then, in 1889, there was no museum. There was not a single museum, there was no lapidarium. And so … back then, in the mind of the administrators, it was a conservation measure, to protect. They always used the words safeguarding, protection, etc. because there was no institution [in Cambodia].[20]

In addition, the transfer of the Harihara head to France in the 1880s, the object of this case study, was reportedly permitted by Cambodia's King Norodom.[21] While few questions are being asked about the circumstances under which the King, subjected to a Protectorate, made this decision, this is used as an argument by France to say that the transfer was not a case of illicit transfer. This argument is potentially further strengthened by France and its institutions having always clearly communicated about these removals.[22] As part of scientific expeditions and conservation work, the removal of statues, their export to France, their study, etc, have always been meticulously documented and openly communicated about. According to the diaries and biographies of early explorers like Henri Mouhot or the experts engaged with the EFEO, there is also no doubt that these were not punitive or (mainly) commercial undertakings.[23] There was also no desire to re-educate the local population or convert them to Catholicism, as was often the case in the African context, for instance. Nevertheless, numerous masterpieces of Cambodian heritage were moved to France, where they remain today, and this happened during a period when the Cambodians themselves – from the King to the worshippers in the villages – had little power or say in the matter.

In 1900, a first decree was adopted by the Governor-General of Indochina introducing a classification system for movable and immovable objects, mirroring the French *loi du 30 mars 1887 pour la conservation des monuments et objets d'art ayant un intérêt historique et artistique* (law of 30 March 1887 for the conservation

[20] Original quote: 'Il envoie ces œuvres en France pourquoi? Parce qu'à l'époque, en 1889, il n'y a pas de musée, il n'y a aucune institution muséale, il n'y a pas de dépôt lapidaire. Et donc … à l'époque, dans l'esprit des administrateurs, c'est une mesure de conservation, en fait, de protection. Ils utilisent toujours les mots de sauvetage, protection, etc. parce qu'il n'y a pas d'institution.' Interview with Pierre Baptiste, Conservator for South-East Asia, Guimet Museum, Paris, France, 28 April 2023.

[21] Mace and Porte (n 3) 105.

[22] This was mentioned by the French interviewees.

[23] Examples are H Mouhot, *Travels in the Central Parts of Indo-China (Siam), Cambodia, and Laos*, 2 vols (London, William Clowes and Sons, 1864); L Delaporte, *Voyage au Cambodge* (Paris, Maisonneuve et Larose, 1999); E Aymonier, *Le Cambodge I: Le Royaume actuel* (Paris, Ernest Leroux, 1900).

of monuments and works of art of historical and artistic interest).[24] The 1900 decree was used to create a 'section of Khmer antiquities of the Indo-China museum' by a subsequent decree in 1905.[25] This second decree stipulated that the museum must accommodate objects whose 'conservation, because of their isolated location, their material or their small dimensions, cannot be properly assured on the very site of the find'. The EFEO, as the scientific and legal regulator of the protectorate's heritage institutions, became responsible for implementing this decree. When the first Khmer museum opened in Phnom Penh in 1905, it was quickly flooded with statues from all regions of Cambodia. In 1921, it became the Albert Sarraut Museum, which would later become the National Museum of Cambodia.

At the same time, archaeological deposits were created in the Angkor area, where the first research and clearing of the temples was carried out. From there, pieces were moved to museums. According to art historian Sophie Biard, this did not create significant problems since the statues and temples had generally been abandoned.[26] However, wherever statues were still part of living traditions, issues arose.[27] The removal of statues was often difficult in remote or isolated sites, such as the Angkor Borei area – from where the Harihara statue was taken – because of their continued local meaning. In this area, extensive ceremonies were reportedly taking place when the statues were removed from the temple and cave areas, indicating a clearly active living culture.[28] In such places, removals were often refused by monks, but were nonetheless still pursued by the French.

The perspective of Kam Doum, a member of the Buddhist Institute in Phnom Penh and an employee of the National Museum, on the mission that took place in 1944 to remove statues from Phnom Da, where they were still being worshipped, to transfer them to Phnom Penh, has been reported as follows:

> They were greeted at the Vietnamese pagoda Chua Thap Son (across from Cave B), where they had to negotiate with the monks in order to proceed with the removal of the sculptures. Torn between the distress and consternation of the Vietnamese community upon seeing its statues being taken away and his instructions from the Phnom Penh authorities, KAM Doum did his best to convince residents that the government was acting out of concern for the conservation of these images. The community asked for a few days' postponement so that the surrounding communities (all the way to the Chau Doc River) might come to pay homage to the images one last time before their departure. KAM Doum was very upset, because he was not able to

[24] Ministère de la Culture, 'Monuments & Sites. Un peu d'histoire', www.culture.gouv.fr/Thematiques/monuments-sites/monuments-historiques-sites-patrimoniaux/un-peu-d-histoire.

[25] Arrêté du 9 mars 1900 'relatif à la conservation en Indochine des monuments et objets ayant un intérêt historique ou artistique', BEFEO, 1, 1901; Arrêté du 17 août 1905 'créant à Phnom Penh la section des antiquités Khmères du musée de l'Indo-Chine', BEFEO, 5, 1905.

[26] Biard (n 13).

[27] Biard (ibid) describes a documented case of another Harihara statue that the monks refused to hand over to the French, and the various steps taken to still obtain it for the museum collection.

[28] Mace and Porte (n 3).

> grant the stay: Pierre Dupont and both the provincial and Phnom Penh authorities had planned a ceremony on September 12 at Angkor Borei to celebrate the collection of all the sculptures for the NMC. Without waiting, the team proceeded on the morning of September 6 to take down a statue of what they thought was Vishnu from the neighbouring temple Chua ong Dai Vuong; in fact this sculpture was the body of the Phnom Penh Harihara.[29]

Hence, at least some of the statues had not been abandoned and they had not lost their religious meaning at the time they were removed. Moreover, those partaking in the removal appear to have been well aware of the continuing, living value of the statues, as Kam further observed: 'A procession with musicians accompanied the removal of each statue to the boat on which they were loaded.'[30] Kam even described how after Phnom Da, the mission continued to remove statues from a living monastery in Angkor Borei. His account noted the monastic community resisting the removal and how French art historian 'Pierre Dupont came from Phnom Penh with a delegation. Gifts were offered to the monastic communities, and elders were given medals, as was the chief of the Angkor Borei village'.[31] The combination of ceremonies and celebrations, with (lengthy) negotiations and 'gifts' demonstrates that these expeditions not only removed statues, but also that despite the awareness of the living nature of these statues, the interest in documenting, studying and preserving Cambodia's heritage – as a material reality – dominated. To feed this desire to preserve material heritage, efforts were made to appease the local communities.

At the same time, it has been argued that the removal of statues mostly concerned those that were fragile or left unattended, and that the French experts sought, as much as possible, to avoid removing pieces that were still being venerated, as well as newer ones.[32] While, there was thus likely an implicit policy not to touch the living heritage, in practice, conservation interests often took the upper hand, resulting in the removal of statues that were still attached to living practices. From the 1960s onwards, almost all statues still in temples were moved to places of deposit, including in particular those from Angkor.

[29] This is the description of Kam's account in Mace and Porte (ibid 106). The authors base themselves on Kam's publication of his account in Khmer: Kam Doum, 'Report on the Transfer of Buddha Statues and a Pedestal from Angkor Borei, Village of Prey Kabbas, Takeo Province' (1945) XVII(1) *Kampuchea Soriya* 1–14; XVII(2) 70–93; XVII(3) 137–55. For a full transcription of Kam Doum's report of the removal of Phnom Da statues, see M Antelme, HC Vicheth, B Porte 'Rapport sur le transfert en septembre 1944 de statues du Buddha et d'un piédestal de la commune d'Angkor Borei, district de Prey Kabbas, province de Takéo, de Kam Doum (Kằm Dŭm)', translated from Khmer by M Antelme, HC Vicheth and B Porte, 'Le « Rapport sur le transfert en septembre 1944 de statues du Buddha et d'un piédestal de la commune d'Angkor Borei, district de Prey Kabbas, province de Takéo », de Kam Doum (Kằm Dŭm)' (2023) 109 *Bulletin de l'École Française d'Extrême-Orient* 237, www.jstor.org/stable/27316657.

[30] Mace and Porte (n 3) 107.

[31] ibid 107–08.

[32] Biard (n 13).

III. The Gradual Removal of Statues from Temple Sites

Tracing the provenance of the Harihara's head all the way to Paris while the rest of its body remained in Phnom Penh is more complex.[33] The statue was found during various stages of research on the Phnom Da site and was brought to different locations, from the late nineteenth century onwards. In 2021, the Cleveland Museum of Art published a catalogue for the 'Revealing Krishna' exhibition, which summarised the main steps in the collection process as follows:[34]

Head	First recorded by Etienne Aymonier in 1882, on the southwestern peak of Phnom Da	Transferred in 1882–89 from Phnom Da to Paris by Etienne Aymonier	Current location: National Museum of Cambodia (but property of Guimet Museum, Paris)
		Transferred from Paris to Phnom Penh in 2016	
Body with legs	First recorded by Henri Parmentier in 1911, 1912 or 1913 in cave F on the northeastern hill of Phnom Da[35]	Transferred in 1911–23 to a new shrine between the two peaks of Phnom Da by local residents	Current location: National Museum of Cambodia
		Transferred from Phnom Da to Phnom Penh in 1944 by Kam Doum, representing Pierre Dupont	
Hand with rosary	First recorded by Henri Parmentier in 1911 at the base of the northeastern peak of Phnom Da, or 'found at the foot of the eastern slope' by Groslier in 1923[36]	Transferred from Phnom Da to Phnom Penh in 1923 by George Groslier	Current location: National Museum of Cambodia
Hand with mace			

[33] It should be noted that the provenance of the dancing Uma statue from Koh Ker, which would see its pedestal sent from Cambodia in exchange of the Harihara's head, is clearer. See n 1.

[34] The table is based on the one presented in an Annex in Mace and Porte (n 3).

[35] ibid, contradicting information (at 131) which mentions that Parmentier recorded the body in cave F in 1913, while referring to the table in the Annex (at 178), which speaks of 1911; Moreover, there is also a reference to 1912 in Dupont (n 4) 43.

[36] Contradicting information in Mace and Porte (n 3) 131, which mentions that Groslier found the arms at the foot of the eastern slope of Phnom Da in 1923, while the table in the Annex (at 178) speaks of a discovery by Parmentier in 1911. Contrary to the latter footnote, in this case, it may well be that the first recording was done by Parmentier and that Groslier then got involved a decade later, removing the arms to Phnom Penh.

The first written records, dating back to the end of the nineteenth century, point to the dispersal of sculpted fragments inside and around the temples and caves at Phnom Da.[37] Starting in 1882, Etienne Aymonier, the colonial administrator, sent the head of the Phnom Penh Harihara to France. The rest of the Phnom Penh Harihara remained on site in Cambodia. Aymonier had received permission from Cambodia's King Norodom to export the object, alongside others, to France for the 1889 Exposition Universelle (World Exhibition) in Paris where they were to be exhibited at the outdoor gallery of the Palais du Trocadéro.[38] That such an agreement was reached in a context of high inequality did not seem to be reflected upon at the time. In Paris, the Lyon-based industrialist Emile Guimet acquired the head, along with other Cambodian artefacts, for his ambitious new museum dedicated to the religions of the Far East, the predecessor of the current Guimet Museum, which eventually became a national museum in 1927.[39]

Several years later, between 1911 and 1913, French archaeologist Henri Parmentier found the headless body of the Harihara statue in Phnom Da, in one of the caves on the northeastern hill, but left it on site. In 1923, another French archaeologist, George Groslier, noted that the statues had been 'recently' transformed into Buddhas by the local community of Vietnamese origin.[40] This explains why the body had been moved without its extra arms/hands and head to another location. He subsequently brought the Harihara's two lower hands, holding a rosary and a mace, to Phnom Penh.

At the end of 1944, yet another French archaeologist, Pierre Dupont, collected a large number of pieces from Phnom Da and Angkor Borei for the museum in Phnom Penh. This included the body (which had earlier been found by Parmentier), with part of the arms and legs of the Harihara statue.[41] By that stage, only the base was likely remaining in Phnom Da, where it is possibly still located today. When the Harihara, alongside other Phnom Da statues, entered the Museum in Phnom Penh, it was prepared to be exhibited in the middle of the south wing.[42] It was set into a concrete base and Dupont fixed the arms that had been transferred earlier by Groslier, to the rest of the Harihara's body. In 1999, another round of (restorative) work followed.

These removals of pieces of the Harihara from Phnom Da to Phnom Penh were part of a much larger campaign in which many sculptures and pieces of sculptures were transferred to the museum in Phnom Penh, designed by Groslier and

[37] ibid 105.

[38] This was emphasised during various interviews conducted for this research.

[39] P Baptiste and T Zéphir, 'L'Art khmer dans les collections du musée Guimet' (2008) *MNAAG/Réunion des musées nationaux* 58–61. See also H McGivern, 'French Museum Reunites Head with Decapitated Khmer Statue', *The Art Newspaper*, 20 January 2016, www.theartnewspaper.com/2016/01/20/french-museum-reunites-head-with-decapitated-khmer-statue; D Fincham, 'Cambodia and Musée Guimet Reunite Khmer Statue', *Illicit Cultural Property*, 21 January 2016, www.illicitculturalproperty.com/cambodia-and-musee-guimet-reunite-khmer-statue.

[40] Mace and Porte (n 3) 103.

[41] ibid 106.

[42] ibid 109.

opened in 1920.[43] During that time, it was not clear that the Harihara head that had already been brought to Paris in the late nineteenth century belonged to the same statue. Just over a decade later, in 1955, Dupont posited that the head in the Guimet collection and the body in the Phnom Penh museum might belong together.[44] This assumption was only further investigated some 50 years later.

IV. Applied Provenance Research and a Legal Hurdle to Overcome

From 1998, Bertrand Porte at the EFEO in Phnom Penh and his colleagues at the EFEO and the National Museum started a series of restorations and de-restorations of the Harihara, alongside other Phnom Da sculptures.[45] Consequently, he realised that there was a connection between the Harihara's body in Phnom Penh and the head in the Guimet Museum.[46] According to Porte, close inspection and comparison of the profiles of the neck and the head, in particular the level where the earlobe was cut, resulted in near-certainty that both pieces belonged together.

Around the same time, while working on the publication of a catalogue of Khmer collections in the early 2000s,[47] Pierre Baptiste and Thierry Zéphir conducted research on the Harihara head in the archives. As a result, they found the documentation describing how it had arrived in Paris. Thereafter, staff at Guimet made a plaster mould of the place where the neck had been cut, which confirmed once and for all that both were part of the same statue. According to Baptiste: 'It is only recently that we were able to make a cast of the upper part of the statue in Phnom Penh and bring it to France to check whether our head actually matched that body.'[48] However, it then still took many years for both museums to come to an agreement about the adequate steps forward. The Guimet Museum confirmed that a long-standing collaboration between the two national institutions was at the basis of the return of the Harihara head:

> The Musée Guimet has always had good relations [with Cambodia], until the 70s. Then there was a rupture of about twenty years, between about '71 and '91. From '91, as soon as Cambodia opened, the Musée Guimet went there and offered its help with education, at the Faculty of Archaeology of Phnom Penh … and then, very soon after the

[43] M Vachon, 'Statue's Head, Body Reunited after Generations', *Cambodia Daily*, 22 January 2016, https://english.cambodiadaily.com/lifestyle/106089-106089.

[44] Mace and Porte (n 3) 131.

[45] B Porte, 'Sculptures transformées, du Phnom Da au Núi Ba Thê' (2016) *Arts Asiatiques* 123, fn 71.

[46] Interview with Bertrand Porte, former Director of the EFEO in Phnom Penh, Phnom Penh, August 2022, and correspondence with Bertrand Porte, October 2024.

[47] It would eventually be published in 2008; see interview with Pierre Baptiste, Conservator for South-East Asia, Guimet Museum, Paris, France, 28 April 2023.

[48] See Vachon (n 43).

re-opening, there was the idea to assist the National Museum in Phnom Penh to restore its collections.[49]

Once it was clear that both pieces belonged together, the museums in Paris and in Phnom Penh, with a prominent role played by the EFEO office, started working to find a way to reunite them. While it is not entirely clear from where the initiative for the return was taken, this largely depends on when one deems that the process really started. According to Chea Socheat, Cambodia's National Museum's Deputy Director of Conservation, the idea came from its Director in 2010.[50] On the French side, both the Guimet Museum and the EFEO saw their role in studying how the pieces fit together as the start of the process. A high-level cultural advisor to the Cambodian authorities mentioned visiting the Guimet Museum with a Cambodian delegation, led by Prime Minister Sok An, when the Harihara case was 'first' discussed, which may have referred to the moment that the political process started.[51] There, thus, seem to be many 'beginnings' to the return process, which demonstrates that it is exactly that: a process.

Indeed, the gradual development of knowledge about the connection between the head and the body of the Harihara, culminating in 2007 in the creation of the mould that confirmed the expected match, were already very much part of the return process. Once the connection between the head and the body was verified on the physical pieces, another part of the process started: finding a way to bring them back together, as it was inconceivable for both the Cambodian and the French experts involved that a statue would remain headless once the matching head was identified.[52] A discussion was thus initiated with the Director of the National Museum at the time, Khun Samen, and eventually with the Cambodian Minister for Culture, Phoeurng Sackona.[53] As such, the rationale for bringing the pieces together was based on both a scientific and aesthetic rationale: the wholeness and integrity of the piece, an argument that is also present in the claim for the reunification of the Parthenon sculptures, for example.

The process thus moved into the legal context applicable to a possible return, as well as into the terrain of museum management and politics.[54] This (largely diplomatic)

[49] Interview with Pierre Baptiste, Conservator for South-East Asia, Guimet Museum, Paris, France, 28 April 2023, in which he also mentioned a joint exhibition and knowledge exchange with French academics having taught in archaeology and art history in Cambodia for decades, as well as the establishment by the French of an art restoration service at the National Museum (which would eventually become part of the EFEO).

[50] Interview with Chea Socheat, Deputy Director of Conservation, Phnom Penh, August 2022.

[51] Interview with a cultural advisor, Phnom Penh, August 2022.

[52] Interview with Pierre Baptiste, Conservator for South-East Asia, Guimet Museum, Paris, France, 28 April 2023.

[53] ibid; however, Pierre Baptiste noted that constructive discussions only advanced with the Cambodian government when Phoeurng Sackona was appointed Cambodian Minister of Culture and Fine Arts in 2013.

[54] Yet, it is understood that the role of the governments, and especially of the French government, remained very limited.

part of the process took many years, until in 2015, an agreement was signed for a permanent loan in two directions in the form of a 'crossed deposits'. Thus the head was eventually returned in 2016, in exchange for the base of a dancing Uma statue from Koh Ker, of which the whole body was at the Guimet Museum. That base was sent to France some time after the head returned to Cambodia, but only because the logistics of moving a massive and very heavy pedestal were more complex than those of the Harihara head.[55]

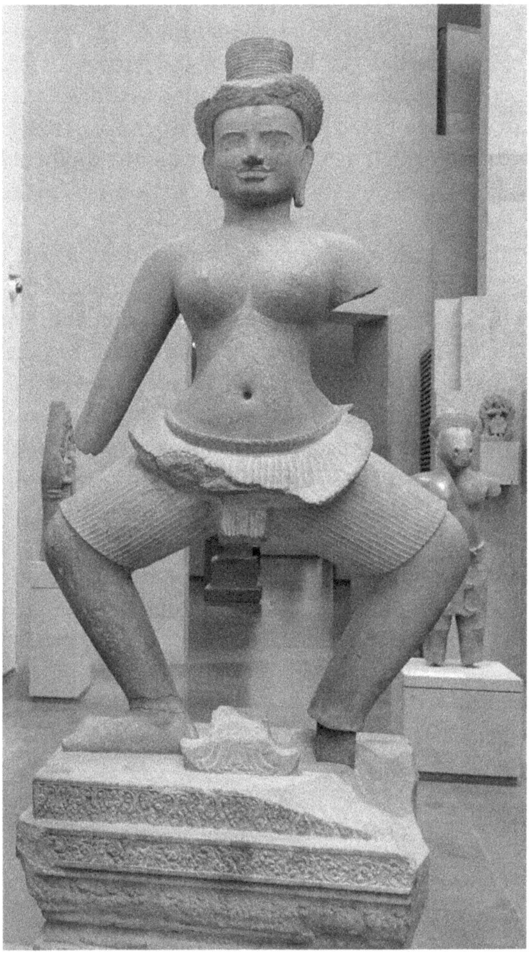

Figure 5.2 Dancing Uma statue at the Guimet Museum in Paris. © Kristin Hausler (2023)

[55] Interview with Pierre Baptiste, Conservator for South-East Asia, Guimet Museum, Paris, France, 28 April 2023: the cost of the transport of both pieces was supported by the Guimet Museum.

While the 1970 UNESCO Convention was ratified by Cambodia in 1972 and by France in 1997, its non-retroactive nature means that it was not relevant for this case. In addition, it appears that the applicable colonial decree at the time did not prohibit the removal of statues from temples; quite the contrary. In addition, the transfer of the statue to France appeared to have been approved by the Cambodian King, even if such agreement may nowadays be questioned given the colonial context in which it was reached. In any case, this return was not led by the states concerned, but by the Guimet Museum and the National Museum of Cambodia. Their longstanding cooperation had fostered a strong foundation of trust between the two institutions. Although legally there was no requirement to return the piece, which was furthermore not deemed looted by the parties, there was a strong will to do so. But while both museums were eager to see the pieces of the statues being reunited, they had a major legal hurdle to overcome to make this possible.[56]

Indeed, the legal context under which the Harihara head was returned to Cambodia was rather different from the legislation in place during the Protectorate, but no less complex in terms of supporting Cambodia. Objects in French public collections, such as the Harihara, are in principle inalienable. According to the French Heritage Code, 'assets constituting the collections of the museums of France belonging to a public entity are part of their public domain and are, as such, inalienable'.[57] Exceptions to de-accessioning must by the object of a decree, as was the case with the law adopted in 2020 for the return of cultural objects to Benin and Senegal.[58]

However, such a decree does not apply to loans, as they do not affect the state ownership of the object being lent. Indeed, loans are often used by museums to exchange objects to feature in temporary exhibitions, for example. Therefore, a

[56] Pierre Baptiste mentioned that, while provenance does not yet seem a major concern for the private sector with France not having ratified the 1995 International Institute for the Unification of Private Law (UNIDROIT) Convention which applies to private market actors, the Guimet Museum now only acquires an object if it can be sure of its lawful provenance, even before the watershed date of 1970 generally referred to in the heritage sector. However, for 90 per cent of the objects on sale, there are issues with regard to their provenance, so they are not purchased by the Museum, which means that they are not studied and disappear into private collections; interview with Pierre Baptiste, Conservator for South-East Asia, Guimet Museum, Paris, France, 28 April 2023.

[57] Translated by the author; see art L451-5 of the Code du Patrimoine (2004), with its original text stating that 'Les biens constituant les collections des musées de France appartenant à une personne publique font partie de leur domaine public et sont, à ce titre, inaliénables' and 'toute décision de déclassement d'un de ces biens ne peut être prise qu'après avis conforme d'une commission scientifique dont la composition et les modalités de fonctionnement sont fixées par décret'.

[58] Loi no 2020-1673 du 24 décembre 2020 relative à la restitution de biens culturels à la République du Bénin et à la République du Sénégal. Another example is the law adopted for the return of cultural objects looted during the Nazi era; see Loi no 2023-650 du 22 juillet 2023 relative à la restitution des biens culturels ayant fait l'objet de spoliations dans le contexte des persécutions antisémites perpétrées entre 1933 et 1945. It should be noted that in 2023, a new report, authored by Jean-Luc Martinez, contains a number of recommendations to advance the return of cultural currently in French collections, including in particular those that were obtained under duress; see 'Patrimoine partagé: universalité, restitutions et circulation des oeuvres d'art', 25 April 2023, www.culture.gouv.fr/fr/Espace-documentation/Rapports/Remise-du-rapport-Patrimoine-partage-universalite-restitutions-et-circulation-des-aeuvres-d-art-de-Jean-Luc-Martinez.

pragmatic approach led to a long-term tacitly renewable loan agreement combined with an exchange: the *'dépôts croisés'* ('crossed deposits') model,[59] which was primarily conceived by the French counterparts, to allow for the return of the Harihara head despite the barrier in the French legislation, which would not have allowed for a permanent return implying a transfer of ownership without the adoption of a decree allowing it.

The long-term loan is automatically renewed until one of the parties terminates the agreement. This format was not new, as France had used it before in cases where returns were legally 'impossible', such as in the case of the Korean imperial manuscripts.[60] However, the case of South Korea has been referred to as an 'imperfect compromise [that] satisfied neither side: The BnF [French National Library] is deprived of custody of items that have formed part of its collections for more than 140 years while technically, and perhaps uselessly, retaining formal legal title; South Korea, meanwhile, has physical custody of the archives while suffering the indignity of being denied ownership over its own national heritage'.[61] This is not unlike the Cambodian solution, although that one even went a step further, with Cambodia lending a piece to the Guimet Museum in exchange for the returned head.[62]

Therefore, the loan involved 'crossed deposits' in which two pieces were exchanged on a long-term basis. The parties indeed agreed that, in exchange for the long-term loan of the Harihara head, the Guimet Museum would receive, also on long-term loan, a piece identified in the collection of the Phnom Penh National Museum, namely the missing pedestal of a tenth-century Koh Ker statue that was in the collection of Guimet. In fact, many pedestals of statues had remained in Cambodia, and since the rest of their statues were missing, they were not considered to be of major value. Both lent pieces remain the property of the lending institution, with due references in the respective catalogues. While the nature of the exchange was an automatically (and tacitly) renewable loan which can be terminated, the lent pieces were nevertheless affixed to the rest of the statue, creating a sense of permanence in their reunification. Although this unification is technically reversible, it is not reversible simple process. Thus, while the parties agreed to a loan to facilitate the return, a loan back would not be a straightforward matter in practice. The French experts involved thus sought a solution that would

[59] The agreement, in French and Khmer, was eventually signed by the Director of the Guimet Museum at the time, Sophie Makariou, and the Director-General for Heritage at the Cambodian Minister of Culture and Fine Arts, Prak Sonara, in 2016. No one was present from the French Ministry of Culture.

[60] D Cox, '"Inalienable" Archives: Korean Royal Archives as French Property Under International Law' (2011) 18 *International Journal of Cultural Property* 409.

[61] ibid.

[62] However, it should be added that in the Cambodian case, the solution was found thanks to the close cooperation between both museums and the EFEO, and that those involved wanted to find a solution. In the South Korean case, most literature speaks of strong objections on the side of the French National Library – for example, Cox (n 60).

be beneficial for Cambodia, as well as feasible within the restrictive French legal context, but not without practical complexities.

Beyond material issues, the 'solution' identified that made it possible to overcome the legal barrier to de-accessioning objects in national collections was not without its administrative hurdles, as even loan agreements need to meet certain requirements, including regarding security. According to Baptiste:

> We have been able to work quite efficiently. In Cambodia and in France, we have been able to convince the relevant authorities within the ministry of culture that we could consider the possibility of crossed deposits.[63]

Despite the pragmatism of the approach, and the best intentions of those involved, there are of course limitations. As discussed, colonial legislation and agreements allowed for France to move the Harihara head to Paris. Arguably, the system of laws and agreements under which the French Protectorate took control over Cambodian heritage, not only with the removal of artefacts but also by controlling the way in which heritage was studied and perceived, remains influential. In France, the return and exchange of Cambodian objects is largely seen as a demonstration of goodwill, while in Cambodia, there is a sense that these objects were taken to France at a time when the country was powerless regarding their transfer and that they should be returned on a permanent basis rather than in the form of a loan, even if long term in nature.

This may explain why in Phnom Penh's National Museum, there is no mention of the Harihara statue having two separate inventory numbers – one in Cambodia and one in Paris – which would highlight that the head is still legally owned by the Guimet Museum. There is indeed a considerable difference between a voluntary loan and restitution based on a legal obligation. In this case, the Cambodian counterpart demonstrated pragmatism as well by accepting an object in return without the transfer of its ownership. Thus, they could voice what mattered to them most: the Harihara was back in Cambodia where it 'belonged', and from that moment onwards, legal ownership was considered a secondary matter.

V. The Spiritual and Living Value of the Harihara

Upon its return, the Harihara's head and body were joined together. 'It was a perfect fit', according to Chea Socheat, who sealed the pieces together.[64] The return was celebrated through a rather formal ceremony. About 200 French and Cambodian government officials, representatives of foreign governments, ambassadors and

[63] Interview with Pierre Baptiste, Conservator for South-East Asia, Guimet Museum, Paris, France, 28 April 2023. Baptiste added that the fact the museum is open on an internal courtyard means that the indoors climate is not controlled and that there are birds and insects moving around in the museum, which was difficult for the French administration to accept at first.

[64] See Vachon (n 43).

officials from the Guimet Museum attended the ceremony to re-attach the head at the National Museum in Phnom Penh. Buddhist monks were also involved. The ceremony was a combination of politics (speeches) and religion (a Buddhist ceremony), which is the typical ceremony organised by the museum when statues are moved or travel.[65] It is difficult to say whether these kinds of event are 'sufficiently spiritual' or not. Such ceremonies, in part due to being held in the formal setting of a museum, are very different from those held within community setting, such as that of the return of a 'living god' to Nepal, which involved exuberant worshipping.[66] Yet, the Buddhist chants and offerings offered to the statue hold important meaning, and in a country where religion has long been banned, this should not be underestimated.

In Buddhist culture, when a statue is made, an 'open-eye' ritual is conducted after which the God's spirit resides in the statue. From then on, one cannot touch the statue, even when it is broken.[67] Bringing the pieces of the Harihara back together was important for ensuring that the God could reside in the statue once again. A Cambodian Ministry of Culture spokesman said that joining the head to the statue felt 'like we are reconnecting the soul of our national heritage'.[68] At the ceremony in Cambodia's National Museum, Deputy Prime Minister Sok An added that '[a]ccording to our Khmer culture, the reunion is symbolic of prosperity'.[69]

The spiritual re-awakening of the Harihara demonstrates the disconnect between 'Western' conservation standards and living heritage values. This disconnect had been introduced by the French under the Protectorate, when heritage moved from being 'alive' and worshipped, to artefacts that were to be studied, preserved and stored in museums, away from those with a living practice attached to them. Whereas the living heritage values persist in Cambodia today, the museum community and the heritage professionals in Cambodia have fully adopted the French (and broader Western) view on the conceptualisation of heritage and its conservation methods. The religious ceremonies, such as that which was carried out upon the return of the Harihara head, tend to be insisted on by both the French and Cambodian experts, and demonstrate an effort to slowly bring living traditions back into the heritage field. Nevertheless, while there is a certain awareness of living heritage values, these are not (yet) integrated in the restoration and preservation practice.

[65] In May 2024, one of the authors attended a similar ceremony in Phnom Penh on the occasion of the upcoming travel of one of its statues. A group of Buddhist monks from the nearby monastery performed a short ritual and prayer, followed by a traditional dance, and a number of official speeches. It was then mentioned that this was the typical ceremony organised whenever a statue travelled to/from the National Museum.

[66] See ch 3 in this volume.

[67] C Hatton, 'Cambodia: Returning the Gods', *The Documentary Podcast*, 12 May 2022, www.bbc.co.uk/programmes/p0c67ghr.

[68] 'Hindu God Statue's Head Returns to Cambodia', *BBC News*, 21 January 2016, www.bbc.co.uk/news/world-asia-35378747#:~:text=The%20statue%2C%20a%20representation%20of,to%20the%20body%20on%20Thursday.

[69] ibid.

What also matters is that upon the return of the Harihara head, no particular efforts were made to involve the 'local community' of the Phnom Da and Angkor Borei area. Its participation did not seem to matter since the piece had been in the museum(s) for so long,[70] and no one from Angkor Borei or Phnom Da seems to have been invited to the ceremony where the head was returned and reunited with the body. Moreover, it appears that returning the statue to the small museum in Angkor Borei, which had recently been upgraded, has not yet been considered.[71] The idea to return the statue to the location from which it had first been removed never appeared to have been discussed among those involved in the return. The general feeling was that this was a major piece of Khmer art and thus belonged in the National Museum in the capital city.[72] The justification was a combination of the preservation and conservation conditions offered by the museum, safety (with less risk of looting), and its accessibility for a larger number of people.

Nevertheless, there is an awareness at the National Museum of the tradition of worshipping what remains of the statues in their original location.[73] Indeed, at the temples and caves in Phnom Da, incense and offerings are placed on the remaining base stones and fragments of sculptures, which appear to have been taken as a justification for not having to return missing pieces of statues to their location of origin (or even copies thereof).[74] At the same time, at the National Museum of Cambodia, religious worshipping takes place regularly.[75] For instance, when an object leaves the museum to partake in a temporary exhibition, this is accompanied with a religious ceremony to ask the spirits for their authorisation to send the statues out of the territory. The same applies to statues that return, which are then reconsecrated. The National Museum is also the place of certain rites linked to traditional festivals: every year – for example, a ceremony takes place for the feast of Pchum Ben, the Cambodian feast of the dead. These ceremonies are usually performed by the monks of the nearby Unalom temple. Beyond these extraordinary events, tributes are also paid to certain statues in the form of offerings of buds of jasmine. The guards of the museum thus invite visitors to place sticks of jasmine in front of the statues, which seems to be popular with tourists. However, these

[70] This was the view of those interviewed in the Cambodian capital for this chapter.

[71] The museum that was initially funded by the EU and opened in 1999, and was refurbished in 2020 with funds from the US government. See S Va, '$4.5 Million Given for Cambodia Heritage Work: Culture Minister', *Khmer Times*, 18 March 2020, www.khmertimeskh.com/702747/4-5-million-given-for-cambodia-heritage-work-culture-minister.

[72] Interview with Visoth Chhay, Director National Museum, Phnom Penh, August 2022.

[73] ibid.

[74] While some recent efforts were made to place copies of statues at Sambor Prei Kuk, Visoth Chhay, the Director of the National Museum, explained that this was undertaken out of a conservation interest, namely to see how the temples had looked with statues in them; as such, it was not because this was valuable to the community or to attract more tourism to those sites. However, in the case of Sambor Prei Kuk, there have been attempts to loot the copies, even if it were only cement copies. Thus, the argument that it is not sufficiently safe to move statues (originals) back to the temples seems to be true. Also, earlier, copies in sandstone had been placed at Banteay Srei. After a few rainy seasons, the sandstone had become weathered, and it had become difficult to distinguish the ancient temples and carvings from the statue copies. Also there, looters had tried to chop off the heads of the sandstone copies.

[75] See Biard (n 13).

latter practices may be more a matter of folklorisation than of the perpetuation of ancient practices.[76]

VI. Conclusion

This chapter has explored how the National Museum in Phnom Penh and the Guimet Museum in Paris came to an agreement of 'crossed deposits', through which they managed to reunite the pieces of two statues, one of which is now in Phnom Penh and another in Paris. The unification through the 'crossed deposits' model was conceived to address some historical 'errors' in which pieces of statues had ended up in separate collections and separate countries, whilst also serving as a practical solution to overcome the restrictive legal context in France. Indeed, in principle, cultural objects housed in French national collections are deemed inalienable, meaning that their de-accessioning is effectively barred unless a specific law is adopted to allow it, which has been the case with a few objects from Benin and Senegal that had been taken under duress, for example.

It is impossible to consider this case without the context of France's involvement with Cambodian heritage. Needless to say, France has and continues to play a major role in the protection and preservation of heritage. This has allowed for extremely detailed documentation, which makes provenance research relatively easy. At the same time, it has also imposed an approach to heritage that was quite far removed from the local culture at the time.

This case of return, which does not amount to restitution since it was achieved on the basis of tacitly renewable loans, could be criticised for the apparent continued French influence in the Cambodian heritage sector and lack of decolonisation within the French museum sector. Moreover, it shows how the 'French model' of heritage governance has been deeply and willingly integrated into the Cambodian context. Yet, that museified approach, especially when compared to the case of a similar context of heritage of spiritual importance in Nepal,[77] has a strong impact on the continuation of living traditions and on the relations between the wider Cambodian community and its heritage.

At the same time, the case also demonstrates the flexibility and innovativeness of both museums and their staff, and the extent to which personal efforts matter in legally complex situations. The 'crossed deposits' solution was an effective and swift way to resolve a matter that legally (and politically) would have been difficult and time-consuming to resolve otherwise. The strong historic bonds between the French and Cambodian institutions and their experts were essential in the elaboration of this solution. While it may not be an entirely satisfying for the Cambodian side, at least for now, it has brought integrity to the Harihara and access to it in Cambodia. Furthermore, it shows that with the necessary effort and creativity, but also compromise, returns are possible, despite legal restrictions.

[76] ibid.
[77] See ch 3 in this volume.

6

Returns and Reparations

*Namibian Objects Returned by Germany**

I. Introduction

Germany controlled South West Africa (present-day Namibia) from the end of the Berlin Conference in 1884/1885 – although missionaries had been present several decades earlier – until the Treaty of Versailles at the end of the First World War in 1919.[1] During this colonial rule, from 1893 onwards, the clashes between German troops and local communities increased and turned particularly violent against the Herero and Nama Indigenous peoples between 1904 and 1907.[2] These colonial wars resulted in the deaths of an estimated 65,000 Herero (up to 75 per cent of the population) and at least 10,000 Nama (about 50 per cent of the population). This period is now widely accepted as the twentieth century's first genocide.[3] Skulls and other human remains were taken back to Germany, but so too were many artefacts and historic records. Most of these found a home in German cultural and scientific institutions, including museums, universities and (research) hospitals. In recent years, Germany has developed guidelines for returning those collections and has made efforts to address its colonial past through a series of political decisions and parliamentary declarations, notably in the case of Namibia.[4]

This chapter focuses on the return by Germany of a series of objects belonging to Hendrik Witbooi (1830–1905), leader of the Nama people in their struggle against the German colonial power. Witbooi was born into a prominent Nama family in 1830. He was baptised and educated at a German Lutheran Mission and was fluent

* Interviews in Namibia were conducted by Kavenaa Tjiworo, Namibian heritage expert. Whenever interviews were conducted in local languages, the translation was provided by Kavenaa Tjiworo.

[1] For a short history of the colonisation, see C Nebe, 'Namibia: A Timeline of Germany's Brutal Colonial History', *DW*, 22 September 2021, www.dw.com/en/namibia-a-timeline-of-germanys-brutal-colonial-history/a-57729985.

[2] H Melber, 'Germany and Namibia: Negotiating Genocide' (2020) 22 *Journal of Genocide Research* 502.

[3] J Zimmerer and J Zeller, *Genocide in German South-West Africa: The Colonial War (1904–1908) in Namibia and its Aftermath* (London, Merlin Press, 2008).

[4] M Grutters and M Muntefering, 'Eine Lücke in unserem Gedächtnis', *Frankfurter Allgemeinen Zeitung*, 15 December 2018, www.bundesregierung.de/breg-de/service/archiv/eine-luecke-in-unserem-gedaechtnis-1561942; Zimmerer and Zeller (n 3).

in a number of European languages. Both his father and grandfather were chiefs of the */Khowese* people, a Nama clan. Hendrik Witbooi inherited that title upon the death of this father. As a chief, Witbooi led his people during their revolution against the German colonial rule from 1893 onwards. Like the Herero people, the Nama – under the leadership of Witbooi – staged a rebellion against the German rule. This uprising resulted in a tragic loss of life and saw many individuals detained in prison camps.[5]

In 1893, during an assault on Hornkranz in which Witbooi was captured by the Germans who also took control of his headquarters, the colonial troops confiscated his family Bible and his riding whip.[6] The taking of Hornkranz was a major turning point in the colonisation of Namibia which would not have been possible without subjugating Witbooi and his people.[7] Consequently, taking away two important symbols of the power of Witbooi turned these objects into symbols for the decades of colonial injustice that followed.

Later, valuable archives belonging to Witbooi were also taken. August Wulff, a German who resided in South West Africa between 1897 and 1913[8] and who would eventually sell his books and letters to a museum in Bremen, described the events as follows:

> When the Witbooi uprising broke out in 1904, the Witboois left the place Gibeon, where I was resident at the time, to gather in Riedmond/Mariental … The population of Gibeon, about 40 whites, spent months entirely on their own. For safety reasons, we burned down all the native villages at that time. Before that, however, we made a cursory search of the huts, and in the process, the two native books and letters came into my hands.[9]

Shortly afterwards, in late October 1905, Hendrik Witbooi died in a skirmish with the Germans near Keetmanshoop. The Nama eventually surrendered to Germany in 1908.

Nowadays, Witbooi is recognised as a national hero in Namibia, making the return of objects relating to him of high political importance. The return of his personal objects is also a clear example of the complexities of engaging communities in return processes that are led by states. Moreover, the case of Namibia's colonisation has been at the forefront of significant political developments in Germany in recent years, entrenching these returns in broader reconciliation discussions with Namibia.

[5] C Erichsen, 'German-Herero Conflict of 1904–07: African History', www.britannica.com/topic/German-Herero-conflict-of-1904-1907.

[6] H Forkl, *Von Kapstadt bis Windhuk. „Hottentotten" oder Khoisan? Die Rehabilitierung einer Völkergruppe* (Katalog zur gleichnamigen Ausstellung, Stuttgart, Linden-Museum) 89, 111.

[7] R Kößler, 'The Bible and the Whip: Entanglements Surrounding the Restitution of Looted Heirlooms' (2019) 12 *ABI Working Paper* 1.

[8] See the entry for the collection of August Engelbert Wulff in Museum-Digital, 'August Engelbert Wulff (1878-1952)', www.global.museum-digital.org/?t=people_to_people&id=172940.

[9] Übersee-Museum Bremen, 'Provenance Research and Repatriations', www.uebersee-museum.de/en/about-us/projekte-positionen/provenienzforschung-und-rueckfuehrungen.

II. Germany and Namibia's Wider Reconciliation Context

To understand the role that the returns of various Witbooi objects played in restoring relations between Germany and Namibia, and, in particular, with the Nama (and Herero) peoples, they must first be contextualised within Germany's gradual steps towards reconciliation with Namibia over the past few decades.

In 1995, during a visit from then German Chancellor Helmut Kohl to Namibia, the Herero demanded, for the first time, reparations for the atrocities committed by Germany during its rule over Namibia.[10] Harring describes how the Paramount Chief of the Herero marched to the German embassy in Windhoek with a petition demanding reparations. Kohl, however, refused to meet the traditional leader. According to Harring, the Herero drew inspiration from the reparations that Germany paid following the Second World War. They sought not only financial compensation but also the recognition that their peoples suffered genocide.

For nearly a decade after this event, nothing much happened until the 100-year commemoration ceremony of the genocide, which took place in 2004 at Waterberg in Namibia. There, Heidemarie Wieczorek-Zeul, the then German Minister for Economic Cooperation, recognised Germany's historical and moral responsibility for the genocide in a speech, stating that 'we Germans recognise our historical, political, moral and ethical responsibility and guilt'.[11] This was not yet a recognition of genocide, and also not a formal apology by the German government, but it was a major step forward. After all, for a long time, beyond its recognition of the Holocaust as genocide, Germany would not recognise other mass killings as genocide if they had happened prior to the adoption of the 1948 Genocide Convention. That position changed in 2015 when Germany recognised the Armenian genocide. Thereafter, German officials also started referring to genocide in the case of Namibia. However, the German government stressed that 'genocide' can also be defined in a 'non-legal' sense, meaning that, despite the change in terminology, there were not necessarily any legal consequences facing Germany if it would refer to the events in Namibia as a case of genocide.[12] Nevertheless, from this moment onwards, a process of negotiations with the Namibian government started, which was focused on addressing the consequences of the genocide against the Herero and Nama peoples.[13]

[10] SL Harring, 'German Reparations to the Herero Nation: An Assertion of Herero Nationhood in the Path of Namibian Development' (2002) 104 *West Virginia Law Review* 393.

[11] 'Germany Asks for Namibians' "Forgiveness"', *DW*, 14 August 2004, www.dw.com/en/germany-asks-for-namibians-forgiveness/a-1298060.

[12] K Brady, 'Germany Refers to Herero Massacre as Genocide', *DW*, 13 July 2016, www.dw.com/en/germany-officially-refers-to-herero-massacre-as-genocide/a-19396892. For more on the non-legal use of the term 'genocide' by Germany and the non-retroactive application of the Genocide Convention, see S Talmon, 'The Genocide in Namibia: Genocide in a Historical-Political or in a Legal Sense?', *German Practice in International Law* (*GPIL*), 23 September 2017, www.gpil.jura.uni-bonn.de/2017/09/genocide-namibia-genocide-historical-political-legal-sense.

[13] H Melber, 'Germany and Reparations: The Reconciliation Agreement with Namibia' (2022) 111 *The Round Table: The Commonwealth Journal of International Affairs* 475.

Of essential importance for this case on the return of Witbooi items is that neither the Herero nor the Nama peoples were involved in these negotiations. This stemmed from Namibian politics, which had since independence strongly focused on national unity and tried to steer away from highlighting the (colonial) suffering of one people over another.[14] This translated into a return process that was government-led, with only a very marginal role for the Witbooi family, the Nama people and the wider civil society.

According to German media:

> The German government will only apologize once the issue of reparations has been settled to its satisfaction. Namibian authorities have done nothing to include in the negotiations representatives of the Herero and Nama critical of the government, while on the other hand, they publicly flirted with a lawsuit against Germany. With due respect for justified frustration at the missing apology, a few representatives of the Herero and Nama have attracted attention by making unrealistic demands and directing verbal attacks at Germany.[15]

Despite tension between the governments of Germany and Namibia and the communities' representatives, negotiations went ahead, mainly as a state-to-state endeavour and, on 15 May 2021, Germany and Namibia issued a Joint Declaration announcing that they were embarking 'upon measures to heal the wounds of the past and create a lasting partnership for the future'.[16] In the Joint Declaration, Germany again acknowledged that it had committed genocide against the Herero and Nama peoples in South West Africa (now Namibia) between 1904 and 1908.[17] It also referred to the human remains, along with cultural artifacts, that had been 'removed unlawfully and shipped to Germany for pseudo-scientific racial purity and eugenic "research" without respect for human dignity, cultural and religious beliefs and practices'.[18]

The forward-looking statement is a rare example of a former colonial power and a former colony issuing a Joint Statement on a state-to-state level.[19] But in another statement made shortly after the Joint Declaration, the then German Foreign Minister Heiko Maas underlined that 'legal claims for compensation cannot be derived from it'.[20] Indeed, the Joint Declaration talks of reconciliation rather than 'reparations'. While it does not provide for compensation, it nevertheless allocates

[14] Kößler (n 7).

[15] D Pelz, 'No Reconciliation without an Apology', *DW*, 29 August 2018, www.dw.com/en/opinion-germany-must-apologize-for-its-genocide-in-namibia/a-45262584.

[16] Joint Declaration by the Federal Republic of Germany and the Republic of Namibia – 'United in Remembrance of our Colonial Past, United in our Will to Reconcile, United in our Vision of the Future' (15 May 2021), para 15.

[17] ibid. However, it should be noted that the term 'genocide' is here to be understood in a historical-political (rather than legal) sense; see S Talmon, 'Reconciliation without Reparation: The German-Namibian Joint Declaration on Our Colonial Past', *German Practice in International Law* (*GPIL*), 20 April 2023, www.gpil.jura.uni-bonn.de/2023/04/reconciliation-without-reparation-the-german-namibian-joint-declaration-on-our-colonial-past.

[18] Joint Declaration by the Federal Republic of Germany and the Republic of Namibia (n 16) para 7.

[19] ibid.

[20] Federal Foreign Office, 'Foreign Minister Maas on the Conclusion of Negotiations with Namibia', 28 May 2021, www.auswaertiges-amt.de/en/newsroom/news/-/2463598.

significant amounts of 'development aid' funding to Namibia for a total of €1.1 billion, as a grant to implement projects in various sectors, including land, natural resources, energy and education.[21] Out of this total amount, €1.05 billion will be 'dedicated to the reconstruction and development support programme for the benefit of the descendants of the particularly affected communities' and the outstanding €50 million will be 'dedicated to the projects on reconciliation, remembrance, research and education'.[22]

However, the measures agreed in the Joint Declaration were not immediately ratified by the German and Namibian Parliaments, with negotiations continuing until December 2024.[23] Despite the approval of few amendments to the initial draft approved in 2021, the Declaration remains unlikely to appease sentiments in Namibia, particularly as it includes a recognition by Namibia that the amount granted by Germany would 'settle all financial aspects of the issues relating to the past addressed in this Joint Declaration'.[24] Furthermore, the 'particularly affected communities' were not sufficiently represented during the negotiations, which has led the 'agreement' to be described as an act of tokenism.[25] While the Herero and Nama peoples had been demanding reparations from Germany for many years, they were largely left out of the government-led negotiations,[26] which led to Germany recognising only a moral duty to repair the past rather than a legal obligation entailing reparations, such as the payment of compensation. Thus, when the Namibian Parliament was to vote on the agreement reached with Germany, protesters who were led by the traditional authorities of the Herero and Nama peoples stormed the parliament building.[27] This sentiment of disenfranchisement was also present during the return process of some of Witbooi's heirlooms.

III. A First Return: The Witbooi Letters

In 1935, August Wulff sold two books with letters and other documents belonging to Hendrik Witbooi to the Übersee-Museum (Overseas Museum) in Bremen. Several decades earlier, in 1904, Wulff had retrieved these documents

[21] As Talmon notes, the amount to be allocated over 30 years is close to the amount that Germany allocated to Namibia in development aid over the past 30 years; see Talmon (n 17).

[22] Joint Declaration by the Federal Republic of Germany and the Republic of Namibia (n 16) para 18.

[23] H Melber, 'Germany's genocide in Namibia: deal between the two governments falls short of delivering justice', *The Conversation*, 7 January 2025, https://theconversation.com/germanys-genocide-in-namibia-deal-between-the-two-governments-falls-short-of-delivering-justice-246719.

[24] Joint Declaration by the Federal Republic of Germany and the Republic of Namibia (n 16) para 20.

[25] Melber (n 13).

[26] However, Talmon noted that: 'Community representatives were included in the Namibian delegation and also acted as advisers to the Namibian delegation leader who was himself Herero.' See Talmon (n 17).

[27] 'Hundreds Storm Namibia Parliament ahead of German Genocide Deal Vote', *Reuters*, 22 September 2021, www.reuters.com/world/africa/hundreds-storm-namibia-parliament-ahead-german-genocide-deal-vote-2021-09-21. See also 'Viewpoint: Why Germany's Namibia Genocide Apology is Not Enough', *BBC News*, 1 June 2021, www.bbc.com/news/world-africa-57306144.

from Witbooi's house before it was set on fire following the community's uprising.[28] The purchase price according to the entry register of the museum was 425 Reichsmarks (RM).[29] In 1994, Bettina von Briskorn, a history student at the time, uncovered the Witbooi documents in the archives of the museum in Bremen:

> There was this room, which was filled up with historical papers and historical files. The museum had no archive, there were no finding aids. I was going through all these papers trying to reconstruct: where did the objects come from? Who were the people who brought them to the museum? What were the circumstances under which they were collected?[30]

During her research, von Briskorn came across letters written by Witbooi, as well as a series of correspondence between the museum and August Wulff, which allowed her to link both sets of documents and identify the Witbooi letters. As the former director of the Namibia National Archives recounted:

> I have been involved in that [the return of the Witbooi letters] since 1978 because then I started to be interested in Hendrik Witbooi and specifically his letters. I started collecting all the letters that I could find that were mentioned somewhere.[31] The diary was in the archives since 1948 or 1949 … But the other two diaries or letter copy books of Hendrik Witbooi had been taken to Germany after 1904 by a private person who got hold of them, were sold to a museum in Bremen where they were forgotten … Then because Bremen has some special connection with Namibia and also because that museum, the Übersee-Museum in Bremen, has historically been advocating the return of stolen objects by its former Director Herbert Ganslmayr [director from 1937 to 1991] in the context of ICOM [International Council of Museums] and ICME [International Committee for Museums of Ethnography], very much advocating the return of [objects], while hardly anybody else in Germany did at the time. So they decided to return it to Namibia and first they made a microfilm, which they sent to Namibia … and then … they repatriated the originals that were actually handed over to president Nujoma on the occasion of a state visit in Germany in 1996. Since then, they are held by the National Archives. That was the first restitution from an official institution to Namibia.[32]

[28] H Gustafsson, *Namibia, Bremen und Deutschland, ein steiniger Weg zur Freundschaft* (Berlin, Aschenbeck und Holstein, 2003).

[29] Übersee-Museum Bremen (n 9). The Reichsmark was the currency in Germany at the time.

[30] Interview with Bettina von Briskorn, Provenance Researcher, Übersee-Museum Bremen, online, April 2023.

[31] It is important to note that the letters in Bremen are not the only ones in German collections. Additional letters that were written by Witbooi to the German army remain in the Adelhausermuseum Natur- und Völkerkunde in Freiburg im Breisgau. The Freiburg letters were digitised (it is assumed that digital copies are in Namibia and originals are still in Germany). For more information, see Freiburger Institutionen, 'Koloniale Sammlungen im Adelhausermuseum Natur- und Völkerkunde', www.freiburg-postkolonial.de/Seiten/Adelhauser-Duerrenberger.htm.

[32] Interview with Werner Hillebrecht, former head of the Namibian National Archives, Windhoek, July–September 2022.

Indeed, following the identification of the documents, the museum, together with the Bremen State Archives, restored the documents and created a microfilm, which was shared with Namibia.[33] At the time, immediately after the 'discovery', the idea was to translate the letters and use them to better understand the collection of the Übersee-Museum. However, interviews revealed that it was quickly decided not to retain possession of the records for Bremen only. Instead, Viola König, the then Director of the museum, and Peter Junge, its then head of the Africa collection, decided that the original documents were to be returned to Namibia.[34] The staff of the museum, as well as the authorities in Bremen at the time, were all very supportive of the return of these documents, and the return itself proceeded in a fast and efficient manner.[35]

Given that the letters had been taken and brought to Germany nearly a century ago, the UNESCO Convention was not applicable to the return process as it is not retroactive. Furthermore, while Germany ratified the Convention in 2007, Namibia has not yet ratified it, despite African states having been instrumental in the adoption of the Convention. At the domestic level, it is unlikely that there was a law that prohibited the export of those objects at the time they left the territory of present-day Namibia.[36] In any case, recourse to local laws were not required given that German authorities were in favour of the return and that German law did not preclude such return: state governments may allow museums to return objects within their collections, provided that there are no budgetary objections.[37]

In this particular case, the personal interest of the people involved in Bremen, combined with an enabling legal context and pre-existing relations between Bremen and Namibia, seem to have stimulated a quick return.[38] Therefore, in 1996, although the then German Chancellor Helmut Kohl had recently refused to meet the Herero leaders in Namibia, the Übersee-Museum in Bremen had already decided to return letters from national hero Hendrik Witbooi. The handover happened on 20 June 1996 at Bremen City Hall. There, on the occasion of a state visit to Bremen by the then Namibian President Dr Sam Nujoma, the Witbooi letters were handed over and subsequently brought to the Namibian

[33] Gustafsson (n 28).

[34] Übersee-Museum Bremen (n 9).

[35] Interview with Bettina von Briskorn, Provenance Researcher, Übersee-Museum Bremen, online, April 2023.

[36] One of the earliest laws identified was the Natural and Historical Monuments, Relics and Antiques Ordinance 13 of 1948 (as amended) in respect of Southwest Africa, repealed by the National Monuments Act 28 of 1969 and itself repealed by the Namibia's Heritage Act, which was adopted in 2004 (Act 27 of 2004); its Archives Act was adopted in 1992.

[37] R Peters, 'Dealing with Collections from Colonial Contexts: Current Developments in Germany' (2022) 8 *Santander Art and Culture Law Review* 371. See also ch 3 in this volume regarding the case concerning Germany and Nepal.

[38] Interview with Bettina von Briskorn, Provenance Researcher, Übersee-Museum Bremen, online, April 2023.

National Archives.[39] While handing over the letters in 1996, Dr Henning Scherf, then Mayor and President of the Bremen Senate, stated:

> The return of these papers is an expression of our deep respect for the uncompromising struggle for the freedom of the people of Namibia and for their leaders. May these documents be a contribution to research into Namibian history.[40]

The Witbooi family, and in particular Hendrik's great-grandson, was informed of the return of the letters 'at an early stage'.[41] However, it appears that the return was not particularly celebrated in Namibia. As mentioned by the former head of the Namibian National Archives, 'there was a ceremony of handing the originals over to the President that was in Bremen, in Germany. But I think nothing in Namibia except then, there was a book launch of the publications and the translations [in Namibia]'.[42] Sources in Namibia remember mostly that the letters were studied and published, with the former director of the Namibian National Archives saying 'I think the biggest impact is the translations and the publications that made them widely known. Otherwise there have been occasional exhibitions with the original, the latest one being I think … two years ago in 2020 in the context of heritage week'.[43]

In Germany, there was a lot of attention given to this official visit by Namibia's President, but the handover of the Witbooi letters was overshadowed by other news relating to the visit.[44] This is also clear when looking at the speech by Dr Henning Scherf at the official dinner for the state visit of President Nujoma, when the letters were handed over. The speech first covered the past cooperation between both entities and joined interests in shipping and fisheries, before mentioning the Witbooi letters and the handover in the concluding paragraphs.[45]

Perhaps the most interesting part of this first return is the ease of the process. Bettina von Briskorn recalled that it seemed quite logical for all involved that the letters should be returned and that a rather smooth process followed, aided by a supportive state government. The current climate in which people tend to refer to political complexities and public opinion seemed completely absent from the process of returning the Witbooi letters. This probably speaks to a time when there was also less political and media attention on the return of cultural objects, allowing for a relatively low-key and 'easy' process which proved relatively uncontroversial.

[39] Gustafsson (n 28).

[40] Translated by the author. The original text is: 'Die Rückgabe dieser Papiere ist der Ausdruck unseres tiefen Respekts vor dem kompromisslosen Kampf für die Freiheit der Menschen in Namibia und vor ihren Führungskräften. Mögen diese Dokumente ein Beitrag für die Erforschung der namibischen Geschichte sein.' The full speech can be found in Gustafsson (n 28) 518–20.

[41] Interview with Werner Hillebrecht, former head of the Namibian National Archives, Windhoek, July–September 2022.

[42] ibid.

[43] ibid.

[44] Interview with Bettina von Briskorn, Provenance Researcher, Übersee-Museum Bremen, online, April 2023.

[45] Gustafsson (n 28).

IV. A Second Return: The Witbooi Bible and Whip

The second set of objects related to Witbooi that were returned took place in a different context. Indeed, efforts had been made to restore relations between both countries. While negotiations were ongoing in terms of addressing the aftermath of the genocide, Germany had returned skulls from the Herero and Nama people to the Namibian government, first in 2011 and then again in 2014 and 2018.[46] These returns were highly complex and politicised. They were first part of a public viewing at the Parliament Garden in Windhoek, during which then Namibian President Hifikepunye Pohamba announced his interest in adding the remains to the Independence Memorial Museum. Although communities and descendants indicated a preference for carrying out traditional rituals and burying the remains, they have thus far been kept in their boxes in a museum depot at the National Museum of Namibia in Windhoek.[47] The repatriation of these human remains was important not only because they were the first remains being returned from German institutions to Namibia, but also because they were part of a broader political process addressing past events. It was followed with the return in 2019 of more objects relating to Witbooi, namely the Bible and whip that had belonged to him, a process which was vastly different from the 1996 return of Witbooi's letters.

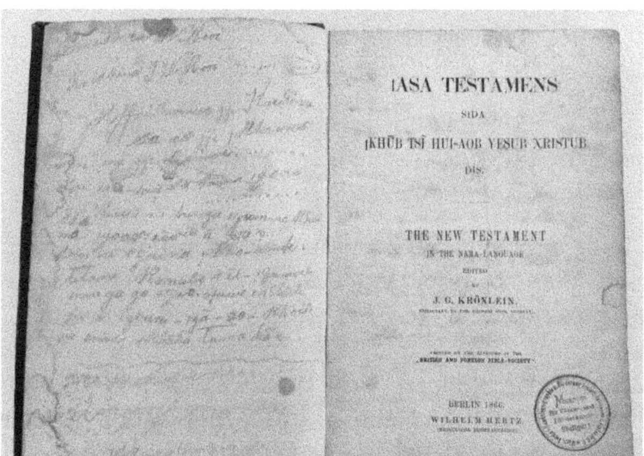

Figure 6.1 Witbooi Bible. © National Archives of Namibia (2022)

[46] AL Bandle, A Chechi, and M Renold, '20 Herero and Nama Skulls – Namibia and Charité Universitätsmedizin Berlin, Germany', *ArThemis Art-Law Centre, University of Geneva*, www.plone.unige.ch/art-adr/cases-affaires/20-skulls-of-colonial-victims-2013-namibia-and-charite-universitatsmedizin-berlin.

[47] VA Shigwedha, 'The Homecoming of Ovaherero and Nama Skulls: Overriding Politics and Injustices' (2018) 4 *Human Remains and Violence: An Interdisciplinary Journal* 67; R Kößler, 'The Restitution of Human Remains and Artefacts: Reflecting on Namibian-German Experiences', 2021, www.kulturgutverluste.de/sites/default/files/2023-04/2021-12-21_HK_Blogbeitrag_Reinhart_Kossler.pdf; 'Viewpoint' (n 27).

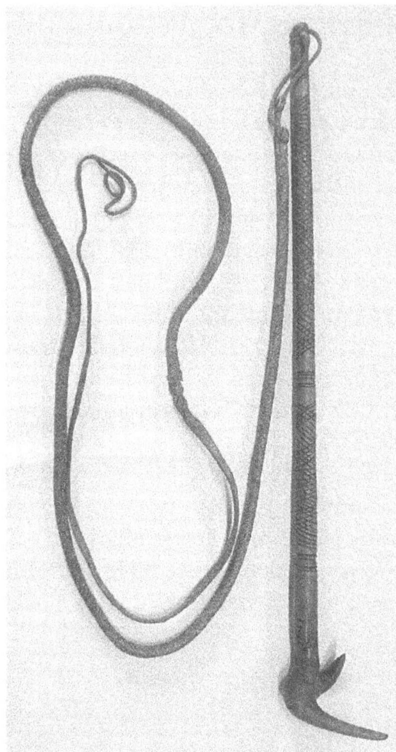

Figure 6.2 Witbooi whip. © Kavenaa Tjiworo (2022)

As Witbooi's bible and whip were important symbols of his power as leader of the Nama people, their return became a highlight of the Namibia-Initiative of the Ministry of Science, Research and Art of Baden-Württemberg,[48] a follow-up to the Engaging the Past, Sharing the Future initiative of the Linden Museum, an ethnographic museum in Stuttgart.[49] The latter is a joint initiative of Germany and Namibia, initiated in 2016, which aims at closer cooperation between researchers in both countries. It is considered an integral part of provenance and restitution initiatives by the Director of the museum:

[48] For more on the Namibia Initiative, see Ministerium für Wissenschaft, Forschung und Kunst Baden-Württemberg, 'Aufarbeitung kolonialen Erbes mit der Namibia-Initiative', www.mwk.baden-wuerttemberg.de/de/kunst-kultur/namibia-initiative.

[49] For more on the project, see Linden Museum Stuttgart Collections Online, 'With Namibia: Engaging the Past, Sharing the Future', www.sammlung-digital.lindenmuseum.de/en/topic/with-namibia-engaging-the-past-sharing-the-future_3181.

> The ethnographic museums in Germany – or some ethnographic museums – are really in the forefront of a changing process. Now for many years, with a new generation of directors, with civil society movements like Black Lives Matter, and also with the Humboldt Forum discussion on what an ethnographic museum should look like in Berlin. And so, restitution for us is one part of this new or changing process of decolonisation, of democratisation of the museums. It is about really sharing authority … So, we have this colonial heir (inheritance). And we think that from this responsibility arises an ethical responsibility. The aim is to create a new partnership with the Global South, with other parts of the world. Restitution is for us one part of this bigger movement.[50]

The Bible that was returned belonged to the Witbooi family and contains handwritten comments by Hendrik Witbooi and other relatives. After having been taken by German colonial troops in 1893, the Bible ended up at the Linden Museum in Stuttgart in 1902, when it was handed to the museum by a German colonial officer called Wassmannsdorf, at the same time as a whip that had also belonged to Witbooi. Despite in-depth provenance research conducted by the museum's staff, the whereabouts of the objects between 1893 and 1902 remain unclear.[51] Nevertheless, a report on provenance research conducted by the Linden Museum indicates that the acquisition had been listed as 'objects of German spoils of war on the occasion of the storming of Hendrik Witbooi's seat of government, Hornkranz, in 1893',[52] thus clearly indicating the circumstances under which these objects had been taken. The return of both objects to Namibia, more than a century later, was meant 'to make a contribution towards healing the wounds of colonial injustice, as far as this is possible today. At the same time, the restitution was intended to mark the beginning of more long-term contacts and exchanges in the realm of science and the arts'.[53]

A. The Return Process: A Strong Moral Case Based on Clear Provenance

Having been in Stuttgart since 1902, Witbooi's Bible and whip had not received much public attention until they became part of an exhibition in 2007.[54] Like the initial entry in the museum's collection, the exhibition catalogue of the 2007 exhibition at the Linden Museum also explicitly referred to 'booty' taken in the raid at

[50] Interview with Ines de Castro, Director of the Linden Museum Stuttgart, online, April 2023.
[51] G Grimme, 'Discomforting Heritage: Dealing with Colonial-Era Objects in Ethnological Museums. Final Report', 2018, www.uni-tuebingen.de/en/77025.
[52] Translated by the author; the original text is 'Deutsche Kriegsbeute-Stücke anlässlich der Erstürmung von Hendrik Witboois Regierungssitz Hornkranz 1893' in Grimme (ibid) 28.
[53] Kößler (n 7).
[54] ibid.

Hornkranz, leaving little doubt that these objects had been obtained forcefully.[55] At the time of the raid, efforts were being undertaken at the international level to prohibit plunder under the laws of war. However, it would only be in 1899, with the adoption of the Regulations annexed to the Convention on the Laws and Customs of War on Land (The Hague Regulations), that plunder would become prohibited under international law. It was then accepted that these rules were only applicable to interstate wars and not for hostilities taking place in a colonial context.[56] Indeed, the practice of European troops at the time that the Bible and whip were taken indicates that the destruction and plunder of cultural heritage continued unabated in colonial contexts overseas.

Despite the absence of any clear legal obligation to return the objects, it was evident how and when these objects had been taken, and whom they had belonged to. Such a clear provenance thus gave rise to a strong moral case for retuning these objects within the enabling German legal framework.[57] Nevertheless, the first efforts to seek the return of the Bible and whip were unsuccessful. First, following the 2007 exhibition, the German-Swiss Committee of the Archives of Anti-colonial Resistance and Liberation Struggle programme in Namibia initiated efforts to repatriate these objects to Namibia.[58] It was followed by 'a minor interpellation (*Kleine Anfrage*) by a deputy of the Green Party in the state parliament (*Landtag*) of Baden-Württemberg'.[59] Reinhard Kössler, a researcher who was involved in various capacities in these early efforts, reports that the time was 'not yet ripe'.[60]

The process that would ultimately prove successful was initiated in 2013. The Namibian government approached the region of Baden-Württemberg through its ambassador in Berlin and officially requested the return of the Bible. According to the Director of the Linden Museum, the decision to return the whip alongside the Bible was taken afterwards. It had seemed logical to return the two objects together since they were both related to Witbooi, taken at the same time, and the provenance was clear with regard to both objects.[61] After negotiations with Namibia and the approval of the governing bodies of the Linden Museum, the State of Baden-Württemberg[62] and the city of Stuttgart, the objects were eventually

[55] Forkl (n 6).

[56] Regulations Respecting the Laws and Customs of War on Land, annexed to the Hague Convention (II) of 1899 and (IV) of 1907 (Hague Regulations), art 23(g).

[57] See also a video on the return: Kashindi Ausiku, 'Gibeon – The Official Return of Kaptein Hendrik Witbooi's Bible and Whip from Germany', *YouTube*, 2019, www.youtube.com/watch?v=Td4-v-3RQXw.

[58] EN Namhila, 'Archives of Anti-Colonial Resistance and the Liberation Struggle (AACRLS): An Integrated Programme to Fill the Colonial Gaps in the Archival Record of Namibia' (2015) 4 *Journal for Studies in Humanities and Social Sciences* 168.

[59] Kößler (n 7).

[60] ibid.

[61] Interview with Ines de Castro, Director of the Linden Museum Stuttgart, online, April 2023.

[62] 'Baden-Württemberg bringt Witbooi-Bibel und Peitsche zurück nach Namibia', 22 February 2019, www.baden-wuerttemberg.de/de/service/presse/pressemitteilung/pid/baden-wuerttemberg-bringt-witbooi-bibel-und-peitsche-zurueck-nach-namibia-1; 'Witbooi-Bibel und Peitsche an Namibia übergeben', 28 February 2019, www.baden-wuerttemberg.de/de/service/presse/pressemitteilung/pid/witbooi-bibel-und-peitsche-an-namibia-uebergeben.

returned to Namibia in 2019.[63] Prior to the return to Namibia, there was a final exhibition organised at the Linden Museum to allow the public to 'say goodbye' to the objects.[64]

In contrast to the 1996 return process, this time the official handover took place in Windhoek and also in Gibeon, the Witbooi family's hometown. Gibeon is a village in the south of Namibia, which received its name from Kido Witbooi, the first Captain of the */Khowese*. Today, Gibeon is still the home to the Witbooi clan. The village is rich in historical sites, including colonial buildings, churches and the remains of the former home of Hendrik Witbooi.

As Ines de Castro, Director of the Linden Museum, recalled enthusiastically:

> The Namibian side organised a tour on the way to Gibeon. We stopped in several communities. So many people had the possibility to see the Bible and whip before the handover and a curator from the National Museum was with me and we both presented it. And it was incredible to see what interest was there for the objects and what importance your objects can have. Sometimes we forget that, and I think that objects are so much loaded with identity, with cultural feelings, with emotions. … Even when we arrived with the plane at six in the morning in Windhoek, there were all these Nama people waiting for us and greeting us and with music and everything. So it was, for me, a very emotional trip that I didn't expect … It was a party, it was emotion, and let's build bridges for the future.[65]

The return ceremony took place on 28 February 2019 in Gibeon. Along with the Director of the Linden Museum, Theresia Bauer who was Baden-Württemberg's Minister of Science, Research and the Arts, and numerous other officials, academics and the press were also present. In Namibia, they were received by the then President of the Republic, Hage Geingob, and the then Minister of Education, Arts and Culture, Katrina Hanse-Himarwa.

Significant efforts were made to bring the objects to Gibeon first, with the return ceremonies attracting large crowds, even in the early morning hours when the plane from Germany touched down in Windhoek.[66] The Nama community, as well as Witbooi descendants, were already present, chanting religious hymns, at the airport, where Namibia's Minister of Education, Arts and Culture lifted the book up to the Nama and Witbooi family representatives, saying 'this is your book. This is our heritage. Finally, and at last, it's back home'.[67]

[63] Peters (n 37).

[64] For a view of the final exhibition, see Linden Museum Stuttgart Collections Online (n 49). For media coverage on the final exhibition, see the short clip from Regio TV, 'Witbooi-Bibel wird nochmal ausgestellt', 12 December 2018, www.regio-tv.de/mediathek/video/witbooi-bibel-wird-nochmal-ausgestellt.

[65] Interview with Ines de Castro, Director of the Linden Museum Stuttgart, online, April 2023.

[66] For comprehensive footage on the return, see the video by A Dieden, 'Stolen Soul. Africa's Looted Art', *DW*, 2020, www.dw.com/en/stolen-soul-africas-looted-art/video-54792198, starting from 16:20 for the event at the airport in Windhoek and from 32:00 for the visit to Gibeon.

[67] ibid, from 16:40.

According to the Director of Namibia's National Museum, 'because of the significance of the objects, the Republic of Namibia decided to make it a national event and more than 1,500 people attended the event in Gibeon',[68] emphasising the local importance and efforts made to include the population of Witbooi's hometown. According to a descendant of Witbooi:

> [T]here were announcements made and the people were made aware and that was a great day … it [the Bible and whip] was not only brought straight to Gibeon but along the B1 road, people that could have access to go and see them and then have that feeling. So, but now for Gibeon people they were invited, and they turned up in large numbers to come and see it.[69]

Afterwards, the Bible was brought to Namibia's National Archive, and the whip was stored in the National Museum, in part because these institutions allow for the best preservation conditions in the country. Both are kept in storage.

B. The Involvement of the Nama Community

Despite the apparent engagement with the community in this second return process, the reality is far more convoluted. The relationship with the Nama community and Witbooi descendants throughout the process illustrates complexities similar to those that arose between the government and the communities during the negotiations on the 'Reconciliation Agreement' with Germany. The process also demonstrates how the return of heritage fits within national politics in post-colonial states.[70] While the return of the Witbooi objects was discussed, Germany and Namibia were negotiating the Reconciliation Agreement at a higher political level. The Herero and Nama communities felt strongly that they were left out of Namibia's negotiations with Germany over their reconciliation, although they had been the primary victims of the colonial rule. Moreover:

> The bible and the whip, then, had been looted under circumstances in which – at least in the eyes of Witbooi (*/Khowesen*) – colonial statehood not only did not exist. What is more, Hendrik Witbooi and his followers resisted this fledgling construction, with all their might and energy … It is therefore hard to see how the looted and now restituted heirlooms could be seen as the property of the Namibian state, which is inevitably the successor of the colonial state.[71]

While it was decided that the objects should be officially handed back over to Namibia in Gibeon, the homestead of the Witbooi clan, it seems that the ceremony

[68] Interview with Nzila Marina Mubusisi, Director of the National Museum of Namibia, Windhoek, July–September 2022.

[69] Interview with Salomon J Witbooi, descendant of H Witbooi, Gibeon, July–September 2022.

[70] For a detailed description of Namibia's post-colonial politics of developing a national narrative and the role of the return of human remains and 'national' treasures within that, see Kößler (n 7).

[71] ibid.

was strongly felt to be an event between the German and Namibian authorities, with little or no role for the Witbooi descendants or for the Nama people. During the ceremony, they were reduced to the status of bystanders observing the celebrations. Nevertheless, the turnout of local onlookers along the trajectory from Windhoek to Gibeon was significant. Moreover, Namibia's government wanted the Bible and whip to be exhibited in the National Archives after the official handover. According to Nzila Marina Mubusisi, the Director of the National Museum of Namibia:

> The communities were involved and … we had some technical committee meetings before we took part in the planning on how the object should be repatriated. The ministry itself did not nominate who should be in the committee meeting. What happened is that the Minister of Education then wrote to the traditional authority [of the Nama] to request for the representations of the traditional authority that there are these objects that are to be repatriated and then the traditional authority gave a nomination of the people who have to take part in the planning of the repatriation. The technical committee together with the ministry's technical team discussed the repatriation and afterward the community at large was informed through national radio and newspapers to create an awareness of the discourse taking place.[72]

On the one hand, it is clear that this interpretation of involvement is rather limited and largely restricted to informing rather than engaging. On the other hand, information obtained from the Linden Museum indicates that there were talks with the Witbooi family in 2018, when the family accepted a return of the objects to the Namibian State, which was confirmed by descendant Salomon Witbooi.[73] Yet, it seems that despite lengthy negotiations between Germany and Namibia, not all stakeholders in Namibia were pleased with the final decision. Kößler reported that:

> Shortly before the envisaged date, obstacles emerged on account of competing claims by the Namibian state on the one hand and the Witbooi community on the other. The Namibian government claimed ownership on account of Hendrik Witbooi's status as a national hero, whereas his descendants insisted that the Bible and the whip were family heirlooms and Namibia had not existed as a territory at the time of the raid in 1893. A working accord was eventually reached, and the return ceremony went ahead at the Witbooi traditional capital of Gibeon in southern Namibia.[74]

The Nama Traditional Leaders Association (NTLA) even wanted to take legal action to stop the return, but the Constitutional Court of Baden-Württemberg concluded that it did not have jurisdiction over the case, which was considered a matter for Namibia's domestic affairs.[75] Clearly, various interests were at play.

[72] Interview with Nzila Marina Mubusisi, Director of the National Museum of Namibia, Gibeon, July–September 2022.

[73] Interview with Salomon J Witbooi, descendant of H Witbooi, Gibeon, July–September 2022.

[74] R Kößler, 'Hendrik Witbooi's Bible', www.africasacountry.com/2019/09/hendrik-witboois-bible-and-the-humboldt-forum.

[75] R Allgöwer, 'Gericht macht den Weg frei: Land kann Witbooi-Bibel zurückgeben' zurückgeben', *Stuttgarter Nachrichten*, 21 February 2019, www.stuttgarter-nachrichten.de/inhalt.gericht-macht-den-weg-frei-land-kann-witbooi-bibel-zurueckgeben.9d9fc8be-e920-4413-abed-21529e61de7c.html.

For instance, according to the NTLA's General Secretary Lazarus Kairabeb: 'The items belong to an individual. If it was part of the household estate, it should have ended in the hands of the church or the family, and the family would have decided what to do with it.'[76] However, as indicated above, a descendant of Witbooi confirmed that the family agreed to have the Bible and whip taken to Windhoek because they felt there was no safe place to keep them in Gibeon,[77] which was also confirmed by the Linden Museum.

Thus, this case highlighted a lack of common voice within a given community, due to a variety of interests. There is no doubt that the National Museum tried to involve 'a local community' through a committee, but this was perhaps only a limited subsection of interested parties. At the same time, public statements by the NTLA reveal that it was not pleased with the outcome of the negotiations, while other members of 'the community' seemed to largely agree with the decision that was taken. On the German side, it also appears to be understood that relations with the community (and family in this case) are among the more complex aspects of a return process, especially when it is to be integrated into state-to-state negotiations. As Ines de Castro further expressed:

> As you know, the very difficult issue is who to restitute to, who should a restitution be made to. I always say that this was like a first try. So, I am very aware that we are maybe doing a lot of mistakes with the restitution process as well, but that we have to try how to do this.[78]

This is perhaps even more complex in this particular case, with objects having belonged to a national hero, and which are, thus, considered as belonging to the nation. But when does an individual stop being an individual and when can the nation claim his belongings? Namibian former Minister of Education, Arts and Culture Katrina Hanse-Hirmawa insisted on the national character of the returns, saying that 'this is a State to State hand-over' to 'the Government and the people of Namibia'.[79] The nationalisation of Witbooi's legacy can be further observed in the decision to inscribe the Witbooi letters on UNESCO's Memory of the World Register.[80] And while treating these objects as national treasures may seem logical from the broader Namibian perspective, it is also apparent that not all interest groups within the hero's descendant family and the Nama community agreed.

[76] D Pelz, 'Namibia: Dispute over Return of the Witbooi Bible', *DW*, 27 February 2019, www.dw.com/en/namibia-dispute-over-return-of-the-witbooi-bible/a-47712784.

[77] Interview with Salomon J Witbooi, descendant of H Witbooi, Gibeon, July–September 2022.

[78] Interview with Ines de Castro, Director, Linden Museum Stuttgart, online, April 2023.

[79] Kößler (n 7) 3–6, quoting Republic of Namibia, Ministry of Education, Arts and Culture press statement by Minister Katrina Hanse-Hirmawa on the return of Witbooi Bible and whip by the Linden Museum, City Council of Stuttgart and the State of Baden-Württemberg in Windhoek, 14 February 2019.

[80] The letters and journals were inscribed onto UNESCO's Memory of the World List in 2005; see www.webarchive.unesco.org/web/20220331145910/http://www.unesco.org/new/en/communication-and-information/memory-of-the-world/register/access-by-region-and-country/na.

C. The Meaning of the Return: Local and State Perspectives

Speaking to a variety of people living in and around Gibeon, it is clear that much importance is attached to the return of the Witbooi objects. It is likely that the public display and the handover ceremony in Gibeon contributed to the local awareness of these returns, and the association with their own history. It is of course difficult to know with any certainty, but it seems unlikely that most people were aware of these objects' whereabouts in Germany beforehand. Hence, the public return surely contributed to this broad awareness.

Many remarks made by local inhabitants highlight the importance of the return and feelings of happiness:

> It's important, it's our history and it's important for the children growing up, they will also get to know what transpired here.
>
> We might seem to be ignorant about that, but we really care, and we really appreciate that the objects were returned to our country because it gives us pride to be associated with something like that.
>
> We felt really happy when the bible and the whip came back because something that belonged to us that was looted by the German administration during the German colonial era but when they came back, we were happy … when they came back to Namibia it was decided that they be stored/kept at the museum, but if we are to have a storage place here like a museum, we would want them to come back here to be kept here and they only went there because we do not have a storage place or a museum.[81]

As with some other return cases, one of the reasons for the Witbooi objects not being stored in Gibeon is indeed that there is no 'appropriate' place to keep them or to make them accessible. The lack of such a facility at the time of the return led the celebration of the return of the Bible and whip to take place in an open area, with all the necessary measures to protect the objects. The area selected was in close proximity to where Hendrik Witbooi used to live.

According to the Witbooi family, plans are currently underway to build a museum in Gibeon, where, once ready, the Witbooi objects might be kept and where his story may be told.[82] The community has identified different buildings that have historical significance and that could be turned into a museum – one is an old postal building, another a former prison. The idea of a museum in Gibeon

[81] All quotes are from fieldwork interviews with community members in Gibeon in July–September 2022.

[82] The idea of a Witbooi museum in Gibeon was already mentioned in the 2005–06 Annual Report of the Museums Association of Namibia; see www.museums.com.na/images/Annual_Report_05-06.pdf. Back in 2005, on the occasion of the centenary of the death of Witbooi, an exhibition was organised in Gibeon, through the Gibeon Unemployed Youth Forum, of which Valencia Karigus was the representative. One of the objectives of the exhibitions was 'to promote the idea of eventually creating a permanent "Hendrik Witbooi Museum" and served as an "appetiser" that suggests what might be possible if funding could be secured to enable Gibeon to renovate or build a suitable building' (Annual Report at 34).

arose shortly after the Witbooi letters had been returned to Namibia. Despite the general enthusiasm for the return, Salomon J Witbooi reflected on it more critically:

> It really left us with mixed feelings because it should not have actually been like that, those things were supposed to be kept here in the hands of our ancestors and the elders and they should have told us that these are the objects that belong to your ancestors. But now these things were looted and taken away … But at the end, we are glad that it could be returned to Namibia and not only to Namibia but that our elders could receive them with their own hands and that they could touch it because most of the elders have already gone to rest but now those who are still alive so we were really very much glad that they could see and us the younger generation that we could also see it and witness the return of these objects.[83]

In Windhoek, a generally positive message resounds, with the Director of the National Museum of Namibia describing the return as follows:

> The returns and restitutions are important because a nation when you know that some of your cultural objects are somewhere [out] there, you don't feel that you are independent, you feel that the people who have stolen from you are continuing stealing from you because those objects have got knowledge which the Namibian community have to benefit from so if we continue keeping those objects outside Namibia, some of those objects are very rare objects, they are very rare cultural material which the Namibian community are not benefiting from which is why we really the cultural objects or the material culture objects of Namibian origin to be repatriated or to be restituted back to Namibia for the local community also to benefit from the knowledge and from the history thereof.[84]

On the German side, the general feeling is also one of a positive achievement, with the Director of the Linden Museum noting her surprise by the general sense of celebration during the return and the absence of openly critical voices, which had been present earlier in the process:

> This was for me a learning process and a very special process and also really seeing all the reactions of the people, young or old. That was for me very important. It showed me that we should continue with this because it is a heavy decision also for a museum director. It is not an easy decision.[85]

The Director hereby highlighted the predominant spirit that was found among most people interviewed on this case – it was not a perfect process and there were difficult decisions to be made along the way, but, overall, all interested parties were satisfied with the outcome. It also demonstrates that while there are always lessons to be learned, the process may be as important as the outcome. The official

[83] Interview with Salomon J Witbooi, descendant of H Witbooi, Gibeon, July–September 2022.

[84] Interview with Nzila Marina Mubusisi, Director of the National Museum of Namibia, Windhoek, July–September 2022.

[85] Interview with Ines de Castro, Director, Linden Museum Stuttgart, online, April 2023.

speeches at the time of the return reflect a similar mindset – that is, that this return is an important step in enhancing relations between both countries:

> At the same time, the restitution of these objects is for us the beginning of a reappraisal of German-Namibian colonial history … Together with our Namibian partners we want to reappraise our colonial history. Therefore, this restitution is not only a view into the past for us, but also the path to a common future: with the Namibia Initiative, we connect our archives, museums and universities through joint projects.[86]

As already mentioned, these returns do fit within a broader context of reconciliation between Germany and Namibia. It is undeniable that Namibia's requests to return Witbooi's Bible and whip also played a role in the adoption of new instruments to support German museums in decolonising their collections. In May 2018, the German Museums Association published its Guidelines for the Care of Collections from Colonial Contexts, which offer recommendations for dealing with collections issued from colonial contexts.[87] In addition to this practical guidance emanating from the museum sector, the German Federal Government, the federal States (Länder), and the German municipal organisations adopted Framework Principles for Dealing with Collections from Colonial Contexts in 2019.[88] This followed a reckoning by the governing political parties a year earlier that 'there is no future without remembrance'[89] and that 'the basic democratic consensus in Germany includes coming to terms with the Nazi regime, the communist era, as well as Germany's colonial history'.[90]

These Framework Principles lay a strong foundation for returns based on ethical (and political) grounds rather than legal ones. Indeed, they affirm that 'identifying cultural objects from colonial contexts which were appropriated in a way which is no longer legally and/or ethically justifiable and enabling their return is a moral and ethical obligation and an important political task', thus pushing for a proactive approach which does not rest on requests from countries or communities of origin.[91] They also point to the requirement to act in a transparent manner and to publish information about collections, which goes hand in hand with provenance

[86] T Bauer, Minister of Science, Research and the Arts Baden-Württemberg, Speech in Gibeon, Namibia, 28 February 2020.

[87] These Guidelines have been subsequently revised, first in 2019 and again in 2021; see German Museums Association, 'Guidelines for German Museums: Care of Collections from Colonial Contexts', 3rd edn, 2021, www.museumsbund.de/publikationen/guidelines-on-dealing-with-collections-from-colonial-contexts-2. See also Peters (n 37).

[88] Federal Foreign Office, 'Framework Principles for Dealing with Collections from Colonial Contexts Agreed by the Federal Government Commissioner for Culture and the Media, the Federal Foreign Office Minister of State for International Cultural Policy, the Cultural Affairs Ministers of the Länder and the Municipal Umbrella organisations', 13 March 2019, www.auswaertiges-amt.de/blob/2210152/b2731f8b59210c77c68177cdcd3d03de/190412-stm-m-sammlungsgut-kolonial-kontext-en-data.pdf.

[89] See Peters (n 37) 373.

[90] Die Bundesregierung, 'Koalitionsvertrag zwischen CDU/CSU and SPD', 12 March 2018, www.bundesregierung.de/breg-de/themen/koalitionsvertrag-zwischen-cdu-csu-und-spd-195906, 167.

[91] See Peters (n 37) 374.

research.[92] In addition, cooperation and dialogue is at the heart of the Principles, highlighting the need to also engage with diaspora communities: 'the responsible handling of collections from colonial contexts depends on dialogue, exchange and cooperation with the countries and societies of origin as well as with their diaspora in Germany'.[93]

Following the adoption of the Framework Principles, a joint Contact Point for Collections from Colonial Contexts in Germany was established in October 2019. This Contact Point is tasked not only with informing and advising states and communities of origin but also with collecting information about colonial collections.[94] Thus, the returns to Namibia not only fit with a bilateral reconciliation process, but also within the development of a decolonisation process for German museums.

V. Conclusion

The case of Germany's return of cultural objects and human remains to Namibia illustrates the potential for these actions to foster reconciliation between nations. However, it also highlights a significant concern: the positive impact on affected communities can be diminished if such returns are limited to state-to-state processes. In this particular case, there had been one clearly identifiable and known owner of the objects, whose descendants are also known: Hendrik Witbooi. This is rare in return cases. And yet, who to return the objects to was not a straightforward question because Witbooi had also become a 'national' figure, which gave his personal, somewhat mundane objects a whole new significance. In this way, the case of Namibia clearly demonstrates that it is not easy to answer the question of 'who' should be involved in a return process and 'who' the returned objects should be returned to.

Namibia itself seems to be learning from these experiences. More recently, 23 objects were brought back from Germany in the context of a project called 'Confronting Colonial Pasts, Envisioning Creative Futures' between the Ethnographic Museum of Berlin (EMB), the Museums Association of Namibia (MAN) and the National Museum of Namibia (NMN), funded by the Gerda Henkel Foundation.[95] This was the result of state-to-state negotiation, but of

[92] R Peters, 'La gestion des biens de collection issus de contextes coloniaux: les évolutions actuelles en Allemagne' in C Bories et al (eds), *Les restitutions des collections muséales* (Paris, Mare & Martin, 2021) 262.

[93] 'Framework Principles for Dealing with Collections from Colonial Contexts' (n 88).

[94] Federal Foreign Office, 'Concept on the Establishment and Organisation of a German Contact Point for Collections from Colonial Contexts', 16 October 2019, www.auswaertiges-amt.de/blob/2262748/5450242f5fdd6b-343b32919aab9c11a6/191016-kol-kulturgueter-pdf-en-data.pdf.

[95] Gerda Henkel Stiftung, 'Confronting Colonial Pasts, Envisioning Creative Futures – Collaborative Conservation and Knowledge Production of the Historical Collections from Namibia Held at the Ethnological Museum Berlin and the National Museum of Namibia, Windhoek',

a collaboration between institutions, which initially led to a long-term loan to Namibia. According to the project's website:

> The objects were selected in close consultation with community representatives in Namibia and will initially be on loan to the National Museum of Namibia, where they will be further researched in the next few years and made available to contemporary artists for creative exploration. This is the first time this type of open-ended cooperative process, one largely determined by the Namibian partners, has been initiated in Germany.[96]

Whilst this process involves objects which ending up in the National Museum, it is an example of collaborative research and of actively engaging Namibians – researchers, artists etc – in the return of these objects.

Finally, these return processes have demonstrated that they do not happen in a political vacuum, but that they may take place along post-colonial reconciliation discussions, even if they do not legally constitute reparations. They also demonstrate that an enabling legal framework, one which does not prevent museums to de-accession objects, plays a crucial role in facilitating return processes, particularly when there is a genuine political will to do so. Additionally, establishing clear provenance significantly bolsters the moral justification for returning items that were acquired within a colonial context of duress.

www.gerda-henkel-stiftung.de/en/confronting-colonial-pasts-envisioning-creative-futures-collaborative-conservation-and-knowledge-production-of-the-histori?page_id=120264; Staatliche Museen zu Berlin, 'Confronting Colonial Pasts, Envisioning Creative Futures', www.smb.museum/en/museums-institutions/ethnologisches-museum/collection-research/research/confronting-colonial-pasts-envisioning-creative-futures.

[96] Staatliche Museen zu Berlin (n 95).

7

The Need for Provenance Research

*The Return of a Dagger from the Netherlands to Indonesia**

I. Introduction

'[T]he dagger's lot was a tale of exile and forgetting.'[1] This is how historian Peter Carey described the fate of Prince Diponegoro's *keris*, an Indonesian word for a ceremonial dagger, in Dutch hands. Indeed, what once may have been a valued possession of one of Indonesia's main leaders against the Dutch colonial rulers fell into oblivion for almost two centuries after it fell into the possession of the Dutch. What unfolded can be interpreted as a narrative of 'not knowing', being 'lost' and perhaps also of insufficient efforts in the quest for the elusive dagger. This story also delves into the complexities of provenance research and highlights the shifting priorities in the return of cultural objects.

This chapter thus focuses on the return, by the Netherlands, of the *keris* of Diponegoro to Indonesia. The return occurred in 2020 after having been postponed for many decades. Throughout this time, it was resoundingly clear that the *keris* was of utmost importance to Indonesia. Indeed, in the 1970s, three decades after Indonesia's independence, the signing of an agreement providing for the transfer of certain cultural objects from the Netherlands had prioritised items that had belonged to Diponegoro. However, the *keris* remained in the Netherlands for several decades thereafter. This chapter delves into the reasons for the delayed return, anchored in provenance research. It also considers the current place of the dagger in the Indonesian context, where it was briefly put back into the spotlight, resulting in a fierce public debate before being quickly transferred to the storage rooms of the National Museum in Jakarta, until being eventually put on display nearly four years later.

* Interviews in Indonesia were conducted by Panggah Ardiyansyah, Indonesian heritage expert. Interviews were conducted in Basha Indonesia and translated by Panggah Ardiyansyah.

[1] P Carey, 'Reflections on the Return of the Diponegoro's Dagger Kiai Nogo Siluman. Suluk Kebudayaan Indonesia', www.langgar.co/reflections-on-the-return-of-the-diponegoros-dragger-kiai-nogo-siluman.

II. From Yogyakarta to the Netherlands: Tracing the Diponegoro's *Keris* Journey

Born in 1785, Diponegoro was the oldest son of the sultan of Yogyakarta, which used to be the capital of the sultanate on the Indonesian island of Java. In the 1820s, a system through which local nobility could rent out land to local farmers was abolished to allow the Dutch colonisers to collect rent instead, which led to the Java War (1825–30). In other words, once the system that had allowed the local nobility to retain a certain level of local control, and income was taken away, the nobility revolted against the coloniser. During this conflict, Diponegoro became the leader of the Javanese resistance.[2] In 1830, after several years of hostilities, Diponegoro had been invited for peace talks, but was captured instead. Around this time, one of his *keris* came into the possession of Dutch Colonel Cleerens. As a prince, Diponegoro would have had several *keris*. It has been said that whenever he engaged in political negotiations, he wore the Kyai Nogo Siluman *keris*.[3] Hence, it is thought that it was the Kyia Nogo Siluman *keris* which was handed over to the Dutch.

Figure 7.1 *Keris* of Diponegoro at the National Museum in Jakarta.
© National Museum of Indonesia, Indonesian Heritage Agency (2025)

[2] D van Reybrouck, *Revolusi. Indonesië en het Ontstaan van de Moderne Wereld* (Amsterdam, De Bezige Bij, 2020).

[3] Interview with Basuki Teguh Yuwono, *keris* expert at the Indonesian Institute of the Arts, Surakarta, April 2022. There are different orthographies in use: *Kyai* or *Kiay* means 'sir' and is usually used for royalty. *Nogo* or *Naga* refers to a mythic snake (usually wearing a crown). *Siluman* (or *Suliman*) refers to spiritual or higher powers.

How exactly the *keris* came into the hands of Cleerens is unknown. According to Carey, Diponegoro voluntarily gave this *keris* to the Dutch Colonel as a sign of trust, prior to departing for peace talks in Magelang (a town in Java, Indonesia).[4] Indeed, according to Basuki Teguh Yuwono, an expert at the Indonesian Institute of the Arts in Surakarta, 'in the palace, the gifting of *keris* was used to build a political legitimacy … between the ruler and his aides, and between kings to build kinship, they could exchange *keris* to build kinship'.[5] However, Basuki Teguh Yuwono does not agree that Diponegoro would have handed over his *keris* voluntarily because a *keris* is a symbol of freedom and honour for Javanese warrior men.[6] Gift giving in a colonial context was rarely without expectations, and local rulers in Indonesia have often been known to give gifts as a sign of subjugation.[7] While little is known about the circumstances in which Diponegoro 'gifted' his *keris*, it is plausible that this was part of any peace negotiations or a strategy to evade imprisonment – both of which failed. It is believed that Cleerens retained possession of the *keris* after Diponegoro's capture rather than following the standard protocol of surrendering it to his superior, Lieutenant General de Kock.[8] Upon returning to the Netherlands, Cleerens eventually donated the *keris* to the Dutch King. Yet, during his journey back, Cleerens did not mention possessing such a significant dagger, which raises questions. If he had intended to donate it to the King, it would be reasonable to expect him to acknowledge travelling with such an important object. This unknown part of the *keris*' journey supports the idea that it had come to symbolise his betrayal of Diponegoro.[9]

While there is no agreement among historians on how exactly the *keris* came into Dutch possession, provenance research revealed that in 1831, the *keris* was donated by Cleerens to the Dutch King. The research conducted by the Wereldmuseum Leiden in 2019 mapped the intermediate journey of the *keris* from the Dutch East Indies to The Hague,[10] using digitised newspaper articles.[11] The first reference to the *keris* in the Netherlands can be found in a letter dated 11 January 1831. On behalf of King Willem I, the Secretary of State – the

[4] Carey (n 1).

[5] Interview with Basuki Teguh Yuwono, *keris* expert at the Indonesian Institute of the Arts, Surakarta, April 2022.

[6] ibid.

[7] J van Beurden, *Treasures in Trusted Hands: Negotiating the Future of Colonial Cultural Objects* (Leiden, Sidestone Press, 2017) 41.

[8] Carey (n 1).

[9] Interviews with Francine Brinkgreve, former Curator at the Wereldmuseum Leiden, and Tom Quist, Provenance Researcher at the Wereldmuseum Leiden, Leiden, June 2022.

[10] The former Museum Volkenkunde (National Museum of Ethnology) in Leiden was renamed Wereldmuseum Leiden (NMVW) in October 2023. The new name of the museum will be used in this chapter, although for most of the period covered, it was called Museum Volkenkunde.

[11] Two newspapers, the *Javasche Courant* and *Opregte Haarlemsche Courant*, mention Cleerens departing from Batavia (present-day Jakarta) on 14 September 1830 on board the ship *Ons Genoegen* and arriving on the Dutch island of Texel on 29 December 1830. There is no explicit mention of the *keris* in these articles; see National Museum van Wereldculturen (NMVW), 'Research Report on the *Keris* of Prince Diponegoro', 27 February 2020, internal document, copy with the author.

highest-ranking civil servant of the Dutch government, acting as an intermediary between the King and his ministers – sent a request for advice on the *keris* offered by Cleerens to the Director-General of the Department of Water Management, Industry, and Colonies. The Director-General replied on 17 January 1831, stating that there were no objections to accepting the *keris*. He advised that the weapon be added to the collection of the Koninklijk Kabinet van Zeldzaamheden (KKZ, the Royal Cabinet of Curiosities). On 25 January 1831, the Secretary of State informed the Director-General of the King's approval. Six days later the *keris* was sent to the KKZ.

Little is known about the *keris* after 1831 until almost two centuries later, except for one event. The weapons from the Dutch East Indies in the collection of the KKZ were exhibited at the Dutch section of the 1876 World's Fair (or Centennial Exposition) in Philadelphia in the US. References to the items on display have been kept, and the description of the *keris* repeats the one in the draft inventory:

> A gold creese, plain scabbard, without engravings, wooden hilt, the blade evidently very old, with gold ornaments. Presented to H.M. by Mr. Cleerens, original from the Pangarang Dipo Negero.[12]

There is one additional phrase compared to the original description: 'without engravings', meaning that the plain scabbard has no engraved decorations. In addition, it speaks of traces of gold remaining. These additional pieces of information were important for the provenance researchers in 2019 because it allowed them to identify the *keris* mostly based on visual traits.[13] Throughout the process, the museum in Leiden examined 112 *keris*, and these elements allowed the researchers to identify just one.[14] Another meaningful event is that the KKZ ceased to exist in 1883, after which its collection was spread across various museums in the Netherlands. A great deal of information was lost in the process, including the whereabouts of the Diponegoro *keris*.

III. Locating and Identifying the Lost *Keris*

According to Basuki Teguh Yuwono, there are more than 4000 *dhapur* or typologies of *keris* in the Indonesian archipelago, with more than 800 decorative motifs for blades and sculpted features near the base.[15] There exist traditional *keris* of different 'levels', with the *keris tayuhan* being the highest, that is, possessing spiritual values, which is the type of *keris* in this case. Other types of *keris* include

[12] See ibid (n 11).

[13] Interview with Tom Quist, provenance researcher at the Wereldmuseum Leiden, Leiden, July 2022.

[14] Interviews with Francine Brinkgreve, former Curator at the Wereldmuseum Leiden, online, June 2022 and October 2024.

[15] Interview with Basuki Teguh Yuwono, *keris* expert at the Indonesian Institute of the Arts, Surakarta, April 2022.

the *keris ageman*, which is the one that is carried as an accessory together with traditional clothes, which is mainly valued for its beauty. Another category is the 'fine art' *keris*, which is more modern. Hence, the typologies and decorative motifs could ultimately be a way to re-identify the *keris* of Diponegoro.

During the times of Diponegoro, 'a *keris* had three functions based on typologies and motifs. First as a weapon. Second, it had a spiritual function. Lastly, it also functioned as a projection of social status'.[16] A Prince like Diponegoro would thus normally have more than one *keris*: 'One could possess his own personal *keris*es as symbols of social status, as well as heirlooms from the parents as symbol of continuity and parents-in-law as symbol of responsibility.'[17] The number of *eluk* (curves) on the blade indicates the importance of its owner, with 11 and 13 curves being the highest rank. The Kyai Nogo Suliman, which means 'his Highness the Invisible King of the Snakes', has 11 curves. Indonesian experts who verified the *keris* described it as follows:

> On the blade there is, in relief, a golden snake which twists along with the curves of the blade. This type of *keris*, which has the name *Nogo Sasra*, has 11 curves, which suggests the owner is someone of high Javanese nobility, which would be the case for Diponegoro.[18]

Furthermore, experts conclude that the animal figures visible at the base of the blade, which earlier experts interpreted as an elephant or a tiger (or lion), is actually an 'invisible serpent', a Nogo Siluman.[19] A similar description was also found in a nineteenth-century letter, where Indonesian painter Raden Saleh had noted that 'the name Nogo (Naga) was given to this *keris* because the gold on it used to represent a snake that ran until the top, as can still be seen from some remnants'.[20]

Though it was assumed for a long time that the *keris* was in the Netherlands, its exact whereabouts were unknown after the dissolution of the KKZ. Yet, the topic came up on several occasions. After Indonesia's independence – declared in 1945 but only recognised by the Netherlands in 1949 – a committee was formed through which both countries agreed on which heritage to return to Indonesia.[21] Already in 1949, there had been a sub-committee during the independence negotiations that focused on culture, which drafted a 'Cultural Agreement'. However, this remained a draft that was never signed. In 1968, a first agreement on culture was eventually signed between both countries.[22] This led to intensified cooperation in the field of archives and the establishment of a Dutch cultural centre in Jakarta. Only

[16] ibid.
[17] ibid.
[18] See NMVW (n 11).
[19] ibid.
[20] Translated from Dutch by the author, with the original text stating '[d]e naam Nogo (Naga) is aan deze kris gegeven, omdat het goud op denzelven eertijds eene slang heeft voorgesteld, die tot aan de punt liep, zoo als nog te zien is, aan enige overblijfselen'; see ibid.
[21] For more on the Dutch-Indonesian cultural negotiations, see C Scott, *Cultural Diplomacy and the Heritage of Empire: Negotiating Post-colonial Returns* (Abingdon, Routledge, 2020).
[22] See van Beurden (n 7) 125–44.

in 1975 did both countries come to an agreement that also included the return of cultural objects, approved by the Council of Ministers of the Netherlands: the Joint Recommendations by the Dutch and Indonesian Team of Experts, Concerning Cultural Cooperation in the Field of Museums and Archives Including Transfer of Objects.[23] By that time, there seemed to be a clear acknowledgement of the importance of returning cultural objects as part of a post-colonisation process. The Joint Recommendations include objects 'which are directly linked with persons of major historical and cultural importance … which are not state owned' (Article II(3)), as well as objects 'of historical emotional value, such as those belonging to Diponegoro' (Article II(4)). A first set of items, consisting of a saddle with stirrups, a bridle, a *pajong* (umbrella) and a spear, that had belonged to Diponegoro were handed over in 1977 during a state visit by Dutch Queen Juliana. At the time, the whereabouts of the *keris* were unknown.

Since the *keris* did not feature in the catalogues of the ethnographic museums in the Netherlands (most of them have today been combined into the National Museum of World Cultures),[24] some assumed that the *keris* had remained in Indonesia. For instance, Francine Brinkgreve, former Curator at the Wereldmuseum Leiden, studied how *kerisses* with important stories or having belonged to leading figures were usually added to the Bataviaasch Genootschap van Kunsten en Wetenschappen (Batavian Society of Arts and Sciences), the predecessor to the national collection in Jakarta, while only other *kerisses* had been brought to the Netherlands during the colonial period.[25] As a consequence, and due to a lack of explicit information indicating otherwise, she assumed that it was likely still in Jakarta or elsewhere in Indonesia.

Some scholars have asked why more efforts were not made to find the *keris*, especially since questions on the *keris* and its fate were regularly raised. For example, in a coded telegram from 1983 the Dutch Ambassador to Indonesia, Lodewijk van Gorkom, wrote that the *keris* was in the Rijksmuseum in Amsterdam, suggesting that the Netherlands return it to Indonesia.[26] Pieter Pott, Director of the Wereldmuseum Leiden at the time, was asked by the Dutch Embassy in Jakarta to search for the *keris*.[27] This request was made in the context of the fortieth anniversary of Indonesia's independence, when it could have been handed back. According to Frans van Dongen, the then Dutch Ambassador to Indonesia, he:

> [W]rote to Director Pieter Pott … and also suggested that the Foreign Ministry in The Hague should make a large gesture and return Diponegoro's kris [*keris*]. It would

[23] ibid; for the full text of the Joint Declarations see at 150–53.

[24] This is composed of the Afrikamuseum (Berg en Dal), the Tropenmuseum (Amsterdam), the Museum Volkenkunde or Museum Volkenkunde (Leiden), and the Wereldmuseum (Rotterdam). All of these were renamed 'Wereldmuseum' in October 2023.

[25] Interview with Francine Brinkgreve, former Curator at the Wereldmuseum Leiden, Leiden, June 2022.

[26] J van Beurden, *The Return of Cultural and Historical Treasures: The Case of the Netherlands* (Amsterdam, KIT Publishers, 2012).

[27] See NMVW (n 11).

> have a symbolic meaning for the whole of Indonesia and a special meaning for its President. But Pott sent me a note that a return was undesirable. I know for sure from my correspondence with Pott that at that moment the kris [*keris*] was in the Museum in Leiden.[28]

It is not clear whether Pott truly found it undesirable. After all, he had searched for the *keris* and had identified a possible candidate among the museum's large *keris* collection. However, according to the Wereldmuseum Leiden, the Dutch Ministry of Foreign Affairs was uncertain about his findings – that is, whether he had identified the correct dagger – and requested further investigation from Pott's successor as director of the museum, van Gulik;[29] yet this follow-up did not take place. And in 1998, Suzanne Legêne found archival records written by Diponegoro's army commander Sentot Alibasya Prawirodirdjo that confirmed that the *keris* had been handed by Diponegoro to Cleerens around the time of the peace talks in Magelang.[30] Not much attention was paid to her research at the time and it seems that the archival records were 'forgotten'.[31] Researcher Jos van Beurden cites Legêne's recollections of that period: 'Museum Volkenkunde (now Wereldmuseum Leiden) was constantly rebuilding. Nobody could do anything with the few characteristics of the kris [*keris*] I had; the staff could help, they said, if I gave them an inventory number … You had to know exactly what you wanted to see, so as an outsider you couldn't really do any object research.'[32] As such, her research into the dagger stopped there at the time. In 2005, questions about the whereabouts of the *keris* of Diponegoro surfaced again during a major exhibition on Indonesia, which took place in Amsterdam.[33] Legêne sought the support of Pieter ter Keurs, then Curator of Indonesia at the Wereldmuseum Leiden, to start the search for the *keris* of Diponegoro anew.[34] Furthermore, Van Beurden also noted having sought cooperation to find the dagger in 2011 and again in 2015.[35] While one may wonder why such a long time passed between Indonesian independence – when Diponegoro objects were given priority for return – and the actual return, it is also the case that in recent decades there was never an explicit request from the Indonesian authorities for the *keris*, whereas

[28] This quote is from an interview with Frans van Dongen by Jos van Beurden; see van Beurden (n 26) 61.

[29] Interview with Francine Brinkgreve, former Curator at the Wereldmuseum Leiden, Leiden, June 2022.

[30] S Legêne, *De bagage van Blomhoff en Van Breugel. Japan, Java, Tripoli en Suriname in de negentiende-eeuwse Nederlandse cultuur van het imperialisme* (Amsterdam, Koninklijk Instituut voor de Tropen, 1998) 290.

[31] It would not be until 2013 that the National Museum of World Cultures would mention having come across this record.

[32] Legêne, cited in J van Beurden, *Inconvenient Heritage: Colonial Collections and Restitution in the Netherlands and Belgium* (Amsterdam, University of Amsterdam Press, 2022) 92.

[33] Savitri et al, 'Kiai Naga Siluman. Dagger Cuts on Both Sides', *Tempo*, 14 April 2020, https://magz.tempo.co/read/interlude/36576/kiai-naga-siluman-dagger-cuts-on-both-sides.

[34] Interview with Tom Quist, provenance researcher at the Wereldmuseum Leiden, Leiden, July 2022.

[35] See van Beurden (n 32) 92.

such requests were made for other collections, and also among those interested in the *keris*, that interest seems to have come and gone with regular flare-ups of attention.

However, while some of this brought the dagger to the attention of the Dutch museum sector, none of this helped place the dagger in Leiden. Moreover, as Francine Brinkgreve explained, it would later become clear that at some point – possibly because of the dissolution of the KKZ – the link between the inventory number and the object was lost and there were a lot of unspecified daggers in Leiden.[36] After the dissolution of the KKZ, Indonesian *kerisses* ended up in different collections, including in Leiden and in the Rijksmuseum in Amsterdam. It is a situation that sketches the constraints of many of Europe's museums with extensive colonial collections and only partial or at best flawed inventories. A lot of information is simply unknown, and resolving some of the puzzles requires an immense amount of effort, without a guaranteed outcome.

That the case was not purposefully ignored is perhaps best demonstrated by the breakthrough that eventually started in 2013. Then, Mirjam Shatanawi, then Curator of Islamic culture with the Wereldmuseum Leiden, rediscovered the archival record in the North-Holland Archive in Haarlem, where the archives of the KKZ are kept, that had already been mentioned by Legêne in 1998.[37] While doing research on a different topic, the curator came across the letter by Diponegoro's army commander, with notes by Javanese painter Raden Saleh. The note gave a detailed description of the *keris* and placed it at the KKZ, which meant that it was likely to have been moved to the Wereldmuseum Leiden when the KKZ was dissolved in 1883.[38] Unlike in 1998, this information re-emerged at a time when other return processes were advancing, which is probably why staff at the Wereldmuseum Leiden paid closer attention to it. Namely, around that time, the Curator of the Rijksmuseum in Amsterdam, Harm Stevens, was involved with the return of the cane of Diponegoro from a private collection,[39] alongside the organisation of an exhibition on the life of Diponegoro at the National Museum in Jakarta in 2015.[40] The same year also saw the 'Bitter Spice' exhibition on the relation between the Netherlands and Indonesia, which included an account of Diponegoro.[41] Two years later, in 2017, instigated by a talk about Diponegoro by Carey at the Rijksmuseum,[42] Stevens and Brinkgreve discussed a possible publication

[36] Interview with Francine Brinkgreve, former Curator at the Wereldmuseum Leiden, Leiden, June 2022.

[37] ibid.

[38] ibid.

[39] Personal account of the return of the staff: H Stevens, *Bitter Spice: Indonesia and the Netherlands from 1600* (Amsterdam, Rijksmuseum Collection in association with Vantilt Publishers, 2015) 157–63.

[40] 'A Tribute to Indonesia's Prince Diponegoro', *Jakarta Globe*, 22 January 2015, www.jakartaglobe.id/features/a-tribute-to-indonesias-prince.

[41] See Stevens (n 39).

[42] See C Driehuizen's tweet on X (formerly Twitter) in 2017 at www.mobile.twitter.com/CDrieenhuizen/status/874731531033563136.

on Diponegoro and agreed to also investigate the *keris* for the occasion.[43] According to staff at the Dutch Ministry of Education, Culture and Science, the initiative for the renewed provenance research was further supported by renewed discussions in the Netherlands about the return of cultural objects. All this also needs to be seen in the broader context of increased provenance research within the museum(s) in general. While this case zooms in on the *keris* of Diponegoro, there were numerous other requests for which provenance research was being conducted.

Aided by the detailed iconographic description by Saleh, all the *keris* that had come from the KKZ, in addition to a series of *keris* with an undefined provenance (and which could thus also have come from the KKZ), were closely examined.[44] Only one *keris* fit the detailed description by Saleh. However, in early 2018, the museum came across the research that had been conducted by Pott in the 1980s, who had identified another dagger as having possibly belonged to Diponegoro. Although at the time of Pott's research, questions had been raised about his findings, the team in Leiden decided to consider both *keris* as potential candidates.

From 2019 onwards, a second stage of provenance research was carried out to seek more information to link either of the identified *keris* to the figure of Diponegoro.[45] It was during this second stage that the researchers discovered that the *keris* had travelled to Philadelphia in 1876, with a detailed catalogue description confirming Saleh's description. Moreover, research on the Philadelphia expo also enabled the identification of the *keris* that Pott had selected as not having belonged to Diponegoro; ruling out the second candidate was an important step in the research process.

IV. Dutch-Indonesian Expert Cooperation

While the provenance research was mainly carried out by a Dutch team, Indonesian experts were involved at various stages of the process, and the Indonesian embassy in The Hague was informed. After all, 'there is the pure research, but there is also the diplomatic side. It is always about the relations between the source country and the country or institution that holds it'.[46] For the Dutch Ministry of Education,

[43] Interview with Francine Brinkgreve, former Curator at the Wereldmuseum Leiden, Leiden, June 2022, who recalls having asked permission to allow staff member Johanna Leijfeldt to conduct that search.

[44] H Lidchi and F Brinkgreve, 'Clues. Research into Provenance History and Significance of Cultural Objects and Collections Acquired in Colonial Situations. Final Report. Pilotproject Provenance Research on Objects of the Colonial Era' (2022) Institute for War, Holocaust and Genocide Studies (NIOD).

[45] This was conducted by provenance researcher Tom Quist, supported by Brinkgreve. All information on this phase comes from an interview with Tom Quist, provenance researcher at the Wereldmuseum Leiden, Leiden, July 2022 and the final report from the NMVW (n 11).

[46] Interview with Francine Brinkgreve, former Curator at the Wereldmuseum Leiden, Leiden, June 2022.

Culture and Science, the role of the Indonesian partners throughout the process was essential:

> It is really important for us that we do not push any restitution on them. The initiative really needs to come from the source country. But because that wish had always been there, at a certain point, the initiative was taken 'we think we found it, do you still want it'?[47]

Yet, given that the further involvement of the Indonesian experts was limited, it is difficult to speak of joint provenance research in this case. There were nevertheless a variety of ways in which Indonesian experts were involved. First, a *keris* expert from Java who lives in the Netherlands was invited to assess the full *keris* collection with the aim of identifying potentially powerful *kerisses*, without specifying that he was looking for the *keris* of Diponegoro.[48] It was assumed that telling him upfront that he was to search for the *keris* of Diponegoro might influence his assessment, in that he would, for instance, look for the most decorated one rather than focusing on the power that he might feel emanating from the dagger. Having gone through a specific fasting ritual prior to assessing the collection, the expert then sought to feel the power that each of the *keris* held. When he held the Diponegoro *keris*, he said it was a *keris* that had belonged to someone from the Javan Court, perhaps even Diponegoro. This further reaffirmed the research team that they had identified the right *keris*. In addition, the Wereldmuseum Leiden also sought the advice of Jani Kuhnt-Saptodewo, a curator of Indonesian descent at the Weltmuseum (World Museum) in Vienna, who confirmed the findings of the provenance researchers.[49]

In early 2019, once the researchers were certain they had identified Diponegoro's *keris*, they informed both the Dutch Ministry of Education, Culture and Science, and the Indonesian Embassy in the Netherlands, which in turn informed the relevant stakeholders in Indonesia. From the Indonesian side, there was a request to not publicise the search and its finding. According to I Gusti Agung Wesaka Puja, Indonesian Ambassador to the Netherlands at the time:

> I understood that the *keris* of Diponegoro is a high-profile case, not only within *keris* experts but also for politicians as well … there was an upcoming presidential election for Indonesia in 2019. I did not want the *keris* to become a political issue or be used for political gains.[50]

This approach was already adopted in 2015, when a staff that had belonged to Diponegoro was returned; the process was also kept under wraps until the staff was exhibited in Jakarta.[51]

[47] Interview with the Dutch Ministry of Education, Culture and Science, Amsterdam, June 2022.

[48] Interview with Francine Brinkgreve, former Curator at the Wereldmuseum Leiden, Leiden, June 2022.

[49] Interview with Tom Quist, provenance researcher at the Wereldmuseum Leiden, Leiden, July 2022.

[50] Interview with I Gusti Agung Wesaka Puja, former Indonesian Ambassador to the Netherlands, Jakarta, April 2022.

[51] L Nicolasen and M Maas, 'Opwinding rond de Staf van Prins Diponegoro', *de Volkskrant*, 25 March 2015, www.volkskrant.nl/nieuws-achtergrond/opwinding-rond-de-staf-van-prins-diponegoro~b82b40ed/?referrer=https%3A%2F%2Fwww.google.com%2F.

In early 2020, after elections had taken place in Indonesia, an official delegation of Indonesians came to assess the *keris*. The delegation included Hilmar Farid, the then Director-General for Culture at the Indonesian Ministry of Culture; Professor Dr Sri Margana, a leading historian at the Gadjah Mada University; and Bonnie Triyana, currently the permanent secretary for the Tim Repatriasi (the Indonesian repatriation committee which was created in 2021). However, they felt strongly that their presence was only there to rubberstamp the provenance research that had already been carried out:

> We came in in the eleventh hour, it was already near the finish line, and we were tasked to manage the return. Before the return, we were given the chance by the Dutch to confirm whether the *keris* belonged to Diponegoro. Due to the time constraint, we very much relied on the research conducted by the Dutch.[52]

The Indonesian experts were well aware of the role they were asked to play in endorsing the Dutch work, whilst regretting not having been given a role that would have been more considerate of their combined knowledge and understanding of Indonesian culture. While the Indonesian team felt that they did not play a crucial role in the process, their presence was considered essential by the Dutch team, especially as they represented not only political power but also the Indonesian intelligentsia.

Nevertheless, one member of the team, Professor Dr Sri Margana, confirmed having been deeply touched when being in the presence of the *keris* for the first time:

> When I first handled the *keris*, time seemed to pause. I felt like I lifted nothing, felt so light. The *keris* of course has a certain weight, but I felt like I was holding nothing, the breathing stopped for a bit. Probably because of my fascination with the *keris*, and not, as Javanese would believe, because of the *keris*' spiritual power.[53]

The situation demonstrates that the implementation of joint provenance research is not a straightforward matter and includes difficult questions, such as at what stages various experts can or should be involved and for what reasons. It also demonstrates that it is often political and not simply a matter of heritage research, which in turn can lead to another series of constraints.

V. A Clear Basis for a Swift Return Process

Once the experts and government officials agreed that the correct *keris* had been identified, a process for its return was initiated. From the onset, it is worth noting as the *keris* had arrived in the Netherlands in the nineteenth century; which meant that the possible application of the 1970 UNESCO Convention to its return

[52] Interview with Hilmar Farid, former Director-General for Culture, Jakarta, April 2022.
[53] Interview with Sri Margana, historian at the Gadjah Mada University, Jakarta, April 2022.

could not even be considered.[54] Already in the seventeenth and eighteenth centuries when the Dutch East India Company controlled trade to the Netherlands, any transfer of cultural objects that was not officially ordered by the Dutch was banned.[55] This was formalised in 1858, with the Batavian Society for Arts and Science being tasked with the protection of objects under the colonial administration, including registering finds.[56] From 1840 onwards, the Dutch colonial administration also started adopting specific laws to protect cultural objects. The first law, in 1840, required the authorisation of the Governor-General to export such goods. At the time of Indonesia's independence in 1945, the Netherlands had used the elaborate system of laws and institutions to protect heritage as a way to counter claims for return,[57] although 'one can conclude that Dutch heritage laws and regulations regarding colonial possessions mainly served the interests of the Dutch State'.[58]

Yet, as per the information available, the *keris* of Diponegoro left the territory before the coming into force of the 1840 law, and at a time when the Dutch East India Company had ceased to exist. Hence, it is likely that no clear legal framework applied at the time to the transfer of the dagger to the Netherlands. Once in the Netherlands, it entered the KKZ collection with the King's approval and thus had become state property. As it had become state property, its return had to be approved by the Parliament.

In this case, the process was facilitated by one main legal instrument:[59] the Joint Recommendations by the Dutch and Indonesian Team of Experts, concerning Cultural Cooperation in the Field of Museums and Archives including Transfer of Objects, agreed by the Dutch and Indonesian governments in 1975.[60] The Joint Recommendations include that:

> Specific objects and specimens which are directly linked with persons of major historical and cultural importance or with crucial historical events in Indonesia should be transferred to the country-of-origin. The two delegations also recognize the desirability to make cultural objects such as ethnographical and archival material available for exhibition and study in the other country in order to fill the gaps in the already existing collections of cultural objects in both countries to promote mutual understanding and appreciation of each other's cultural heritage and history.

As Diponegoro was a national hero in Indonesia, objects that had once belonged to him had priority for return (referred to as 'transfer'). According to the Ministry of Education, Culture and Science, the Joint Recommendations governed the return of the *keris*, which meant that the case was 'separate from the policy for

[54] In any case, while the Netherlands accepted the treaty in 2009, Indonesia is not a party to it.
[55] See van Beurden (n 7) 123–24.
[56] ibid.
[57] See the discussion on the Joint Declaration above.
[58] J van Beurden, 'Hard and Soft Law Measures for the Restitution of Colonial Cultural Collections – Country Report: The Netherlands' (2022) 8 *Santander Art and Culture Law Review* 407, 412.
[59] For more details on the Dutch legal context, see ibid.
[60] See van Beurden (n 26) 150–53.

the treatment of colonial collections and the National Commission for Colonial Collections under the Culture Board'.[61] The same press release also makes clear that compliance with the Joint Recommendations was at the basis of this return. In this particular case, as soon as the museum was convinced that it had found the *keris*, it requested the Minister to allow for its return to Indonesia.

Around the time of the dagger's return, the Netherlands also adopted the 2016 Erfgoedwet (Dutch Heritage Act),[62] which allows for the de-accession of national collections – that is, those owned by the Dutch state.

The 2016 Act, which has since been essential for returns, is a merger of six earlier laws, each pertaining to a specific subset of heritage matters, including two earlier laws which were concerned with the return of cultural goods: the 2008 Wet tot teruggave cultuurgoederen afkomstig uit bezet gebied (Law on the Return of Cultural Goods Coming from Occupied Territories)[63] and the 2013 Uitvoeringswet UNESCO-verdrag 1970 inzake de onrechtmatige invoer, uitvoer en eigendomsoverdracht van cultuurgoederen (Implementation Act UNESCO 1970 Convention on the Unlawful Import, Export and Transfer of Ownership of Cultural Property).[64] However, neither of the laws applied to objects brought to the Netherlands under Dutch colonial rule. This gap was addressed in the 2016 Act, which not only combined a set of previous laws, but also addressed some gaps, such as the return of colonial objects. The 2016 Act addresses the matter only very broadly as it allows for the de-accession of any object or collection. Part of this had already been addressed in the earlier laws, but, as per the 2016 Act, this became applicable to all objects in Dutch collections.[65]

[61] Translated from Dutch by the author; the original text in Dutch is 'gescheiden van de beleidsvorming rond de omgang met koloniale collecties en de commissie Nationaal kader koloniale collecties onder de Raad voor Cultuur'. See, Rijksoverheid, 'Nederland geeft dolk van Javaanse verzetsheld terug aan Indonesië', 4 March, 2020, www.rijksoverheid.nl/actueel/nieuws/2020/03/04/nederland-geeft-dolk-van-javaanse-verzetsheld-terug-aan-indonesie.

[62] The Netherlands, 2016, Act of 9 December 2015, comprising an inventory and adaptation of regulations pertaining to cultural heritage ('Heritage Act'); for an English version, see www.english.cultureelerfgoed.nl/publications/publications/2016/01/01/heritage-act-2016#:~:text=The%202016%20Heritage%20Act,%2C%20archaeologists%2C%20own-ers%20and%20administrations%20.

[63] Overheid.nl Wettenbank, 'Wet tot teruggave cultuurgoederen afkomstig uit bezet gebied', https://wetten.overheid.nl/BWBR0021656/2008-08-01.

[64] Overheid.nl Wettenbank, 'Uitvoeringswet UNESCO-verdrag 1970 inzake onrechtmatige invoer, uitvoer of eigendomsoverdracht van cultuurgoederen', https://wetten.overheid.nl/BWBR0025996/2013-01-01.

[65] It is only following the October 2020 report of the Adviescommissie Nationaal Beleidskader Koloniale Collecties (Advisory Committee National Policy on Colonial Collections) and the consequent creation of an Adviescommissie teruggave cultuurgoederen uit koloniale context (Advisory Committee for the Return of Cultural Objects from a Colonial Context) in 2022, and the development of the 2021 Beleidsvisie collecties uit een koloniale context (policy for collections from a colonial context) by the Ministry for Education, Culture and Science that a specific system for colonial collections has been put in place; however, all these came after the return of the *keris* of Diponegoro. See Adviescommissie Nationaal Beleidskader Koloniale Collecties, 'koloniale collecties en erkenning van onrecht', October 2020, Raad Voor Cultuur;, Rijksoverheid, 'Beleidsvisie collecties uit een koloniale context', 29 January 2021, www.rijksoverheid.nl/documenten/kamerstukken/2021/01/29/rapport-beleidsvisie-collecties-uit-een-koloniale-context.

The procedure for return is clearly described in the Heritage Act and was put into action by the Ministry of Education, Culture and Science. De-accession involves: (1) a public announcement by the minister or another relevant authority (section 4.17); and (2) an independent commission that advises on the de-accessioning (sections 4.18–4.20). This independent commission is meant to 'advise on whether the object concerns a cultural object or collection of particular cultural-historical or scholarly significance or that is irreplaceable and indispensable as part of the Dutch cultural heritage' (section 4.19), but does not advise on the question of return itself. It is mobilised whenever the request for de-accession concerns an object that is likely to be of particular importance for the Dutch heritage collections. This commission is composed of independent experts.[66] As its role is only advisory in nature, the final decision is to be taken by the Ministry. Also in the case of the *keris*, the decision to return it was publicly announced.[67] Yet, in this specific case, while the 2016 Act was applied, it was mainly governed by the Joint Recommendations. It is important to note that in 2023 and 2024, major returns to Indonesia have taken place within this framework.[68]

As for the *keris*, on 3 March 2020, it was formally handed over by Ingrid van Engelshoven, the then Minister of Education, Culture and Science, to I Gusti Agung Wesaka Puja, the then Indonesian Ambassador to the Netherlands, during a ceremony at his embassy in The Hague.[69] At that point, an agreement was signed between both governments and the Indonesian Ambassador gave the Dutch Minister a €1 coin in return.[70] This exchange was part of a tradition, as recalled the former Indonesian Ambassador to the Netherlands:

> In terms of ritual from traditional knowledge, we exchanged the *keris* with a coin. I was inspired by the event in November 2016 when the Prime Minister (PM) Rutte handed the Bugis *keris* to the Indonesian president, at the time we were not aware of the local custom to be followed, that after the *keris* was handed, we should give a coin as an exchange (to the PM). We were panicking, looking for a coin, and finally someone had a one thousand rupiah coin. We then put the coin in a badge holder. Rutte seemed confused when he received the coin, since he was not briefed before. The president Joko Widodo explained it to him, and he laughed. That is why I exchanged the *keris* with a one euro coin. The Dutch minister of culture was also a bit confused before I explained

[66] Guidelines for the de-accession of museum objects Museumvereniging, 'Leidraad afstoten museale objecten' (LAMO 2023), https://commissie.kolonialecollecties.nl.

[67] https://zoek.officielebekendmakingen.nl/stcrt-2020-13002.html.

[68] On the 2023 returns, see https://leiden.wereldmuseum.nl/nl/over-museum-volkenkunde/pers/persberichten/koloniale-collecties-terug-naar-indonesie-en-sri-lanka. On the 2024 returns, see www.government.nl/latest/news/2024/09/20/for-second-time-cultural-artefacts-to-be-returned-to-indonesia and https://leiden.wereldmuseum.nl/nl/opnieuw-culturele-objecten-terug-naar-herkomstland-indonesie.

[69] See Rijksoverheid (n 61).

[70] According to Hilmar Farid, the former Director-General for Culture at the Indonesian Ministry of Culture who signed the agreement alongside the Ambassador and the Minister, it confirmed the item in question to be the *keris* of Diponegoro and that it was handed over to Indonesia on 3 March.

> it to her. Then, Francine [Brinkgreve] called me to explain the meaning of this exchange since the coin has come into the museum collection.[71]

Following this exchange, the Wereldmuseum Leiden deemed that the coin was now part of the history of the *keris*, and thus requested its handover from the Ministry:

> The coin was officially handed over to the museum on 7 July [by the Ministry], after which it has been added to the museum's collection, since it is an important part of the story of the *keris*. By chance, I Gusti Agung Wesaka Puja, former Indonesian Ambassador to the Netherlands, visited the museum on 7 July and reconfirmed that exchanging the *keris* for the coin was indeed a Javanese tradition. Specifically for the exchange of *kerisses*, a coin is exchanged as a counter-gift, in order to ensure that the relations between both parties continue.[72]

In Leiden, the *keris* had been in storage, so its departure had little impact on the public display. Nevertheless, the exchanged coin, now in the collections of the Wereldmuseum Leiden, provided a sense of continuity for the story of Diponegoro in the Netherlands. While an object has left its collection, another entered. With regard to the *keris*, the Netherlands understood that, from the moment of handover, it was fully up to the Indonesian authorities to decide what happened to it. Hence, there were no further demands included in the agreement. The day following the handover, on 4 March 2020, Indonesian Ambassador Puja personally accompanied the *keris* to Jakarta, together with Francine Brinkgreve. He recalled his concerns during the return journey:

> After we arrived at Jakarta airport, I was really worried. There were four of us at the time, me, Francine, the cultural attaché, and a staff from the embassy. During the security check, the other three were directed to the green line, but I was led to the red line. I said that I am an Indonesian Ambassador, but they did not care and insisted that I went to the red line. I asked the immigration officers if they needed to check all the baggage. They said no, only the blue suitcase, which was the one containing the *keris*. I was really worried if they saw that I brought a *keris*. But when the suitcase already passed the x-ray machine, the officers stayed still. And when I picked up the suitcase, they allowed me to go … Those are the stories behind the scenes, whether you want to connect them with something mystical, that is up to you. But that is definitely out of my expertise.[73]

Despite some concerns, the transportation of the *keris* was completed without any hurdles, and it was transferred to the National Museum in Jakarta. After its arrival in Jakarta, the return was eventually publicised.

[71] Interview with I Gusti Agung Wesaka Puja, former Indonesian Ambassador to the Netherlands, Jakarta, April 2022.

[72] Interview with Francine Brinkgreve, former Curator at the Wereldmuseum Leiden, Leiden, June 2022.

[73] Interview with I Gusti Agung Wesaka Puja, former Indonesian Ambassador to the Netherlands, Jakarta, April 2022.

A *keris* is a highly important object, which in Javanese tradition is ascribed spiritual values. As already discussed, this power was said to be felt by the Javanese expert who was first invited by the Wereldmuseum Leiden to assess the *keris* collection. Keeping this in mind, the return was accompanied by certain ceremonies. For instance, when it was later exhibited in Surakarta (the historic capital also known as Solo), rituals were performed. Two interviewees confirmed that:

> The museum conducted a special ceremony as a symbolic event for those individuals who wanted to perform a ritual. Also, we need to minimise the amount of contact between *keris* and the water used in a ritual to minimise the damage in the material. It would not be feasible as well to have all ritual equipment within the exhibition space.[74]

Separate individual rituals were also conducted:

> An interesting fact is that many *keris* enthusiasts including myself performed a thanksgiving ceremony separately in their own house when we heard that the *keris* of Diponegoro was being returned to Indonesia. It was an extraordinary event for us within the world of *keris*. Though we would not publish this activity in the media, since it was a more personal event.[75]

VI. From One National Collection to Another

Once it arrived in Jakarta, the *keris* entered Indonesia's National Museum collection, where it remains to this day. The *keris* was initially exhibited at the Bogor presidential palace in Jakarta during the state visit of the Dutch King.[76] It was later exhibited in the National Museum in Jakarta for a special exhibition called Pamor Sang Pangeran, which was held in November 2020. This exhibition was dedicated to the life of Diponegoro and included a film about his capture in 1830.[77] According to Nusi Isabila Estudiantin, Curator at the National Museum in Jakarta, the interest in the *keris* grew exponentially:

> From the beginning, we had scheduled a small exhibition on Diponegoro after receiving the *keris*. This was immediately followed by requests we got from the public to show the *keris*. So, the exhibition grew bigger over time … The director general [for culture]

[74] Interview with Basuki Teguh Yuwono, *keris* expert at the Indonesian Institute of the Arts, Surakarta, April 2022.

[75] ibid.

[76] See further below, section VIII.

[77] For local media sources, see 'A Prince's Legacy Part I: The Diponegoro Exhibition at the Indonesian National Museum', *Independent Observer*, 21 November 2020, www.observerid.com/a-princes-legacy-part-i-the-diponegoro-exhibition-at-the-indonesian-national-museum; NN Wira, 'National Cultural Week 2020 to Feature Exhibitions on Affandi, Prince Diponegoro', *Jakarta Post*, 27 October 2020, www.thejakartapost.com/life/2020/10/27/national-cultural-week-2020-to-feature-exhibitions-on-affandi-prince-diponegoro.html.

> responded positively to this initiative and he asked that the exhibition should be part of national cultural week.[78]

Subsequently, there was also an exhibition in Surakarta that featured the *keris*.[79] However, since then, the *keris* had been mostly kept in storage at the National Museum. At the time of our research, curator Nusi Isabila Estudiantin said 'we will include the *keris* in the new display for the B building, after the renovation, on the fourth floor'.[80] The museum was thereafter damaged by a fire in 2023, and at its re-opening in October 2024, the *keris* was featured at the centre of a display on Diponegoro. At the time of writing, it is not yet clear whether this new temporary exhibit will become the permanent Diponegoro display.

It is the Indonesian government that decided that the *keris* would become part of the collection of the National Museum, even if it could not immediately be exhibited there, and even though towns like Surakarta are famous as centres of *keris* making and would have had the infrastructure to showcase the *keris* upon its return. Moreover, since 2019, there is a 'Diponegoro Room' dedicated to the Prince and his capture at the History Museum in Jakarta, where the *keris* could have been put on display right away alongside other exhibits related to Diponegoro, but this is not a national-level museum.[81] Nonetheless, Indonesia decided resolutely for the item to remain in the collection of the National Museum. According to the former Director-General for Culture:

> That is because the return happened in the context of bilateral cooperation between two countries. So, the most competent institution is the National Museum. We do not see other alternatives considering the logistics and jurisdictions. This issue might become crucial in the future because some objects in the Dutch collection have significance for living communities. The sultanate might be gone, but there are descendants, and we need to check their lineages. And to avoid confusion on different claims because the return would be conceived by the government, the responsibility for the storage should fall into a state institution. If the communities wanted access, then it is a matter of agreement between the National Museum and these communities. And that the communities would not be included in the (bilateral) agreement. If they insisted that the objects should be returned to the communities, they could process the repatriation themselves. We (the government) are open to that idea. It is a question whether the

[78] Interview with Nusi Isabila Estudiantin, former Curator at the National Museum, Jakarta, April 2022.

[79] RS Prabowo, 'Ini Wujud Keris Pangeran Diponegoro yang Dipamerkan di Museum Keris Solo', *Suara Surakarta*, 22 November 2021, www.surakarta.suara.com/read/2021/11/22/142402/ini-wujud-keris-pangeran-diponegoro-yang-dipamerkan-di-museum-keris-solo.

[80] Interview with Nusi Isabila Estudiantin, Former Curator at the National Museum, Jakarta, April 2022.

[81] News Desk, 'Prince Diponegoro Chamber Expected to Attract More History Buffs to Jakarta History Museum', *Jakarta Post*, 7 April 2019, www.thejakartapost.com/news/2019/04/07/prince-diponegoro-chamber-expected-to-attract-more-history-buffs-to-jakarta-history-museum.html; '395th Anniversary of the Former Batavia Stadhuis, Now the History of Jakarta Museum', *Independent Observer*, 16 February 2022, www.observerid.com/395th-anniversary-of-the-former-batavia-town-hall-now-the-history-of-jakarta-museum.

> Dutch would be willing to engage the communities directly. There was (a claim) already from Balinese (royals) helped by Dutch (expatriate) stating in a letter that it would not be appropriate if the return came to the National Museum and rather should come to them directly. (I said) they could directly ask for the regalia from the Dutch. So, when the objects are to be returned within the framework of this (bilateral) agreement, they should go to the National Museum.[82]

Other officials agreed with this point of view, highlighting the role of Diponegoro as a national hero:

> The most important thing to me is to register the object as national heritage. The official custodian is the national museum, and local museums can then borrow the object. The legal matter has to be done right from the beginning. But this debate would be more complicated when we are talking about families of the owner, or the descendants … we still need to formulate the internal procedure in Indonesia. As for the *keris* of Diponegoro, I think it is appropriate to store it in the national museum.[83]

Diponegoro is indeed an important figure in Indonesian history. Panggah Ardiyansyah, an Indonesian heritage researcher, describes how his persona was made to represent the country's independence struggle and played an important role in the development of a shared national identity.[84] His popularity in post-colonial Indonesia was further aided by being 'hated' by the Dutch and, in 1967, he was officially recognised as a national hero.[85]

While an alternative could have been to return the *keris* to the family of Diponegoro, the family itself did not request it. Indeed, his descendants appear to agree with the decision of the authorities and that, as Diponegoro is a national figure, objects related to him should be made available to the nation. For that reason, they do not want the *keris* – or any other Diponegoro objects in the national collection – to be returned to the family. When asked where the *keris* should be kept, Roni Sodewo, a descendant of Diponegoro, answered: 'at the national museum, we should let Diponegoro belong to this country'.[86] Nevertheless, while he agreed on the national character of Diponegoro's heritage, he also felt that there was a lack of engagement with the family, which was not formally invited to see the *keris* at the National Museum; 'no contact from the ministry. And even I have not seen the kris [*keris*] directly until today'.[87]

In this case involving an object having belonged to an important national historical figure, the decision to move the object to a national institution seems logical. The lack of engagement with the descendants, as well as the decision

[82] Interview with Hilmar Farid, former Director-General for Culture, Jakarta, April 2022.
[83] Interview with Bonnie Triyana, Permanent Secretary of the Indonesian Repatriation Committee, Jakarta, April 2022.
[84] P Ardiyansyah, 'Restitution and National Heritage: (Art) Historical Trajectories of Raden Saleh's Paintings' in L Tythacott and P Ardiyansyah (eds), *Returning Southeast Asia's Past: Objects, Museums and Restitution* (Singapore, NUS Press, 2018) 168.
[85] ibid.
[86] Interview with Roni Sodewo, descendant of Diponegoro, April 2022.
[87] ibid.

not to display the *keris* (at least for the first four years after its return), may be questioned. Although there seems to be general agreement about the final destination of the *keris*, there was little to no debate, or even public engagement, in that decision-making process. From the Dutch side, the decision was clearly left to the Indonesian authorities. In Indonesia itself, policy regarding the return of cultural objects has only developed recently. Its regulation on museums adopted in 2015 makes no reference to restitution, nor does it provide explicitly for the transfer of returned objects to the National Museum.[88] In 2021, its former Director-General, Farid, said that he was focusing repatriation efforts on Indonesian objects in Dutch collections 'obtained in an inappropriate manner based on historical research', with high priority being given to 'objects that are closely related to the formation of our historical identity'.[89] Part of this new approach involved the creation in 2021 of a Repatriation Committee, composed of seven experts, headed by I Gusti Agung Wesaka Puja with Bonnie Triyana as the Secretary, which is tasked with conducting research, advising the government, as well as supporting return processes.[90] These recent changes in Indonesia were explicitly linked to advances in the Netherlands, in particular the report issued by the Advisory Committee National Policy on Colonial Collections – often referred to as the Gonçalves report after the Committee's president – in October 2020.[91] The report stated that in order to rectify historic injustices, the Netherlands should unconditionally return objects taken in former colonies, if the source country so requests. The report also referred to the desire of source countries to be more explicitly involved in provenance research. The Indonesian efforts, combined with those of the Dutch, have led to two major rounds of returns in recent years, demonstrating that the approach works.

VII. Controversy Following the Return

While its eventual location in the National Museum was rather uncontroversial, the dagger gave rise to some controversy upon its return, which must be considered in view of the (symbolic) value of the return process in restoring relations between both countries. The return occurred at the same time as an official state visit by the Dutch King to Indonesia. This was not fortuitous, but instead the revealing of the return of the *keris* was planned to coincide with this visit.

[88] Database Peraturan, 'Peraturan Pemerintah (PP) No. 66 Tahun 2015', www.peraturan.bpk.go.id/Details/5642/pp-no-66-tahun-2015.

[89] Quote translated from Indonesian; for the original text, see D Maulipaksi, 'Repatriasi, Upaya Indonesia Kembalikan Benda Cagar Budaya dari Belanda', *Kementerian Pendidikan dan Kebudayaan*, 11 January 2021, www.kemdikbud.go.id/main/blog/2021/01/repatriasi-upaya-indonesia-kembalikan-benda-cagar-budaya-dari-belanda.

[90] ibid.

[91] See Adviescommissie Nationaal Beleidskader Koloniale Collecties (n 65).

Thus, on 10 March 2020, immediately after its return, the *keris* was first exhibited in Jakarta at the Bogor Palace, where it was viewed by Indonesian President Joko Widodo and Dutch King Willem Alexander and Queen Maxima. This was when the Indonesian public and the media were officially informed about the return of the *keris*. Since the *keris* had already been formally handed over and returned, there were no official ceremony or speeches. According to Brinkgreve, 'it was absolutely not the case that the King carried a nice present for the president. But it was to show the Indonesian people that the *keris* was back … But the real handover was between the minister and the Ambassador in The Hague'.[92] After all, the *keris* had been part of a Dutch state collection rather than a royal collection. Hence, its official handover was a matter for the government, not the King. However, this distinction was lost on the Indonesian media and public. The particularities of Dutch administration involved nuances that was overlooked, resulting in an apparent misunderstanding of the lack of recognition of the handing over, with Triyana, the Permanent Secretary of the Indonesian Repatriation Committee, saying that:

> The Dutch do not want to say that the return was a gift, or even handed over. The moment felt flat, like the *keris* just dropped from the sky. So, this heritage, this object, is like a battlefield between Indonesia against the Dutch and the Dutch against themselves. It is a contestation arena to interpret the past. The king is wrestling with himself and his people, the same goes for the president as well. (In this context) the *keris* became the arena for battle. So, it was a ceasefire, to stay silent.[93]

In view of restoring relations in a post-colonial context, a different approach could perhaps have been considered. However, as the former Indonesian Ambassador to the Netherlands recalled, the non-politicisation of the event was deliberate:

> That was something that was consciously avoided. When we had the hand-over, it would show to the public in Indonesia who was the colonial master and who was the colony. We should avoid for the sake of the Indonesian public to show that now we are standing on equal footing. That was different when we compare it with the Prime Minister Rutte in November 2016 for the collection from the Nusantara museum in Delft. We have agreed on the transfer and one of them is the Bugis *keris*, since it was a less controversial museum object and was decided by the Dutch themselves for the PM Rutte to bring and hand over the *keris* himself. It has a different context with the *keris* of Diponegoro. For the *keris* of Diponegoro, it is politically sensitive and very high profile. So, we wanted to avoid the return being dragged into politics.[94]

[92] Interview with Francine Brinkgreve, former Curator at the Wereldmuseum Leiden, Leiden, June 2022.

[93] Interview with Bonnie Triyana, Permanent Secretary of the Indonesian Repatriation Committee, Jakarta, April 2022.

[94] Interview with I Gusti Agung Wesaka Puja, former Indonesian Ambassador to the Netherlands, Jakarta, April 2022.

During the same state visit, the Dutch King expressed regret for the violence that had occurred during the Indonesian revolution, but did not mention the return of the *keris*, or the issue of restitution in general. It is unclear to what extent 'the silence' of the Dutch King on the matter of the return of the *keris* further fuelled controversy in Indonesia regarding its authenticity. As already discussed, Diponegoro had more than one *keris*. Hence, the *keris* that was returned was one of many that had belonged to Diponegoro. From the provenance research, it seemed certain that the returned *keris* had belonged to him, but it remained possible that a mistake was made with its identification. Confusion arose when one of the Indonesians who verified the *keris* spoke of recognising a lion on the dagger. This would mean that the *keris* did not have the typical Nogo Siluman iconography, prompting public scepticism about whether the Netherlands had returned the correct *keris*.[95] Nevertheless, the provenance is not contested by any of the Indonesian experts that were involved in the process and had access to the thorough provenance research:

> Everyone agrees, no dissenting voice. Even though, when the *keris* arrived in Indonesia, it opened up a public debate, and it is open because the identification has used the fully available historical data. For those who do not agree with the identification, it is up to them, but they need to give the counterproof as well.[96]

The debate broke out on social media and seems to have been steered by *keris* experts who had not been involved in the process,[97] and were only informed of its shape and iconography, but not to the historic records associated therewith. There was also a degree of political opposition involved. Yet, as Bonnie Triyana notes:

> The appetite to discuss the *keris* in public was really big, I saw a lot of discussions being held. They do not really care about the process of the return, but more on the *keris* itself. So, the *keris* continues to live on, and has new meanings.[98]
>
> Sometimes they, people from the political opposition, need a media controversy to bring attention to themselves. But we have a strong foundation for the identification, including the three letters. So now the burden of proof falls to the doubters.[99]

At the very least, the public debate and (political) controversy demonstrates not only the importance of Diponegoro-related objects for Indonesians at large, but also the importance of being mindful of local sentiments throughout the process.

[95] In April 2020, an article was published on the controversy, with *keris* and traditional weapons experts questioning whether it was the correct one, since it was not of the correct type; see Savitri et al (n 33) 28–33.

[96] Interview with Hilmar Farid, former Director-General for Culture, Jakarta, April 2022.

[97] The Dutch (and Belgian) media also started reporting that the Netherlands may have returned the wrong *keris*; see, for example, E Brassem, 'Indonesische experts: Nederland gaf de verkeerde kris terug', *Trouw*, 21 April 2020, www.trouw.nl/gs-b42b3451; P Mijlemans, 'Nederland geeft verkeerde dolk terug aan Indonesië', *De Standaard*, 23 April 2020, www.standaard.be/cnt/dmf20200423_04932234.

[98] Interview with Bonnie Triyana, Permanent Secretary of the Indonesian Repatriation Committee, Jakarta, April 2022.

[99] ibid.

VIII. The Return of Cultural Objects as Part of Restorative Justice?

Despite the controversy, Indonesian media referred to the return of the *keris* as 'an acknowledgment of the right of Indonesians to have fought for their freedom as well as a right of the Indonesian people to have access to the objects that are part of the legacy of one of their most important heroes as part of Indonesian heritage'.[100] There is indeed a dual meaning to the return. First, it relates to the symbolism involved with the Netherlands returning objects taken from Diponegoro specifically while he was standing up against colonisation. Second, it highlights the importance of Indonesians having access to their own history and the material heritage that relates thereto. Linking both is the importance of restoring relations between the two countries, thereby acknowledging past wrongs. In that sense, the Dutch King's regrets for the violence committed in Indonesia could have been associated to the return of taken objects, whether directly expressed or not. According to heritage scholar Cynthia Scott:

> Dutch officials persistently linked cultural property return with both the establishment of good post-colonial cultural relations, and more importantly, an ongoing Dutch presence in Indonesia's cultural life. This linkage limited the range of responses officials could make to Indonesian demands for returns … In other words, in the absence of good cultural relations, officials could not let returns be seen as gestures of surrender, nor of remorse, or admissions of wrongdoings.[101]

More recently, van Beurden criticised ongoing developments in the Netherlands for being Eurocentric and downplaying the capacities of the former colonies. In addition, the current approach is said to be overly reactive (rather than proactive) by putting a lot of emphasis on the need for the former colonies to demand the returns. This can be particularly challenging given that the content of the Dutch national collections does not appear to be entirely clear even to their staff, as exemplified by the case of *keris*.[102] At the same time, Farid stressed the importance of Indonesia playing a more active role in those processes: 'there is a tendency by the Dutch that they think they could help us making choices, which for me is unacceptable'.[103]

Elsewhere, questions have been raised about Indonesia's approach to restitution and its systematic decisions to nationalise returned objects, even if these are of high local importance or part of a living culture.[104] While these are general

[100] See 'A Prince's Legacy Part I' (n 77).
[101] See Scott (n 21) 11-12.
[102] See van Beurden (n 58).
[103] Interview with Hilmar Farid, former Director-General for Culture, Jakarta, April 2022.
[104] E Smith, R Ristiawan and T Sudarmadi, 'Protection and Repatriation of Cultural Heritage – Country Report: Indonesia' (2022) 8 *Santander Art and Culture Law Review* 383.

approaches, some of which were only being developed around the time of the restitution of the *keris* or after, it seems likely that both the Netherlands and Indonesia will continue to approach restitution as a bilateral engagement, which has thus far left little room for any community engagement; as understood by Brinkgreve at the Wereldmuseum Leiden, 'there is the pure research, but there is also the diplomatic side. It is always about the relations between the source country and the country or institution that holds it'.[105] This leaves the following key question: if the return of cultural objects is to contribute to restorative justice, then who benefits from such a high-level process?

The Dutch government also confirms that these kinds of symbolic acts are important in improving relations with the former colony:

> In fact, this kind of restitutions work best if they are also a strengthening of the bilateral relations. Restitution is beyond the physical transfer, primarily a symbolic act, and that symbol needs to be positive. The current policy is therefore focused on following a truly joint process. We are, at this moment, in the possession of the objects, so there is a certain inequality in the relationship when considering the request, logically, so you have to agree with each other on how you can do this well.[106]

In Indonesia, Farid spoke of the importance of using such cases of return to increase awareness of decolonisation:

> Yes, [this should be conveyed through] the publication, display, research, and the conclusion on one object can be used for education. Rather than learning about historical chronology in three years … they can learn history from the objects. That is the direction we would like to take into the future.[107]

It is clear that wider opportunities to use the dagger's return for restoring relations between both countries have not fully been used on either side.

IX. Conclusion

The return of the *keris* of Diponegoro exemplifies the importance of thorough provenance research and a proactive approach thereto, as well as the complexities and limitations of such research. The case cannot be considered without questioning the many decades during which no search for the *keris* was conducted, despite the existence of an agreement to return cultural objects from the Netherlands to Indonesia, signed back in 1975, which even prioritised those objects that had belonged to national figures like Diponegoro. There is no doubt that the whereabouts of the *keris* were unknown, but there had also been many pointers and

[105] Interview with Francine Brinkgreve, former Curator at the Wereldmuseum Leiden, Leiden, June 2022.

[106] Interview with Dutch Ministry of Education, Culture and Science, Amsterdam, June 2022.

[107] Interview with Hilmar Farid, former Director-General for Culture, Jakarta, April 2022.

requests by researchers that were not sufficiently considered. At the same time, this case has to be considered in the broader context of museums often housing very large collections, with many objects not being adequately inventoried, and having limited resources to respond to numerous requests – whether formal or informal – for provenance research into singular objects or collections.

Once concerted efforts started, it still took several years to identify the *keris*, which is an indication of how complex provenance research can be and how necessary it is for museums to invest in it. Moreover, as is often the case with historical research and despite considerable evidence, all the work conducted did not answer every question that had been raised. While there is little doubt that the identified *keris* had indeed belonged to Diponegoro, everyone involved also accepted that it was always possible that more information could appear in the future, potentially leading to another conclusion. While the integration of Indonesian experts in the provenance research process was crucial, it raises two important points. First, there is the question of when 'joint provenance research' should start. Many seem to agree that the Indonesian involvement was insufficient, and high-profile Indonesians felt like they were used to sign off a process that had been largely led by the Dutch. Indeed, the embassy in The Hague was involved early on, but that is at the political level and it does not equal the involvement of academics or museum professionals. It is thus understandable that they felt that their role was insufficient at best. On the other hand, for a significant period of time, there was nothing much in which to involve an Indonesian team, which demonstrates that such decisions are not straightforward. Yet, some of these issues may have been avoided if the Dutch collections would have been more accessible to Indonesian researchers and if there had been an existing process to engage with Indonesian researchers from the onset. Yet, easier access requires better inventories, but drawing these up requires much investment and research as well, and the lack of resources is often the main reason why these museums have not yet been able to do so. A second interesting aspect of the Indonesian involvement in the provenance research is that several among them referred to the spirit of the *keris* and the power that they could feel. This intangible link with the past and its objects is something that could have been overlooked, but was given a particular place in this process. The seriousness with which this aspect was approached reflects a significant level of respect for the culture on behalf of the Dutch researchers involved.

Once the object was identified with sufficient certainty, the Dutch legal framework enabled a swift process, despite the object having become the property of the Dutch state. Of essential importance in this case were the Joint Recommendations by the Dutch and Indonesian Team of Experts, concerning Cultural Cooperation in the Field of Museums and Archives including Transfer of Objects of 1975, which called for the return of Indonesian objects, especially those that had belonged to Diponegoro. This was combined with the applicable Dutch Heritage Law, which allows for de-accession, upon the approval of the Ministry of Culture, following the advice of a committee.

However, returns are about much more than following recommendations and adhering to a legal framework. From a transitional point of view, a number of opportunities may have been missed. This starts with the insufficient involvement of Indonesian experts in the provenance research and the absence of engagement with the descendant family and the wider Indonesian public in the return, and continues with the Dutch King's visit, during which no explicit link was made to the return of cultural heritage. The (social) media controversy that emerged highlighted the flawed process, but also underlined how important the object remains in Indonesia. The case ends – for now – with the *keris* having eventually been put on display at the National Museum, after several years in storage.

8

The Return of the Makonde Mask from Switzerland to Tanzania

The Role of Third Parties in the Return of Cultural Objects

I. Introduction

In 1984, a wooden Makonde mask was stolen at the Museum and House of Culture in Dar es Salaam, Tanzania's largest city and principal port.[1] At the time, the theft was reported to all the relevant authorities at the national and international levels, including the Tanzanian police, the International Criminal Police Organization (INTERPOL) and the International Council of Museums (ICOM). Purchased from a well-known Parisian art dealer in September 1985 by Jean-Paul Barbier-Mueller, a Swiss collector, the mask entered the collection of the private museum he had established in 1977 with his wife Monique, the daughter of collector Joseph Mueller, to showcase their collection of traditional arts from different world cultures.[2]

In 1988, Professor Enrico Castelli, an expert in East African art at the University of Perugia, was asked by the Barbier-Mueller Museum to help with the preparation of a catalogue for one of its upcoming exhibitions on African art.[3] The following year, in 1989, he mentioned to the Barbier-Mueller Museum that he had found an old photograph of a display of a very similar mask, which had been taken in the National Museum in Dar es Salaam. Having

[1] It may have been part of a group of 16 other objects stolen at the time, but these objects have not been recovered.

[2] The Barbier-Mueller collection was first created in 1907, with the acquisition by Joseph Müller of a painting by Swiss painter Ferdinand Hodler; see V Noce, 'Masterpieces from the Barbier-Mueller African and Oceania Collection to Be Sold at Christie's in Paris', *The Art Newspaper*, 6 February 2024, www.theartnewspaper.com/2024/02/06/christies-to-auction-masterpieces-from-the-barbier-mueller-african-and-oceanic-art-collection-in-paris; See also the website of the museum www.barbier-mueller.ch/en/historique-eng. It should be noted that the Association of Friends of the Musée Barbier-Mueller also annually publishes *Arts & Cultures*, a specialist magazine of non-Western arts.

[3] E de Roux, 'L'affaire du masque makondé du Musée Barbier-Mueller', *Le Monde*, 14 February 1998, www.lemonde.fr/archives/article/1998/02/14/l-affaire-du-masque-makonde-du-musee-barbier-mueller_3655103_1819218.html.

purchased the mask in good faith,[4] Jean-Paul Barbier-Mueller contacted ICOM in July 1990, immediately after he was made aware of the possible origins of the mask.[5] By 1996, although no responses had been received from inquiries made in Tanzania, ICOM suggested that the mask be returned. However, a formal request for return was not raised and no guarantee regarding security or conservation measures was presented to address the concerns that had been raised.[6] Despite some negotiations over the next decade, no agreement could be reached between the parties,[7] which finally led to the involvement of the UNESCO Intergovernmental Committee for Promoting the Return of Cultural Property to its Countries of Origin or its Restitution in Case of Illicit Appropriation (ICPRCP).

Before considering the roles played by the ICPRCP and ICOM in the return of the mask, and the possible impact of the case of the Makonde mask on the parties involved, this chapter delves into the legal status of the mask and any possible legal obligation to return attached thereto. This requires an analysis of the domestic laws of both Tanzania and Switzerland, as well as their international legal obligations. The chapter concludes with a reflection on the current circumstances of the mask, the wider impact of its return on laws and policies, as well as possible future developments in the field. To understand the importance of the case for Tanzania in particular, it starts with a historical overview of the contextual backdrop, that is, the museum from which the mask disappeared in the 1980s, a product of colonialism, but also of regained independence.

II. The National Museum of Tanzania: The Building of a National Identity

The theft of the Makonde mask occurred at the Museum and House of Culture, part of the National Museum of Tanzania, which consists of a consortium of five institutions that, together, seek to preserve and exhibit the country's history and natural environment.[8] The National Museum inherited the collections of its

[4] According to Maître Yves Jeanrenaud, legal representative for the Barbier-Mueller Museum, interview, online, 29 June 2023, as the object was bought from a well-known Parisian art dealer, the purchaser deemed that due diligence would have been conducted by such art dealer as to the lawful origin of the object.

[5] See de Roux (n 3).

[6] ibid.

[7] It is worth noting that, in 1999, the Director-General of the National Museum of Tanzania expressly underlined his appreciation of the steps taken by the Barbier-Mueller Museum for respecting the ICOM Code of Professional Ethics.

[8] The other four museums which make up the consortium are the Village Museum in Dar es Salaam, the National History Museum and the Arusha Declaration Museum in Arusha, and the Mwalimu Julius K Nyerere Memorial Museum in Butiama.

predecessor, the King George V Memorial Museum, which had been established through a Museum Ordinance Act in 1935,[9] at a time when the UK administered Tanganyika – which together with Zanzibar forms present-day Tanzania – under a League of Nations mandate.[10] The creation of the museum was thus part of the colonial rhetoric, honouring the memory of the recently deceased King whilst seeking to educate the local population about its own heritage.[11]

Following its public opening in 1940, efforts were put into growing the collections of ethnographic materials, which were then seen as the last remnants of disappearing cultures.[12] The arrival of the Makonde mask into the museum's collections in 1949 was part of these efforts at showcasing the country's cultural diversity.[13] Upon entering the collections, the Makonde mask quickly gained the nickname 'handsome boy'.[14] It is an example of a 'lipiko' mask, meaning 'helmet mask' in the language of the Makonde people, an ethnic group which lives principally in southern Tanzania and in northeastern Mozambique, as well as in Kenya.[15] These masks are used at initiation ceremonies, with the dancers looking out through the mouth opening.[16] Made of lightwood, human hair, pigment and wax, it is 30.5 cm tall. The figure, which wears a hat, could represent a convert to Islam and thus possibly acknowledge the links between the Makonde people and the Eastern slave traders who operated along the coast.[17] It is likely that the mask belonged to an individual member of the Makonde people and that it was collected by a scholar associated with the University of Dar es Salaam as part of those early initiatives aimed at expanding the museum's collections, which would soon be used to support the country's post-independence development.

[9] Museum Ordinance No 40 of 1935. Its establishment is largely due to the impetus of Sir Harold MacMichael, the Governor of Tanganyika between 1933 and 1937, who had an interest in archaeology; see 'News and Views' Sir HA MacMichael, KCMG (1937) 140 *Nature* 1003, 1004.

[10] It should be noted that Tanganyika was first colonised by the Germans in the 1880s when it became part of German East Africa, and then by the British in 1919 (first as a League of Nations mandate, before being held as a UN trust territory following the Second World War).

[11] In 1940, the museum was eventually opened to the public. On the origins and history of the museum, see A Staniforth, 'Returning Zinj: Curating Human Origins in Twentieth-Century Tanzania' (2009) 3 *Journal of Eastern African Studies* 153.

[12] ibid 160.

[13] Inside, the mask bears the catalogue reference BMG 1027-49 in reference to the year it was entered into the collection.

[14] This nickname appears on the note attached to the mask.

[15] S Phelan, 'Learn More: Makonde Mask 3', *Pacific Lutheran University*, 2015, www.plu.edu/africanartcollection/masks/makonde-mask-3/learn-more-makonde-mask-3.

[16] KC Ani Casimir, OS Nwakego, and E Umezinwa, 'Masking Traditions and Their Behavioral Functions in Accounting for Stability and Order: A Critical Exposition of Select Study of West, East and Central African Masks' (2015) 5 *Open Journal of Political Science* 115, 124–25.

[17] ICOM, 'Makonde Mask – Signing of an Agreement for the Donation of the Barbier-Mueller Museum of Geneva to the National Museum of Tanzania', press release, 10 May 2010. It should be noted that slavery was only abolished in 1922 in Tanganyika.

Figure 8.1 The Makonde mask at the Museum and House of Culture, National Museum of Tanzania, Dar es Salaam © Kristin Hausler (2023)

In 1961, Tanganyika gained its independence and ceased to be a British Trust Territory, becoming a republic in 1962. A year later, in 1963, the Museum Ordinance was repealed in favour of a new piece of legislation which turned the King George V Memorial into a national museum.[18] And in 1964, Tanganyika formed a union with Zanzibar to become known as the United Republic of Tanzania. These political developments generated a need for building a national identity, a process which could be bolstered by the National Museum. In 1965, a major new exhibition opened at the museum entitled the Hall of Man, which was meant to reclaim the country's history. Its opening was attended by the first President of independent Tanzania, Julius K Nyerere, who was photographed along the star exhibit of the new Hall: the *Zinjanthropus boisei* skull (known as 'Zinj'), which had once been considered the 'earliest remains of man ever found'.[19]

Discovered in Olduvai Gorge in 1959 by Mary Leakey, wife of paleoanthropologist Louis Leakey, the skull had been brought back to their Kenyan base, a common practice at the time, with scientists regularly taking their discoveries

[18] The National Museum Act (No 23 of 1963), enacted by the Parliament of Tanganyika, established the National Museum, and the objects which were then vested in the trustees of the King George V Memorial Museum were thus transferred to the trustees of the newly created National Museum. This Act was repealed and replaced in 1980 with the National Museum of Tanzania Act (No 7 of 1980).

[19] Zinj is an old name for East Africa. It is now known as Paranthropus boisei or Australopithecus boisei; see C Broderick, 'The Discovery of "Zinj"', *The Leakey Foundation*, 12 July 2019, www.leakeyfoundation.org/the-discovery-of-zinj.

across the border to Kenya or even much further for study. Yet, following independence, the country was keen to regain the missing elements of its original story. However, by the time it was returned from Nairobi's Coryndon museum in 1965, 'Zinj' was no longer considered a direct ancestor of humankind and had thus lost most of its scientific value. Nevertheless, the publicity around its return turned it into a symbol of national unity based on a common (pre)history, a symbol that still appears on the logo of the museum.[20] Indeed, Tanzania was among the first independent African nations to actively work towards a national identity, away from tribal identities.[21] Decades later, a consequence of this approach is that cultural heritage is largely governed at the national rather than the local level.

Throughout the following decades, the museum played a central role in the building of a national identity, with former President Nyerere even donating his desk to it.[22] By 1984, when the Makonde mask was stolen, the National Museum of Tanzania, at first a small colonial institution, had metamorphosed into a consortium of several museums staffed by nationals rather than temporary foreign employees.[23]

III. Protecting Tanzanian Heritage: The Makonde Mask's Legal Status

Shortly after having established the King George V Memorial Museum, the British colonial administration enacted the territory's first legal instrument to protect cultural heritage: the 1937 Monuments Preservation Ordinance, which allowed the governor to declare monuments and sites of archaeological, scientific and historic significance as reserved areas.[24] A governmental antiquities division was eventually established in 1957, as part of the Ministry of Education.[25] In 1962, the day after becoming President of then Tanganyika, Nyerere created the Ministry of National Culture and Youth, declaring that:

> [C]ulture is the essence and spirit of any nation. A country which lacks its own culture is no more than a collection of people without the spirit which makes them a nation. Of all the crimes of colonialism, there is none worse than the attempts to make us believe we had no indigenous culture of our own.[26]

[20] See Staniforth (n 11) 155.

[21] See in general MV Gorham, 'Displaying the Nation: Museums and Nation-Building in Tanzania and Kenya' (2020) 63 *African Studies Review* 487.

[22] ibid.

[23] See Staniforth (n 11) 166; LA Mbughuni, *The Cultural Policy of the United Republic of Tanzania* (Paris, UNESCO Press, 1974) 34–35.

[24] Monuments Preservation Ordinance of 1937 (amended 1949).

[25] See the webpage of the United Republic of Tanzania, Ministry of Natural Resources and Tourism, Antiquities Division: www.mnrt.go.tz/index.php/sectors/antiquities-division; correspondence with Wilson Jilala, forensic anthropologist at the National Museum of Tanzania, 29 January 2024.

[26] See Mbughuni (n 23) 16.

In addition to addressing the nation's identity in the post-colonial context, there was at the same time a need to address the growing trade in cultural objects.[27] Thus, in 1964, Tanzania repealed the Monuments Preservation Ordinance and replaced it with the Antiquities Act.[28] By regulating excavations and associated discoveries, the Antiquities Act also ensured that the national government maintained oversight over finds made on its territory. Until then, objects found on the territory were frequently sent abroad for scientific research and exhibitions, but, at the time of independence, there was a growing interest in the National Museum and its collections to build the national identity of the newly established United Republic of Tanzania.[29] A national culture to reaffirm pride in a way of life that had been suppressed in the process of colonisation was deemed a 'necessity'.[30]

The Antiquities Act, which was amended in 1979,[31] adopts a wide definition of antiquity as it includes immoveable objects such as monuments, as well as movable objects such as relics and protected objects. Relics are the oldest as they refer to:

> [A]ny movable object made, shaped, painted, carved, sculptured, inscribed or otherwise produced or modified by human agency in Tanganyika before the year 1863, whether or not it shall have been modified, added to or restored at a later date and includes any human or other vertebrate faunal fossil or botanical fossil or impression, found in Tanganyika.

While the Act also adopts the term 'ethnographical objects' for all other objects produced after 1863,[32] only those produced prior to 1940 are considered 'protected objects' and thus antiquities under the Act.[33] The sale and export of relics and protected objects are prohibited under the Act, unless a licence has been obtained from the Director of Antiquities.[34]

At the time the mask entered the museum's collections in 1949, there was no law classifying objects as 'protected'. In light of the Antiquities Act, an object must have been produced before 1940 to fall under the category of 'protected ethnographical object' or before 1863 to be considered a 'relic'. While the mask was certainly produced before 1949, it is possible it was only produced after 1940 and therefore may not be considered an antiquity under the Tanzanian Antiquity Act, but rather an ethnographical object.[35] However, in addition to the age threshold

[27] ibid 36.

[28] Antiquities Act (No 10) of 1964, Cap 333, amendment No 22 of 1979.

[29] See Staniforth (n 11) 166–67.

[30] See Mbughuni (n 23) 14.

[31] Antiquities (Amendment) Act (No 22) of 1979.

[32] The arbitrary date of 1863 was selected for defining relics because it was 100 years before the adoption of the Antiquities Act in 1964.

[33] Section 2 of the United Republic of Tanzania, Antiquities (Amendment) Act of 1979 defines 'protected objects' as ethnographic objects or wooden doors or door frames 'carved in Tanganyika in any African oriental style, before the year 1940, and includes any object declared to be a protected object under section 90(a)'.

[34] ibid ss 14–15.

[35] ibid s 2, which defines ethnographical objects as moveable objects 'made, shaped, painted, carved, inscribed or otherwise produced or modified by human agency in Tanganyika after the year 1863;

which may offer automatic protection, the Antiquities Act also provides the Minister responsible for antiquities with the power to 'declare any object or class of objects discovered or made in Tanzania and being of palaeontological, archaeological, historical or natural interest to be a protected object'.[36] This is generally the case for objects that have entered the collections of the National Museum of Tanzania, with the Minister following the view of its Chief Curator.[37] Therefore, the Makonde mask was likely considered a 'protected object' under the law when it was stolen due to being part of a national collection.

Before going further, it is worth noting the possible issue raised by the classification of an object depending on a specific date, rather than a time period. In this case, an object was considered a relic when it was over 100 years old, with the relevant year of 1863 specifically noted when the Antiquities Act was originally adopted in 1964. In addition, the category of otherwise 'protected objects' refers to ethnographical objects produced before 1940, which corresponded to 24 years prior to the adoption of the Antiquities Act. So, for example, in 2024, 60 years after the adoption of the Act (and given the amendment of 1979 did not change the year for categorising objects), this meant that to be a relic, an object had to be 160 years old rather than 100 years old. Similarly, to qualify as a protected ethnographical object, an object had to be 84 years old rather than 24.[38]

In any case, its protected status at the domestic level meant that the Makonde mask could not be lawfully exported without a licence – in addition to the fact that it had been stolen from the National Museum. Furthermore, Tanzania had also ratified the 1970 UNESCO Convention at the time it was stolen and illegally exported,[39] and according to its Article 3: 'The import, export or transfer of ownership of cultural property effected contrary to the provisions adopted under this Convention by the States Parties thereto, shall be illicit.' Thus, in order for this provision to be triggered, state parties must adopt provisions to protect cultural property from trafficking, such as prohibiting their export without a licence.[40] Furthermore, they must also prohibit the import of an object that was stolen from a museum in another state party.[41] And in cases where a cultural object has been stolen, the 1970 UNESCO Convention provides for the restitution of the object in question.[42]

However, as already mentioned in earlier chapters, the 1970 Convention is not retroactive and thus only applies if it has already entered into force in both the states

for use in any social or cultural activity whether or not it is still being used by any Community in Tanganyika', but does not include objects 'for sale as a curio'.

[36] ibid s 9(1).

[37] Correspondence with Wilson Jilala, forensic anthropologist at the National Museum of Tanzania, 29 January 2024.

[38] This should be borne in mind by legislators when adopting laws that associate an age threshold with increased levels of protection: a number of years may be preferable to a specific year.

[39] Indeed, Tanzania became a party to the 1970 UNESCO Convention in 1977. However, it should be noted that until 2023, it did not comply with its art 16, which provides for the reporting of state parties.

[40] 1970 UNESCO Convention, art 6.

[41] ibid art 7(b)(i).

[42] ibid art 7(b)(ii).

concerned prior to the object's import. While Tanzania was already a party when the object entered Switzerland, the latter only became a party to the 1970 UNESCO Convention in 2003, implementing it domestically with the Federal Act on the International Transfer of Cultural Property (also known as the Cultural Property Transfer Act (CPTA)) in 2005.[43] Until then, an object could only be claimed within the five-year period following its loss, a period which had already lapsed when the mask was identified in Geneva by Professor Castelli in 1990.[44] Thus, the good-faith purchaser had become the legitimate owner of the stolen mask under Swiss law. Furthermore, neither Tanzania nor Switzerland had ratified the 1995 International Institute for the Unification of Private Law (UNIDROIT) Convention on Stolen or Illegally Exported Cultural Objects, the treaty adopted to strengthen the 1970 UNESCO Convention that imposes a due diligence obligation on the purchaser.[45] Therefore, given the lack of applicable treaty and the likely difficulties in obtaining redress before a Swiss court,[46] Tanzania could only realistically pursue an alternative means of dispute resolution to seek the return of the mask – that is, negotiations.

IV. The Role of the ICPRCP in the Negotiation Process

Jean-Paul Barbier-Mueller, the Swiss collector who had purchased the mask, was passionate about acquiring objects from all cultures so that they would not be forgotten or destroyed. He had not only become the lawful owner of the mask under Swiss law, but he was reportedly also generally 'opposed to the return of artefacts to their countries of origin' and the efforts of UNESCO in supporting those returns out of fear that this might lead to their loss.[47] However, in this specific case, he had immediately contacted ICOM upon learning that the mask in its possession could have been the object of a theft. Indeed, there seems to have also been an immediate willingness to return the object as the Barbier-Mueller Museum offered to return it as a permanent loan in 1998 already. A year later, the Tanzanian government indicated its wish to regain ownership of the mask rather than it being the object of a loan. As a result, in February 2002, the Barbier-Mueller

[43] Acceptance on 3 October 2003.

[44] It should be noted that this period has now been extended to 30 years; see CPTA, art 9(4).

[45] Switzerland signed (but did not ratify) the 1995 UNIDROIT Convention in 1996.

[46] In principle, Switzerland does not automatically enforce foreign export laws unless it has entered into a bilateral agreement with the state in question (as is now provided under the CPTA); see FD Strebel, 'The Enforcement of Foreign Judgements and Foreign Public Law' (1999) 21 *Loyola of Los Angeles International and Comparative Law Review* 55, 96. However, this is not necessarily excluded; see M Weller, 'Iran v Barakat: Some Observations on the Application of Foreign Public Law by Domestic Courts from a Comparative Perspective' (2007) *Art Antiquity & Law* 279. On the question of recognition of national ownership of antiquities, see also P Gerstenblith, 'Schultz and Barakat: Universal Recognition of National Ownership of Antiquities' (2009) 14 *Art Antiquity & Law* 21, 21–48.

[47] V Noce, 'Jean-Paul Barbier-Mueller, Museum Founder and Collector Who Opposed the Return of Artefacts to Their Countries of Origin', *The Art Newspaper*, 1 February 2017, www.theartnewspaper.com/2017/02/01/jean-paul-barbier-mueller-museum-founder-and-collector-who-opposed-the-return-of-artefacts-to-their-countries-of-origin.

Museum agreed to transfer its ownership of the mask to Tanzania under the aegis of ICOM, but under certain conditions, which included: a symbolic compensation, the undertaking to take all the necessary measures to safeguard the security of the returned mask, and the recognition that the museum had acted with the required due diligence.[48] The Tanzanian government did not respond formally to this offer;[49] instead, by 2005, it had submitted the case to the ICPRCP for information purposes, a process which is meant to encourage bilateral negotiations.[50]

Despite having informed the ICPRCP of its ongoing dispute, negotiations remained at a standstill,[51] which led Tanzania to file a formal request for the return of the mask with the secretariat of the ICPRCP in 2006. According to the statute of the ICPRCP:

> A request for the restitution or return by a Member State or Associate Member of UNESCO may be made concerning any cultural property which has a fundamental significance from the point of view of the spiritual values and cultural heritage of the people of a Member State or Associate Member of UNESCO and which has been lost as a result of colonial or foreign occupation or as a result of illicit appropriation.[52]

Thus, Tanzania had to prove that the mask had left its territory without the consent of its owner. Furthermore, and in accordance with the ICPRCP Rules of Procedure, Tanzania also had to demonstrate that it had initiated bilateral negotiations, which had 'made unsatisfactory progress, have been suspended or have failed' and that the mask was missing from a national collection.[53] Finally, the mask had to have a 'fundamental importance', which could be argued on the basis of having been part of the collection of the National Museum of Tanzania. From 2007 onwards, the case was thus listed as 'pending' before the Committee.

[48] According to Maître Yves Jeanrenaud, legal representative for the Barbier-Mueller Museum, interview, online, 29 June 202, at the time, the museum asked for a payment of €3,800 to support its costs and fees. See also ICOM (n 17).

[49] It should be noted that on 22 June 2002, the Director-General of the National Museums of Tanzania indicated that a formal decision would soon be reached.

[50] See ICPRCP Rules of Procedure, r 37. See also the Report on the 2004–05 activities and the thirteenth session of the ICPRCP (23 August 2005) 33 c/rep/15, para 4: 'Members of the Committee (Canada, Croatia, Eritrea, Ethiopia, Greece, Iraq, Mali and Switzerland) and Observer States (Italy, Niger and the United Republic of Tanzania) provided updates on national activities relating to the return/restitution of cultural property. In particular, Ethiopia reported extensively on the very good progress concerning the return of the Aksum obelisk from Italy to Ethiopia, and Italy expressed its wish that UNESCO be involved in the process. The United Republic of Tanzania also reported on a case with Switzerland concerning a request for restitution to Tanzania of a Makonde mask.' At the time, the Committee included a Swiss member, as well as an observer member from Tanzania.

[51] It was reported that the Swiss museum wanted to retain ownership of the mask, even after its return to Tanzania; see F Shyllon, 'Return of Makonde Mask from Switzerland to Tanzania: A Righteous Conclusion' (2011) 16 *Art Antiquity & Law* 79, 80.

[52] Statutes of the ICPRCP, adopted by 20 C/Resolution 4/7.6/5 of the 20th session of the General Conference of UNESCO (24 October–28 November 1978), art 3(2). See also the Operational Guidelines for the implementation of para 104 of the 1970 UNESCO Convention, according to which a request may be submitted to the ICPRCP when no treaty, including the 1970 Convention, is applicable to the dispute.

[53] ICPRCP, Rules of Procedure, adopted by the First Session of the ICPRCP (May 1980) and revised by the Twenty-Second Session of the ICPRCP (September 2021), r 34.

Given the intergovernmental nature of the ICPRCP, Switzerland became a party in the case.[54] Since the object had entered its borders lawfully and its current (private) possessor had become its legitimate owner, the Swiss government's room for action was limited. Nevertheless, the Swiss representative expressed his country's 'willingness to facilitate negotiations with a view to restitution'.[55] Indeed, the Swiss delegate to UNESCO was always present at the meetings and regularly provided updates regarding its government's discussions with the Swiss museum.[56]

Taking note of the negotiations between Tanzania and the representative of the Barbier-Mueller Museum, and of the offer made by Switzerland to act as a facilitator in any additional negotiations between the two, the ICPRCP encouraged both states 'to continue their efforts to resolve this dispute in a positive manner'.[57] However, the filing of the formal request before the ICPRCP had the opposite effect as it led to a breakdown of the negotiations between the Swiss museum and Tanzania. In turn, the Barbier-Mueller Museum filed a formal complaint against the United Republic of Tanzania with the Federal Office of Culture of Switzerland.[58]

In 2009, during the fifteenth session of the ICPRCP, the then Director-General of UNESCO, Mr Matsuura, 'offered encouragement to the Committee and Member States with respect to their work in the restitution of cultural property [and] expressed his wish for progress in the negotiations … between the United Republic of Tanzania and Switzerland concerning the Makonde Mask'.[59] The ICPRCP noted that 'discussions were under way' and that:

[54] Report on the 2006–07 Activities of the Intergovernmental Committee for promoting the return of cultural property to its countries of origin or Its restitution in case of illicit appropriation (28 August 2007) 34 c/rep/14, para 10: 'The parties concerned by the three cases pending before the Committee, the Parthenon Marbles, the Boğazköy Sphinx and the Makonde Mask, submitted recent information on ongoing bilateral negotiations. Each of the three cases was the subject of a Recommendation presented jointly by the parties concerned, namely, Greece and the United Kingdom of Great Britain and Northern Ireland, Turkey and Germany, the United Republic of Tanzania and Switzerland.'

[55] ibid para 11: 'In connection with consideration of these cases, Greece informed the Committee of the forthcoming opening, in late 2007, of the Acropolis Museum. The representative of Switzerland emphasized that the case of the Makonde Mask had not formally been brought before the Committee since the Swiss State did not hold the object requested; he nevertheless expressed Switzerland's willingness to facilitate negotiations with a view to restitution.'

[56] Interview with Etienne Clement, former head of the UNESCO offices in Cambodia and the Pacific, 1 March 2023.

[57] See Report on the 2006–07 Activities of the Intergovernmental Committee (n 54), recommendation no 3.

[58] Interview with Maître Yves Jeanrenaud, legal representative for the Barbier-Mueller Museum, online, 29 June 2023. See also ICOM (n 17); AL Bandle, R Contel and M-A Renold, 'Affaire Masque Makondé – Tanzanie et Musée Barbier-Mueller', *ArThemis Art-Law Centre University of Geneva*, www.plone.unige.ch/art-adr/cases-affaires/masque-makonde-tanzanie-et-musee-barbier-mueller.

[59] Report on the 2008–09 activities and the fifteenth session of the Intergovernmental Committee for promoting the return of cultural property to its countries of origin or its restitution in case of illicit appropriation (24 August 2009) 35 C/REP/14, para 10: 'The Director-General of UNESCO, Mr Matsuura … offered encouragement to the Committee and Member States with respect to their work in the restitution of cultural property, citing the return of the Aksum Obelisk to Ethiopia. He expressed his wish for progress in the negotiations between Greece and the United Kingdom regarding the Parthenon Marbles, between Turkey and Germany with regard to the Boğazköy Sphinx and between the United Republic of Tanzania and Switzerland concerning the Makonde Mask.'

> [T]he Swiss authorities were in regular contact with the owners of the museum in possession of the mask. In that respect, Switzerland played a pivotal role as facilitator in the negotiations between Tanzania and the Barbier-Mueller Museum. For its part, Tanzania gave its written assurance that the Makonde Mask would be well protected.[60]

Thus, recognising the 'constructive negotiation process which is carried out with a view to the return of the Makonde Mask', the ICPRCP again encouraged 'the United Republic of Tanzania and Switzerland to continue their efforts to resolve this matter in a positive manner'.[61]

A few months later, in September 2009, the Tanzanian Ministry of Natural Resources and Tourism informed the Barbier-Mueller Museum of its decision to accept the conditions laid out by the Swiss museum in 2002, including the payment of some compensation, the acknowledgement of the return as a donation (thus recognising the Swiss museum's ownership title) and a guarantee that the mask would be securely stored.[62] On 6 November 2009, a Tanzanian governmental delegation met the representatives of the Barbier-Mueller Museum in Geneva to pave the way for the return of the Makonde mask to Tanzania. The agreement was eventually signed by the parties in Paris on 10 May 2010.[63]

In 2010, during its sixteenth session, the ICPRCP noted that 'several African countries and the Committee Chairperson welcomed this successful restitution and expressed the hope that the example would be an inspiration for the Committee's future work'.[64] However, at the time of writing, the case of the Makonde mask remains the only one brought before the ICPRCP by an African state that has been

[60] ibid para 16: 'The third recommendation adopted at the fourteenth session pertained to the Makonde Mask. Discussions were under way and the Swiss authorities were in regular contact with the owner of the museum in possession of the mask. In that respect, Switzerland played a pivotal role as facilitator in the negotiations between the United Republic of Tanzania and the Barbier-Mueller Museum. For its part, the United Republic of Tanzania gave its written assurance that the Makonde Mask would be well protected.'

[61] ibid para 13: 'The parties concerned by the three cases pending before the Committee, the Parthenon Marbles, the Boğazköy Sphinx and the Makonde Mask, submitted the most recent information on ongoing bilateral negotiations. Each of the three cases was the subject of a recommendation prepared under the auspices of the Committee with the help of the Secretariat, and presented jointly by the parties concerned, namely Greece and the United Kingdom of Great Britain and Northern Ireland; Turkey and Germany; and the United Republic of Tanzania and Switzerland.' See also recommendation no 3.

[62] See Shyllon (n 51), who cites the *Daily News of Tanzania*, 14 May 2010. According to Maître Yves Jeanrenaud, legal representative for the Barbier-Mueller Museum, interview, online, 29 June 2023, the compensation eventually amounted to €5,000. It should be noted that being stored securely did not imply being stored in a strong room; indeed, it was foreseen that a plate recognising the donation would be affixed alongside the exhibited mask upon its return.

[63] According to Maître Yves Jeanrenaud, legal representative for the Barbier-Mueller Museum, interview, online, 29 June 2023, while the agreement was subject to arbitration in Paris, the Swiss museum did not pursue communication with Tanzania to verify whether all the return conditions had been met, although it was aware that sometime after its return, the mask had still not been exhibited with a plate recognising the donation.

[64] ICPRCP, 'Final Report of the Sixteenth Session' (21–23 September 2010) para 17.

resolved.[65] More globally, the return of the Makonde mask also remains one of the few 'success stories' of the ICPRCP thus far.

To strengthen its role in the resolution of disputes over cultural objects and given the preference of states for alternative modes of resolving disputes over cultural property, the ICPRCP formalised its mediation and conciliation procedure during the same (sixteenth) session.[66] Thus, any return or restitution request submitted to the ICPRCP may now be resolved through mediation or conciliation if the parties to the dispute so agree. However, these procedures have not been used so far, which may be due to states' preference for more informal negotiation processes.[67] Nevertheless, the ICPRCP has encouraged UNESCO Member States and Associate Members to consider those procedures and requested its Secretariat to develop some tools to facilitate their use.[68] In addition to these formalised mediation and conciliation procedures, it is worth noting that the issue of restitution is debated in other fora within UNESCO, in particular given that this is an issue that now attracts widespread interest and support among its Member States, as demonstrated by the adoption of the MONDIACULT Declaration. Beyond UNESCO, there are other bodies which may play an important role in this area, such as ICOM when a museum is directly involved in a dispute like the one over the Makonde mask.

V. The Role of ICOM in the Return of the Mask

As it closed the case, the ICPRCP noted that:

> [A] solution had been found to the case of the Makonde Mask through the good offices of Switzerland in Bern and in Paris and to the fact that the discussions had been facilitated by the UNESCO Secretariat. After 20 years of negotiations between the parties, the mask had been presented to the government delegation of the United Republic of Tanzania by representatives of the Barbier-Mueller Museum, under the auspices of ICOM, which stressed the importance of its Code of Ethics.[69]

[65] Pending cases concern the Broken Hill Skull (brought by Zambia) and the Ife Bronze Head (brought by Nigeria).

[66] UNESCO, 'Rules of Procedure for Mediation and Conciliation in accordance with Article 4, paragraph 1, of the Statutes of the Intergovernmental Committee for Promoting the Return of Cultural Property to its Countries of Origin or its Restitution in Case of Illicit Appropriation' (October 2010) CLT-2010/CONF.203/COM.16/7. It should be noted that while only UNESCO Member States and Associate Members may use these procedures, they may represent the interests of their nationals and of public or private institutions located in their territories.

[67] ICPRCP, 23rd session (18–20 May 2022) ICPRCP/22/23.COM/9, para 2. It should be noted that in 2013, Greece invited the UK to enter a mediation procedure regarding its dispute over the Parthenon sculptures, but the UK refused to do so.

[68] ibid.

[69] See ICPRCP (n 64) para 17.

The role of ICOM was thus also underlined.[70] As a member of ICOM, the Barbier-Mueller Museum had sought its advice once it had been informed that the mask could have been stolen at the National Museum of Tanzania. ICOM then followed up with the National Museum of Tanzania, thus also acting as a facilitator, before recommending to the Barbier-Mueller Museum to return the mask.[71] ICOM also organised the exchange ceremony, which took place in Paris, where the parties signed the return agreement.[72]

As the global organisation in the museum field, ICOM has developed ethical (non-legally binding) standards for museums, including on the return of 'cultural property'. Thus, according to the ICOM Code of Ethics for Museums, which was also mentioned by the ICPRCP in relation to this case:

> [M]useums should be prepared to initiate dialogue for the return of cultural property to a country or people of origin. This should be undertaken in an impartial manner, based on scientific, professional and humanitarian principles as well as applicable local, national and international legislation, in preference to action at a governmental or political level.[73]

Therefore, it favours dialogue involving the concerned museum rather than negotiations at the interstate level, such as those foreseen by the ICPRCP, an intergovernmental body. Furthermore, the ICOM ethical code encourages a proactive approach to the return of cultural property, with museums invited to 'initiate dialogue' rather than simply respond to requests for return. By contacting ICOM upon the raised suspicion about an object in its collection, the Barbier-Mueller Museum thus abided by the ethical guidelines of its professional organisation.

In terms of de-accession from museum collections, the ICOM Code of Ethics also provides that removing an object from a museum collection 'must only be undertaken with a full understanding of the significance of the item, its character (whether renewable or non-renewable), legal standing, and any loss of public trust that might result from such action'.[74] This is in line with its ethical principle

[70] There are already synergies between the ICPRCP and ICOM, as representatives of ICOM may participate in the meetings of the ICPRCP in an advisory capacity; see ICPRCP Rules of Procedure, r 6.3.

[71] This is in line with its purpose; see ICOM Statutes (2023), art 2.

[72] See ICOM (n 17). The museum had required the agreement to be signed under the aegis of ICOM; interview with Maître Yves Jeanrenaud, legal representative for the Barbier-Mueller Museum, online, 29 June 2023. It should be noted that ICOM also funded the return ceremony held at Hotel Raphaël in Paris.

[73] The ICOM Code of Ethics for Museums (adopted 1986 and revised 2004), 6.2. At 6.3., the Code of Ethics further states that: 'When a country or people of origin seeks the restitution of an object or specimen that can be demonstrated to have been exported or otherwise transferred in violation of the principles of international and national conventions, and shown to be part of that country's or people's cultural or natural heritage, the museum concerned should, if legally free to do so, take prompt and responsible steps to cooperate in its return.' It is worth noting that the ICOM Code reflects 'principles generally accepted by the international museum community as base-line standards for the museum sector worldwide'; see the Checklist on Ethics of Cultural Property Ownership compiled by ICOM, the ICOM Ethics Committee, and the Koordinierungsstelle Magdeburg: www.icom.museum/wp-content/uploads/2018/07/110825_Checklist_print.pdf.

[74] ICOM Code of Ethics for Museums, 2.13.

according to which museums 'have particular responsibilities to all for the care, accessibility and interpretation of primary evidence collected and held in their collections'. Therefore, the seeking of information and certain guarantees by the Barbier-Mueller Museum before agreeing to return the object was in line with the standards established by ICOM.

According to the ICOM Code of Ethics, museums must therefore strike a delicate balance between their duty to preserve their collections and responding to requests for return. It is only in the case of restitution – that is, when an object has been 'exported or otherwise transferred in violation of the principles of international and national conventions, and shown to be part of that country's or people's cultural or natural heritage' – that the ICOM Code of Ethics states that a museum should 'if legally free to do so, take prompt and responsible steps to cooperate in its return'.[75] The question of returns falling outside of the law is not dealt as clearly by the Code, which refers to impartiality, as well as 'scientific, professional and humanitarian principles'.[76] Recognising the complexities raised by requests for return, ICOM compiled a checklist on ethics of cultural property ownership in 2011.[77] However, while the checklist was meant to improve the guidance to museums dealing with such issues, it only reiterates the ethical principles contained in the Code, along with the provision of some contacts within ICOM who may in turn offer further advice on specific queries. Unless this void has been filled by guidelines at the national level, museums are left largely alone in dealing with such requests and establishing their own guidelines for cases falling outside the law.

Nevertheless, it is worth noting that the ICOM Code of Ethics does provide ethical guidelines for acquisition, as it states that:

> [E]ffort must be made before acquisition to ensure that any object or specimen offered for purchase, gift, loan, bequest, or exchange has not been illegally obtained in, or exported from its country of origin or any intermediate country in which it might have been owned legally (including the museum's own country). Due diligence in this regard should establish the full history of the item since discovery or production.[78]

While the conditions of the sale of the Makonde mask in Paris are somewhat unclear, the vendor was certainly not able to provide a full history of the item. However, although the Makonde mask was an example of the purchase of a cultural object where the conduct of due diligence falls short of the current ICOM ethical guidelines, at the time of the mask's acquisition, these guidelines had not yet been adopted. That being so, there is a need for clearer guidelines from ICOM still, as many objects have entered museum collections at a time when ethical (and legal) standards were not yet adopted or widely accepted.

[75] ibid 6.3.
[76] ibid 6.2.
[77] See Checklist on Ethics of Cultural Property Ownership (n 73).
[78] ICOM Code of Ethics for Museums, 2.3.

VI. The Return and its Impact

Like the rest of the process, the actual return of the mask was an affair of institutions, states and international organisations. The exchange ceremony held in Paris was not public and was only attended by a few individuals, including representatives of the Tanzanian Ministry of Natural Resources and Tourism, the co-founder of the Barbier-Mueller Museum and its director, as well as the director of ICOM. At the time, a Tanzanian representative reportedly stated that 'the nation marks a historic day as we receive one of the country's cultural heritage treasures', even if the mask, a typical Makonde mask, was not necessarily considered a national treasure before its return.[79]

In Dar es Salaam, there was no special ceremony to celebrate the return of the mask, which has been housed in the museum's strong room since its return in 2010, along with other items also considered national treasures. While researchers can request to view the mask, the strong room is generally not accessible to the public. Contrary to 'Zinj', the returned mask has not become an object of pride for the museum and there is no indication of its presence in any of the publicly accessible areas of the museum. With security having been a condition for its return,[80] the museum has thus decided to house the mask, indefinitely, in its strong room to avoid any possible future embarrassment. As such, with the mask hidden from view, its return story is not told anywhere within the walls of the museum. Rather than a national treasure, the first exhibit welcoming any visitor inside the courtyard of the House of Culture is a US-funded memorial for the hundreds of victims of the 1998 terrorist attacks against the US embassies in Tanzania and Kenya.[81]

There are many possible reasons for the lack of celebrations in Tanzania, which contrasts with some other examples given in this book. Indeed, the mask returned had not been directly stolen from a community, but from a national museum, which made the entire process one of institutions and states, with a striking absence of other local stakeholders. Thus, the status of the mask as a somewhat ordinary museum object likely made the return less prone to celebration, as might have been the case if the mask had been an object that still had strong community ties or an object that had belonged to a national hero figure.

The lack of ceremonies in Tanzania may also derive from the return having been labelled as a 'donation' in recognition of the good faith of the Swiss collector and the impact this had on the Tanzanian sentiments surrounding the case. Folarin Shyllon, a leading African scholar in the fight against the illicit trafficking of cultural objects, strongly criticised the terms of the agreement for the return of the mask, insisting that the return amounted to restitution rather than donation,

[79] Shyllon (n 51) 82.

[80] ibid 81. It should be noted that Shyllon reports messages from Jean-Paul Barbier-Mueller, who indicated having received a guarantee that the mask would be housed in a secured showcase.

[81] The memorial was erected for the twentieth anniversary of the attacks in 2018.

a term 'indicative of the patronising posture of the museum'.[82] He argues that the receiving state, Tanzania, was forced to agree to the conditions imposed by the Swiss institution in order to have the mask back.[83] In addition to labelling the return as a donation, the compensation that had to be provided to the Swiss museum may have further irritated the sentiments of the Tanzanians.[84]

In any case, the return of the Makonde mask did not lead to any cultural cooperation between the Barbier-Mueller Museum and the National Museum of Tanzania: the two institutions have had no contact and neither of the two institutions publicly acknowledge the 'successful' return of the Makonde mask.[85] Indeed, at the Barbier-Mueller Museum, there is no trace of the Makonde mask having ever been part of its collection. But while it has not publicised any general return policy, it is worth noting that some of its African collection has been exhibited on African soil with some long-term impact: its gold artifacts collection led to the establishment of the Gold of Africa Barbier-Mueller Museum in Cape Town in 2001, where most of its collection was exhibited until it moved to Pretoria in 2019.[86] In addition, a few months before the mask was returned, Jean-Paul Barbier-Mueller launched a cultural foundation seeking to study 'neglected populations that are in danger of disappearing',[87] which prohibits those involved in its research from acquiring or receiving objects from the populations concerned.

In Switzerland, despite some calls for the adoption of legal instruments to address questions of provenance research and restitution, there is at present no domestic law beyond the legislation that implements the 1970 UNESCO Convention.[88] Interestingly, when considering a parliamentary motion to adopt measures to support institutions faced with a request to return colonial objects specifically, the Swiss Federal Council commented that it is an issue that requires a coordinated international approach (rather than a national one) and that, therefore, principles pertaining to the return of such objects should be preferably developed by UNESCO.[89] Nevertheless, in a message issued in 2020, the Federal Council

[82] See Shyllon (n 51) 80.

[83] ibid 82.

[84] ibid 81, where he refers to '"maintenance" costs for the warehousing of the mask over the years'. He is also very critical of the initial return offer, which sought to avoid the transfer of ownership.

[85] This was confirmed by the current director of the Barbier-Mueller Museum, Anne-Joëlle Nardin, email communication, 18 July 2023.

[86] Javett-UP, 'The AngloGold Ashanti Barbier-Mueller Gold of Africa Collection', 24 September 2019–16 December 2025, www.javettup.art/exhibitions/the-anglogold-ashanti-barbier-mueller-gold-of-africa-collection.

[87] See Cultural Foundation, 'Launch of the Fondation Culturelle Musée Barbier-Mueller at the Musêe du Quai Branly in Paris on 24 March 2010', www.fondation-culturelle-barbier-mueller.org/en/launch-of-the-fondation-culturelle-musee-barbier-mueller-at-the-musee-du-quai-branly-in-paris-on-24-march-2010.

[88] See, for example, the parliamentary motion Wermuth 18.4236 on a common strategy for provenance research and restitution of cultural objects dating from the colonial period, which was presented in 2018 and rejected in 2019: www.parlament.ch/fr/ratsbetrieb/suche-curia-vista/geschaeft?AffairId=20184236.

[89] ibid.

underlined the importance of a responsible legal and ethical approach to looted heritage.[90] Although it has so far mostly focused its efforts on Nazi-looted art, the Swiss confederation has adopted several measures which are relevant to cultural objects taken in other circumstances, including the provision of financial support to Swiss museums for provenance research and the adoption of guidelines.[91] It was precisely to explain the measures already undertaken that a report was published in 2022, following another unsuccessful parliamentary motion seeking the adoption of a federal procedure for Swiss museums to engage in the restitution of cultural property taken during the colonial era.[92] While the report does not mention the role of the Swiss government in the return of the Makonde mask, it underlines that the Federal Office of Culture can act as a coordinator and facilitator in return processes.[93]

In the absence of national legislation and guidelines for the return of cultural heritage beyond Nazi-looted art, some Swiss museums have adopted their own strategy, including in particular with regard to objects taken in the colonial context.[94] In addition, Switzerland has expressed its commitment to providing its good offices to the parties to a dispute involving objects housed in Swiss collections, as well as supporting the role of the ICPRCP.[95] The Federal Council has also supported a parliamentary motion which sought the establishment of a platform for provenance research.[96] And finally, in 2023, the Swiss Federal Council decided to establish an independent expert Commission for Cultural Heritage with a Problematic Past, which will be managed by a newly created Looted Art and Provenance Research department within the Federal Office of Culture.[97]

With the mask having been housed in a strong room since its return, the impact it has had on the National Museum of Tanzania has been minimal. However, in the museum's strategic plan for the period 2021–26, one of its objectives includes the establishment of an inventory of cultural treasures located outside the country, as

[90] Swiss Federal Council, 'Message for Culture for the Period 2021–2024', FF 2020 3037 3112.

[91] Federal Office of Culture, 'Provenance Research in Switzerland', www.bak.admin.ch/bak/en/home/cultural-heritage/looted-art-from-the-nazi-period/provenance-research-in-switzerland.html.

[92] See Report of the Federal Office of Culture to the Science, Education and Culture Committee of the Council of States on the work undertaken in relation to cultural property from a colonial context (2 March 2022), which followed parliamentary motion Sommaruga 20.3754.

[93] ibid 10, where the report refers to the return of a statue of God Ekeko to Bolivia.

[94] In 2022, the Swiss Museum Association published a booklet on provenance research focused on the colonial context; see VMS AMS, 'Recherches de provenance dans les musées II: Collections liées aux contexts coloniaux. Notions de base et introduction à la pratique', 2022, www.museums.ch/admin/data/files/media/file_fr/424/vms_standard_provenienz_koloniale-sammlungen_f_web.pdf?lm=1700553846. For more on the practice of Swiss museums, see K Kuprecht, 'Colonial Loot and Its Restitution – Country Report: Switzerland' (2022) 8 *Santander Art and Culture Law Review* 457, 460–61, 463–64, 467–68.

[95] Federal Office of Culture, 'Alternative Dispute Resolution', www.bak.admin.ch/bak/en/home/cultural-heritage/looted-art-from-the-nazi-period/alternative-dispute-resolution.html.

[96] See motion 22.3023 of the Science, Education and Culture Committees, www.parlament.ch/fr/ratsbetrieb/suche-curia-vista/geschaeft?AffairId=20223023.

[97] See the ordinance on the independent commission, which came into force on 1 January 2024, which followed the partial adoption of a parliamentary motion, Pult 21.4403, www.fedlex.admin.ch/filestore/fedlex.data.admin.ch/eli/oe/2023/89/fr/pdf/fedlex-data-admin-ch-eli-oe-2023-89-fr-pdf.pdf.

well as the development and implementation of a restitution plan by June 2026.[98] According to Wilson Jilala, a forensic anthropologist at the National Museum of Tanzania, 63 foreign institutions have already been identified as having Tanzanian objects within their collections.[99] Curators of the National Museum of Tanzania have started to collaborate with some of the institutions currently housing those objects to gain further information. Indeed, before considering requesting the return of any object, the National Museum seeks to assess not only the physical condition of the objects but also its 'cultural' or 'community value' – that is, whether its return would be of sufficient benefit for the museum or its community of origin.[100]

At the time the Makonde mask was returned, the Tanzanian representative was reported pointing out that 'Tanzania has the right to reclaim the stolen cultural artefacts and other items of artistic value spirited out of the country';[101] however, it has not been involved in any other high-profile request for return since the case of the Makonde mask. The Antiquities Division, which falls under the Ministry of Natural Resources and Tourism, has not yet adopted a specific policy concerned with the return of cultural heritage but developments are underway.[102] Nevertheless, Wilson Jilala mentioned that even if all the objects identified in foreign collections by the National Museum were requested and returned, 'we will know what to do, it's ours'.[103] In response to security concerns, he underlined that they should not be an excuse to withhold an object as 'the reality is wherever you keep this object, whether in Europe, whether in Africa, whether in the Americas, the criminals are there, they are everywhere, and they do it if they need it'.[104] He added that a lack of infrastructure should equally not be used as an excuse not to return heritage. Indeed, he believes that former colonies have a role to play through the provision of reparations, which should include the financing of infrastructures to house returned objects, and that this would in turn provide value for a society which continues to suffer from the consequences of colonialism. He sees the inclusion of heritage provisions within reparations as a means of redressing 'barbaric actions', noting that:

> [I]t is up to the colonial masters [*sic*] and us to sit down and discuss what means of reparations can help us … they have benefited millions in money, millions of objects from this country. They should see the humanity, they should see the reason for feeling pain in these individuals.[105]

[98] National Museum of Tanzania, 'Strategic Plan 2021/22–2025/26' 5.

[99] Interview with Wilson Jilala, forensic anthropologist at the National Museum of Tanzania, Dar es Salaam, 3 October 2023, who noted that Germany has been identified as the most important holder of paleontological remains from Tanzania, with 500 crates having been taken from Southern Tanzania before the First World War.

[100] ibid.

[101] See Shyllon (n 51) 82.

[102] See further above.

[103] Interview with Wilson Jilala, forensic anthropologist at the National Museum of Tanzania, Dar es Salaam, 3 October 2023.

[104] Interview with Wilson Jilala, forensic anthropologist at the National Museum of Tanzania, Dar es Salaam, online, 25 September 2023.

[105] Interview with Wilson Jilala, forensic anthropologist at the National Museum of Tanzania, Dar es Salaam, 3 October 2023.

Jilala believes that many African countries are willing to negotiate and focus on the future rather than past mistakes, without forgetting the pain: 'apologising is a key for opening the discussion … we apologise to show respect'.

In relation to infrastructure, one may even go further and question such a need altogether. A Tanzanian contemporary artist who was asked to participate in a cultural project linked to the return of cultural objects stated: 'we don't need museums. That is not how we use those objects in Tanzania'.[106] Thus, although former colonial powers may support the existence of museums elsewhere in the world, they should not be imposed as a condition to obtain cultural heritage in return.

Thus far, Tanzania has not been as vocal about cultural reparations as some other African states, in particular West-African states such as Nigeria.[107] However, it has established a commission tasked with the development of a national plan for the return of cultural heritage. Much of the debate is now focused on addressing the consequences of the colonial era.[108] Several German museums have initiated provenance research projects and return processes with regard to objects of Tanzanian origin within their collections, including in particular objects looted during the Maji Maji War.[109] As part of its two-year exhibition of looted objects which will be returned to Tanzanian at its conclusion, the Humboldt Forum has invited contemporary Tanzanian artists to 'dialogue' with the masks in its collections, including with the carving of new masks.[110] Thus, provenance research and

[106] Interview with Rachel Kessi, Director of Muda Africa/Contemporary Dance, online, 16 October 2023.

[107] According to Rachel Kessi, Director of Muda Africa/Contemporary Dance, interview, 16 October 2023, this may be in part a legacy of former President Nyerere.

[108] With regard to looting during the colonial era, Germany had only legally been required, under the Treaty of Versailles which followed the conclusion of the First World War, to return the skull of Sultan Mkwawa, the Hehe tribal leader who had led the rebellion in German East Africa. After having been located within the collections of the Übersee-Museum in Bremen, it was transferred to the British government, which administered Tanganyika at the time, which eventually returned it to its community of origin in 1954. For the full story, see J Desplat, 'The Skull of Sultan Mkwawa', *The National Archives*, 15 August 2019, www.blog.nationalarchives.gov.uk/the-skull-of-sultan-mkwawa. See also PM Bushozi, 'Towards Sustainable Cultural Heritage Management in Tanzania: A Case Study of Kalenga and Mlambalasi Sites in Iringa, Southern Tanzania' (2014) 69 *South African Archaological Bulletin* 136, 137. It should be noted that beyond the Treaty of Versailles, there has not been any other legal obligation for Germany to return objects looted during its colonial rule.

[109] For example, with partners at the National Museum of Tanzania, the Humboldt Forum has developed an exhibition of looted objects, which will be returned at the close of the exhibition; see Staatliche Museen zu Berlin, 'Ethnologisches Museum: Restitutions to Namibia and Tanzania', 29 June 2022, www.smb.museum/en/whats-new/detail/ethnologisches-museum-restitutions-to-namibia-and-tanzania/#:~:text=The%20Restitution%20of%20Objects%20to%20Tanzania&text=The%20pilot%20project%20Tanzania%2FGermany,Maji%20Memorial%20Museum%20in%20Songea. See also 'Germany to Send Back All Artifacts it Stole during Maji-Maji Warfare', *Tanzania Times*, 29 June 2022, www.tanzaniatimes.net/germany-sends-back-all-artifacts-it-stole-from-tanzania-during-maji-maji-warfare. For more in general on collaborative research, see K Weber-Sinn and P Ivanov, '"Collaborative" Provenance Research: About the (Im)Possibility of Smashing Colonial Frameworks' (2009) 18 *Museum and Society* 66. For an introduction to the Guidelines for dealing with artefacts acquired from colonial contexts adopted in Germany in 2018, see ch 6 in this book.

[110] Humboldt Forum, 'Vinyago – Dancing beyond Colonial Biographies', 23 November 2022–8 January 2023, www.humboldtforum.org/en/programm/laufzeitangebot/dance/vinyago-58145.

the return of cultural objects can become part of a larger cultural cooperation project, which may in turn support the cultural and creative sector.[111]

VII. Conclusion

The return of the Makonde mask was the result of nearly two decades of negotiations. It is interesting to note that an agreement was finally reached when the parties met in person privately, in Geneva, after years of written correspondence and formal meetings within the framework of the ICPRCP. From a legal standpoint, while the mask had been stolen and illegally exported from Tanzania, the 1970 UNESCO Convention was not applicable as it was not in force in Switzerland when the mask entered the collection of the Barbier-Mueller Museum. This showcases the limitations of treaty law, which in principle does not apply retroactively, in addressing this type of claims. It also highlights a current lack of bilateral agreements for the return of cultural objects. The importance of bilateral agreements was indeed specifically noted by the ICPRCP, including for cases falling outside the scope of the 1970 Convention. And while Switzerland has already concluded nine bilateral agreements, it does not have any with a Sub-Saharan country yet.[112]

While the legal landscape changed considerably in Switzerland during the negotiations for the return of the mask, these discussions did not weigh heavily on its ratification of the 1970 UNESCO Convention. And although the case of the Makonde mask did not lead to a surge in cases brought before the ICPRCP, its resolution certainly demonstrated that placing such a dispute under an international (and intergovernmental) spotlight could put pressure not only on the country party to it, but also on a private possessor falling under its jurisdiction. While Tanzania had sought the return of the mask since 1996, it is only since its formal request before the ICPRCP that significant steps were made towards its return. Indeed, after having been officially pending before the ICPRCP at its 2007 and 2009 sessions, the mask was eventually returned in 2010. Therefore, it may be inferred that the intergovernmental committee, and the political pressure it can add to requests for return, can usher parties to a dispute to come to an agreement, even in the absence of legal requirements to do so. As foreseen with the establishment of the ICPRCP, this mechanism may, thus, be particularly beneficial for claims over objects taken during the colonial rule, which may not be otherwise

[111] However, it should be noted that there may be legitimate concerns in participating in such projects. Rachel Kessi, the Director of MUDA, a contemporary dance company in Tanzania, believes that reputational risks may be associated with working with a European institution which some call to boycott: interview, 16 October 2023.

[112] It should be noted that Switzerland is examining the possibility of concluding further bilateral agreements, including with African countries; interview with Marco Eichenberger, scientific collaborator at the Swiss Federal Office of Culture, online, 12 October 2023. For a list of current agreements, see Federal Office of Culture Specialised Body for the International Transfer of Cultural Property, 'Bilateral Agreements', www.bak.admin.ch/bak/en/home/cultural-heritage/transfer-of-cultural-property/bilateral-agreements.html.

supported by any applicable legal provision. This rationale led the ICPRCP to formalise its mediation and conciliation procedure in 2010, the year the mask was returned. While it has not yet been put into effect, most states support it, as noted in the MONDIACULT Declaration adopted in 2022. Furthermore, the immediate willingness of the Barbier-Mueller Museum to return the mask was somewhat beneficial for its image,[113] and provides another example of the positive disposition of a museum to return an object despite the benefit of a legal title over it.

Finally, the requirements of the Barbier-Mueller Museum for returning the mask, the legitimacy of which may in themselves be questioned, were largely respected. As agreed, the Tanzanian government compensated the museum for some of the fees it incurred as a result of the dispute and financed the return of the mask, since the collector had purchased the mask in good faith and initiated the steps to facilitate its return. Nevertheless, the payment of compensation appears to have had a negative impact on the way in which the return is generally seen in Tanzania. Also, while the security requirement attached to the return of the mask can be explained by the theft of the mask that resulted in its acquisition by the Swiss collector, it has led to it remaining locked up in the strong room of the museum. While it had been collected for all to learn about the Makonde culture, it is currently not readily available for all museum visitors to enjoy, which significantly reduces the potential impact and meaning of the return. Without a security requirement attached to its return, it is likely that the return of the mask would have had a greater impact in Tanzania. This begs the following questions: was the imposition of such a requirement worthwhile? And, if so, who should bear the cost of an increased security infrastructure?

While there is a need to further engage local communities in heritage governance, there is also a need for training relevant stakeholders in order to curb the illicit trade in cultural objects.[114] A visit to a local arts market appears to suggest that Dar es Salaam continues to be a stop on the route of traffickers.[115] According to Wilson Jilala, there is still insufficient knowledge and capacity within the police and custom department to curb the trafficking in cultural objects.[116] Despite being stored in a secure environment, the benefits of having had the mask returned are minimal for the nation, especially for the community of origin of the mask, which is located hundreds of kilometers away and which had no part in the return process. As public engagement and education around the mask could enrich the understanding and appreciation of its cultural significance, museum staff hold aspirations that the mask will be displayed more prominently in the future, suggesting that its narrative is far from concluded and that another chapter has yet to be written.

[113] Interview with Maître Yves Jeanrenaud, legal representative for the Barbier-Mueller Museum, online, 29 June 2023.

[114] See Bushozi (n 108) 137, 140.

[115] W Jilala, and N Lwoga, 'The Illicit Trade in Cultural Objects in Tanzania: An Investigative Report' (2024) 4 *Journal of the Kenya National Commission for UNESCO* 1.

[116] Interview with Wilson Jilala, forensic anthropologist at the National Museum of Tanzania, Dar es Salaam, 3 October 2023.

9

Conclusion

Lessons Learnt from Past Return Processes

The return processes discussed in the preceding chapters are very diverse, with major differences stemming from their respective contexts and jurisdictions. But despite their many idiosyncrasies, several commonalities emerge, which allow for the identification of the lessons learnt and recommendations that are presented in this final chapter. While applicable to a majority of cases, it is worth noting from the outset that not all findings are pertinent to all of the cases analysed. Therefore, they should not be treated as generalisations that are necessarily applicable to all return processes, but rather as considerations which may inform other current or future return processes, support further developments in the area, and enrich the debate on the return of cultural objects by bringing different, longer-term and often unheard perspectives thereto. Indeed, while the cases presented in this volume can be described as exploratory, the research into these past processes and the fate of returned cultural objects was equally exploratory.

All the return processes detailed in this volume consisted of the first overseas return process of a certain type of object or between certain categories of parties. This meant that, for the return to happen, a number of questions had to be answered and hurdles overcome along the way. Moreover, the parties involved had to demonstrate flexibility and adapt their own personal views or institutional policies in order to achieve a result that was satisfactory for both parties. This was generally the case when negotiations were conducted in good faith, with a mutual intention to reach an agreement. While the cases considered in this book all resulted in the return of the objects claimed, the processes that led to this were difficult to foresee and plan for, often depending on the goodwill and tenacity of individuals and institutions alike. The lack of predictability in the return processes was largely due to their pioneering character. The absence of applicable legal or policy frameworks was another factor that confounded those processes, which thus had to rely heavily on ethical considerations, without much external guidance or support being available to the individuals or institutions involved in those processes. Yet, these return processes also illustrate that despite the lack of applicable rules to direct them, or even in spite of legal obstacles, returns have nevertheless been possible in a manner that brought (at least some level of) satisfaction to both parties.

Since research for this volume started, several new laws and guidance documents have been adopted at the domestic level to bring some clarity, if not certainty, to those involved in processes aimed at the return of cultural objects. The development of some of these instruments was informed by the exploratory return processes analysed in this volume and the innovative solutions they devised to resolve complex problematics. But while some of these processes inspired more structured and systematised approaches, others have not done so – or, at least, not yet. At present, although the laws and guidance that have been adopted thus far have advanced the ways in which return processes are approached in some jurisdictions, they have still not led to a fundamental shift across Europe. Return processes remain in principle reactive rather than proactive, a matter of exception rather than the norm. There is significant work ahead to ensure that responses to return claims, as well as return processes, become both more predictable and satisfactory for all stakeholders involved. By pointing to possible lessons learnt from a variety of past processes, this volume seeks to offer valuable insights that can inform and shape future developments in this area.

I. Ethical, Legal and Institutional Frameworks

A. Ethical Values and the Wider Historical Context

The circumstances which surrounded the removal of the cultural objects from their contexts can offer a sufficiently firm ethical basis for allowing their return, in the absence of a clear legal basis providing for the return of the items in question. In some of the cases examined, the export and subsequent import of the objects into Europe was lawful because there was no legal restriction that was applicable to their transfers at the time. Even if the removal of the objects from their contexts had amounted to theft, their extended stay in European collections meant that the latter had lawfully obtained titles to them, becoming their recognised owners within their jurisdictions. In other instances, the removal of the objects was deemed explicitly lawful from the start due to the colonial laws or policies which were then applicable, or because of an apparent authorisation to remove the object, obtained in a situation of inequality or duress. In such cases, even if the removal of the object may have been contrary to a local or traditional law, such a rule was not taken into account.

Thus, the requests for the return of specific cultural objects, as well as the decisions and processes followed for their return, were not based on legal provisions, but were guided by ethical values such as fairness, justice, equity, compassion, respect or accountability. When applying these ethical values, the parties involved considered the wider historical context surrounding the removal, along with the originally intended use of the object and the circumstances under which they were taken. In some cases, the decision to return an object can be viewed as part of a reckoning of past wrongs, even in the absence of any direct or recognised responsibility for the historical injustices that framed the removal and transfer of the object. Furthermore, in some instances, a comprehensive understanding of the wider context also often necessitated to take into account contemporary borders and nations that did not exist at the time the objects were appropriated. In two of the processes examined, the establishment of independent statehood had even led to a greater appreciation of the objects in question in the country of origin. This was the case for objects which had once belonged to individuals who have since become national heroes due to their resistance against colonial powers: Witbooi in Namibia and Diponegoro in Indonesia (see Chapters 6 and 7, respectively). The return of their belongings can be situated within a broader context of reconciliation between Germany and Namibia, and between the Netherlands and Indonesia. Therefore, changes in the contexts of origin and shifts in perspectives regarding past events should be considered when evaluating the future of objects in cultural collections, a consideration which may give rise to a solid ethical basis for returning these objects.

In the case of the G'psgolox pole covered in Chapter 2, the removal and export of the totem pole was authorised by the Canadian government at a time when First Nations were forcibly controlled by the government. The decision of the Swedish museum to return it was principally rooted in the profound meaning it held for the claimant and its originally intended purpose, which led the returning party to eventually accept that it could be laid to rest in its natural environment, destined to disintegrate, rather than being preserved indoors for posterity. There is little doubt that the wider historical context also played a role in the decision of the Swedish museum. It was certainly a ground for requesting its return on the part of the claimant community. The absence of legal requirements to return cultural objects in the face of past wrongs and continued inequalities has led the Canadian Museum Association to recommend that the duress imposed on First Nations should be taken into account when considering their repatriation claims, and that the time period during which duress was imposed should be considered as extensive, possibly extending to the present day. This approach reflects the current practice of some museums, which already apply a low threshold when deciding whether to return a cultural object. Indeed, these museums focus on whether the claimant is the adequate entity or person to return the object to rather than whether there are any legal obligations requiring the object to be returned. This demonstrates a particularly clear consideration of the wider historical context, which could apply to all objects removed from their contexts of origin during certain periods.

With regard to the church bells discussed in Chapter 4, although they had been legally acquired and exported from Chile, their connection to an immense human tragedy in Santiago also provided an ethical basis for their return. While the fire that had destroyed the church where they had hung was not linked to a historical wrong, their donation by Welsh parish communities was still deemed the 'right thing to do'. Thus, their return was driven by a sense of compassion for the people of Chile, despite the bells having been integrated into the cultural fabric in and around Swansea for nearly 150 years. While the uniqueness of this case may not have inspired ethical guidance like in other jurisdictions, it nevertheless strongly influenced to another, similar return shortly afterwards.

When there is no legal basis for a return or when existing legal frameworks appear unjust in light of the wider historical context, an ethical approach can thus help shape responses to claims and any subsequent return process. However, it is worth noting that, given the untested nature of the return processes examined in this book, the ethical values that could be applied were not always evident and often had to be identified along the way. In some cases, those who returned cultural objects simply reported having acted out of a moral imperative to 'do the right thing' in the light of a wider context, without necessarily pointing to specific ethical values. To improve this ethical reasoning, there should be a clearer articulation of the values and principles that can guide contextual analyses in return processes. This should also encompass the reconciliation and weighing of potentially conflicting or competing ethical values by the parties involved. For example, as evidenced in several cases such as the return of the G'psgolox pole, the ethical claims of a country or community of origin can sometimes clash with museum conservation ethics. While the exploratory processes analysed in this volume may provide valuable insights for developing further ethical guidance, they certainly highlight the importance of ethical values and the challenges associated with their identification and application when addressing claims for the return of cultural objects.

B. Enabling Legal Frameworks and Alternative Dispute Resolution

While the application of ethical values alone may suffice in resolving return claims to the satisfaction of all parties involved, an enabling legal or institutional framework can significantly facilitate return processes. With the exception of the case of the dagger of Diponegoro which was returned following the Joint Recommendations adopted decades earlier by Dutch and Indonesian representatives, the return processes explored in this volume could not be anchored in a clear policy or legal instrument. In fact, in many cases, the applicable legal framework posed significant obstacles that the parties had to navigate in order to successfully complete a return process. For instance, in the case of the church bells returned to Chile, legal restrictions limited the disposal of assets of the Welsh church community that wished to return them. It was only due to the advanced legal knowledge of one of the individuals involved, and an expansive interpretation of the law, that this barrier was overcome, allowing for the swift return of the bells. Conversely, in the case of the totem pole, such a flexible interpretation was not possible. As a result, the return was delayed, partly due to the authorisation required from the government to return an object that had become state property by being incorporated into the collection of a national museum. Similarly, in the case of the

Khmer statues (see Chapter 5), the inalienability of French collections rendered ownership transfer impossible, thus requiring a creative approach from the parties involved. In turn, this seemingly fostered some resentment from the Cambodian side, which has yet to openly acknowledge France's continued ownership of the head of a statue that was, at least temporarily, returned.

In other instances, such as in Germany, there was a legal framework that enabled the respective museums to return an object within their collections if they deemed it adequate to do so. Thus, while a legal basis is not strictly necessary for the return of an object overseas, an enabling legal framework can alleviate unnecessary hurdles when ethical grounds for such returns are established. And in the Netherlands, while the return of the Diponegoro dagger was primarily grounded in the Joint Recommendations made following independence, the country had since adopted additional legal provisions which further facilitated its return.

Beyond an enabling legal framework, the cases examined here have prompted a critical examination of the need for legal requirements to return cultural objects acquired under circumstances of inequality or coercion, even in cases where no formal laws were in place at the time of removal or transfer. While legal obligations for the restitution of items taken during the Holocaust have been adopted, similar measures have been implemented only in rare instances concerning objects taken in other contexts of duress or inequality. While returns should not be compelled upon a country or community of origin, the development of clear legal requirements for a proactive evaluation of cultural items within collections warrants serious consideration.

It is also important to recognise that while international law has not created significant obstacles to the return of cultural objects, it has also not provided substantial support for such processes. In particular, the 1970 UNESCO Convention offers a wide-ranging framework, but it has proven to be largely irrelevant in the cases we analysed. Many of these cases involved the removal of cultural objects prior to the Convention's adoption or involved countries that had not yet ratified it. Nevertheless, it has certainly influenced perceptions of ownership concerning cultural property, emphasising national interests over international ones.

In terms of the processes involved in the return of cultural objects, it is notable that all documented returns resulted from alternative dispute resolution, specifically negotiation, rather than arbitration or mediation. While the intergovernmental sphere has sought to play a role in resolving disputes over cultural objects through the ICPRCP, established under the aegis of UNESCO, this committee played only a marginal role in one instance: the return of the Makonde mask. Although bringing the case before an intergovernmental committee may have bolstered Tanzania's negotiation position, the ICPRCP merely encouraged constructive dialogue between the parties without direct intervention. Consequently, in nearly all the analysed cases, negotiations were conducted directly between the entity seeking the return and the returning party, whether a state, museum or religious institution. Notably, none of the cases utilised the mediation procedure integrated into the functioning of the ICPRCP in 2010. While this procedure may play a more significant role in the future, it is only applicable to UNESCO Member States and Associate Member States, thereby supporting state-led processes that may not always adequately address the concerns of all stakeholders. Alternatively, mediation facilitated by a non-governmental organisation could prove more effective to ensure that relevant communities and individuals are actively involved.

Regardless of the format, engaging third parties as mediators could possibly be advantageous for all involved in the return processes. Presently, European museums often find themselves at the centre of a public debate that has become increasingly polarised in recent years. The cases documented in this volume largely unfolded away from public scrutiny, allowing the involved parties to manage the complexities of the return process without the pressures of public opinion, until a resolution was achieved. Where returns received more visibility, such as in the case involving the Netherlands and Indonesia, or in Namibia, strong opposition or criticism emerged. In the case of the dagger of Diponegoro, the public debate focused on the authenticity of the returned object. In Namibia, the discussion was more localised between national authorities and communities. Such controversies highlight the shortcomings of certain processes, but also risk dampening the willingness to engage in future return processes. As returns are increasingly in the public eye, the involvement of third parties may provide a welcome buffer for those engaged in these discussions.

C. From Existing Institutional Relationships to Fortuitous Circumstances

Although some of the return processes in this book resulted from fortuitous circumstances, established institutional relationships played a crucial role in facilitating several returns. For instance, the return of objects to Namibia benefited from pre-existing connections with the German museum, allowing for the swift return of the Witbooi letters. Similarly, although the French legal system bars the transfer of ownership of items that have become part of a public collection, the long-standing relationship between French and Cambodian cultural actors not only facilitated the 'crossed deposits' of parts of two statues, but it served also as a platform that fostered the discussion about the exchange in the first place. Therefore, while an enabling legal framework can ensure the absence of unwanted hurdles once ethical grounds for returning an object are established, an institutionalised relationship can promote constructive dialogue over the return of cultural objects, whether on a temporary or permanent basis. Close cooperation between museums through research and other forms of regular engagements has resulted in more straightforward return processes. Such relationships has led to innovative solutions, demonstrating the willingness of individuals on both sides to find workable resolutions, even amidst a proscriptive legal context.

Finally, several of the return processes analysed in this volume were propelled by the determination of the requesting parties and serendipitous circumstances.

For example, the church bells were brought to the attention of Chilean representatives by individuals in the UK who had a personal interest in their story, which in turn piqued the interest of the Chilean government. In the case of the idols returned to Nepal, the return happened after a visitor fortuitously identified the Uma-Maheshwor in Berlin (see Chapter 3). Similarly, the Makonde mask was not identified in a museum in Geneva by someone actively searching for it, but rather by an expert who happened to have photographed it years earlier in the National Museum of Tanzania before it was stolen (see Chapter 8). In the case of the totem pole, the Haisla Nation was made aware of its presence in Scandinavia through hearsay, prompting a Haisla delegation to take the opportunity of a trip to the region, made for entirely different reasons, to go to Stockholm to verify whether the pole was in fact theirs. Overall, the return processes analysed were typically not the result of proactive initiatives by the institutions which held the objects in question. A proactive framework could ensure that the return of cultural objects would not solely rely on chance or the initiative of particularly active claimants. A first step towards a proactive institutional approach involves investing in provenance research, making collections (especially those not on display) accessible to researchers from countries of origin, and ensuring that inventories are available online when appropriate. Institutions holding cultural objects in their collections should also consider whether these objects should be returned and, if so, contact those who may have an interest in the object(s) being returned. To facilitate this, relevant institutions should be provided with the financial means to adopt such as proactive approach, which may derive from a legal obligation to act proactively, as mentioned above.

II. Practical Challenges and Obstacles

Beyond the applicable legal frameworks, which in several cases constituted major hurdles to completing a return process desired by both parties, the processes considered brought several additional challenges to light, including securing the financial resources required to complete a process, engaging all the possible rights holders to an object being returned, and the attachment of conditions to the return of an object.

A. Addressing the Financial Implications

Aside from legal barriers, the financial costs associated with returning objects often pose significant obstacles. The need for financial resources typically begins with the provenance research required to adequately address a claim. Although there is a growing trend encouraging museums to adopt a proactive approach to returning cultural objects, this has not been accompanied by the necessary financial support to facilitate such efforts. During interviews, several museum professionals mentioned that provenance and repatriation work must be prioritised within existing budgets, often at the expense of other activities, in a sector where resources are increasingly scarce. Moreover, requests for returns are not only increasing but are also becoming more complex and costly – for instance, when involving researchers and experts from the countries of origin at an earlier stage. In the cases analysed, such involvement was rare – not necessarily due to a lack of interest, but rather due to the challenges and costs associated with it. Additionally, a proactive approach should not be confined to provenance research or verification; it should also encompass outreach to potentially interested entities or individuals. However, many institutions find themselves limited in their ability to engage fully due to resource constraints. In the current climate, this results in museums often facing criticism for not doing enough by default.

Similar, and frequently more substantial, financial limitations exist in the countries of origin, which may have to cover part of the return costs or face the financial implications of receiving and re-integrating the object into their collections. Particularly in cases where conditions are attached, meeting these requirements can be financially burdensome for the receiving party. The case of the G'psgolox pole exemplifies this, as the financial burden of returning an object often falls primarily on the claimant; for smaller communities, this can effectively prohibit or at least delay a return. Communities and states that have lost their cultural heritage under duress should not have to bear the financial burden of its return. In several analysed cases, funding for the return of objects was secured through external sources, such as in-kind donations for transportation, while other costs were supported by charitable organisations or individual museum benefactors. However, the return of objects should not hinge on the goodwill of external parties. A state that has benefited from housing an object, whether in a public museum or private museum, should bear the financial responsibility for its return when justified. Furthermore, it should allocate resources to enable its museums to adopt a more proactive approach, as well as support the communities seeking the return of their cultural objects.

B. Engaging Heritage Holders Beyond the Claimants

In all analysed cases, the party that sought the return of an object was the one to which the object was ultimately returned. Notably, none of the returning institutions or countries opted to return the object(s) to another party than the claimant. This pattern held true regardless of the type of claimant, whether they were a government or a community. While this seems straightforward, it has occasionally raised questions, especially in instances where an object was returned to a state despite its significant ties to a specific community or even a family. For example, in Namibia and Indonesia, objects were returned to the respective governments, despite the fact that the original individual owners were identified. Yet, since these individuals had become national heroes, the objects are now housed in national collections rather than held by their heirs or communities of origin. Although the relevant community or family may have accepted this outcome, their interests were not always adequately represented during the return process. Communities often lack the necessary capacity or network to navigate the intricate procedures involved in requesting or negotiating a return, or they may not even be aware of ongoing high-level diplomatic discussions regarding their cultural heritage. As highlighted by the G'psgolox case, a community needs to be particularly resilient in order to pursue a claim for the return of a cultural object. However, a possible lack of capacity should not lead to the dismissal of the legitimate interests of a community or individual in an object.

Even when a government spearheads a return process, it can still consider community interests once an object has been returned. For example, in Nepal, the Patan Museum appears poised to relocate the revered relief back to its original site. More broadly, there has been a reckoning in the country that returning idols to their communities for worship may be preferable to their sterile preservation within museum walls. This recognition has led to a surge in returns to Nepal, accompanied by vibrant community celebrations each time an idol is restored to its original location. Such returns resonate particularly deeply for spiritually important objects, yet this intangible meaning is not systematically considered. In the case of the Harihara statue in Cambodia, for instance, despite the awareness of its spiritual value among all the parties involved, it remains housed in the National Museum, primarily due to the material-focused approach to preservation that has been deeply entrenched within the national conservation culture in Cambodia.

The cases in this volume demonstrate the importance of ensuring that multiple perspectives are represented throughout the return process, extending beyond those who formally claim the object. When considering the varied interests and groups that may be connected to an object, it is also crucial to acknowledge its intangible dimensions – for example, its role in worship or traditional ceremonies. In line with a human rights approach, the community concerned should be actively engaged in the return process, which should not be confined to government representatives. Both the returning and receiving parties must recognise the potential for diverse, multi-layered interests in an object. Conducting broad consultations, possibly including relevant diaspora communities through the application of a human rights lens, could enhance perceptions of the process and the parties involved, fostering a sense of ownership among all stakeholders. In addition to ensuring that the voices of local heritage holders are both heard and thoughtfully considered during return processes, their informed consent should in some cases also be sought in relation to the re-integration of an object. This is particularly important when the object is not returned to its local place of origin, but instead to a central governmental entity. Doing so can establish a more equitable framework for the return of cultural heritage.

C. Making Returns Conditional

While this volume predominantly features cases where the returning entity allowed the country, institution or community of origin to decide on the fate of the returned object, there are notable cases where the return was contingent upon specific conditions being fulfilled by the requesting party. Although agreeing to such conditions facilitated the return, they systematically proved challenging, if not impossible, to implement, resulting in a generally negative perception of the return process among claimants. For instance, the return of the Makonde mask (see Chapter 8) was granted on the stipulation that it would be securely stored to prevent theft, leading to its storage in a strong room that is not directly accessible to the museum's visitors. While this arrangement satisfied the condition imposed by the returning party, it fell short of being a wholly satisfactory outcome for the National Museum of Tanzania, which currently lacks the means to upgrade its security infrastructure, as well as for the Tanzanian public, which cannot readily view the returned mask. Similarly, the return of the totem pole to the Haisla Nation was conditional on its continued preservation for future generations in a climate-controlled facility. Although this requirement was initially agreed upon, it eventually became evident that meeting it would be overly burdensome, particularly because of the financial implications of constructing such a facility. Ultimately, the Swedish museum relinquished this condition, recognising that allowing the pole to disintegrate in nature, in accordance with Haisla tradition, was the most appropriate course of action. Thus, the conditions attached to the return of the pole complicated and prolonged negotiations, with the only benefit being the understanding gained by museum staff. These examples also illustrate that once an object has been returned, the receiving entity often tends to comply with the terms of the agreement, at least until the stipulated conditions become overly challenging to fulfil.

Conditions tied to the return of objects may extend beyond security or conservation requirements; they can also shape the format of the return itself, which may not necessarily entail a full transfer of ownership. For example, the National Museum of Cambodia would have likely preferred to obtain legal title over the head of the Harihara statue to ensure its permanent return. However, due to French legislation, it had to accept its return as a loan, without transfer of ownership and on a temporary basis. Moreover, this loan was accompanied by a reciprocal arrangement in the form of a 'crossed deposit', wherein the Cambodian side permitted a foot piece to complete another Khmer statue still housed in the Guimet Museum in Paris.

Other conditions may be prerequisites for the return of an object, such as the making of a replica. In the cases examined, the making of a replica was never imposed, but was offered to jump-start stalled negotiations. The Haisla Nation offered a replica of the G'psgolox pole, understanding that it might ease the de-accessioning of an object that had become state property by providing a 'like for like' replacement. This offer was well received by the Swedish museum and its visitors, who were able to witness Haisla culture in action during the final stages of the pole's carving within the museum. Today, visitors continue to appreciate this ambassador of a distant culture. However, the Haisla community largely views the creation of the replica negatively, feeling it was a forced compromise. Some community members emphasised that a totem should not be duplicated, as it should remain unique, asserting that producing an exact replica contradicts their beliefs.

Given these complexities, attaching a condition to the return of an object should be considered carefully and avoided wherever possible, particularly when it may adversely affect the process or its perception. This includes the creation of replicas, which may not align with cultural practices, and could be replaced by the commissioning of a new piece instead. Both parties must assess the feasibility of conditions and consider whether additional support may be necessary to meet them. Ultimately, such conditions should be evaluated not only in light of the receiving institution or community's capabilities, but also their values and the underlying principles guiding the return process.

III. Return Processes as Opportunities

A. Platforms for Reconciliation and Cooperation

While considering the historical circumstances under which an object was removed from a context may support the decision to return it, the act of returning cultural objects may itself constitute a step towards reconciliation and the redress of past wrongs. Although none of the processes considered in this volume was part of judicial or quasi-judicial means of reparations resulting from the establishment of responsibility for a wrongful act, some occurred alongside broader efforts seeking to address, if not repair, a colonial legacy. In those instances, the return of cultural objects offered a concrete opportunity for parties to come together and begin addressing historic grievances. Restoring culturally significant objects to peoples formerly subjected to domination can contribute to empowering them, whether as a nation or as a community. Even when the return of an object does not constitute restitution within a reparative framework, it can still complement and possibly provide leverage for broader reconciliation efforts. In some contexts, these processes may also include cultural revitalisation initiatives, with the returned object acting as a potent symbol of reclaimed identity, as illustrated by the case of the G'psgolox pole. Therefore, it appears essential for processes to engage the communities associated with the objects in question, as well as with the historic wrongs being addressed, and to transcend state-led processes.

This can be further illustrated by the case of the return by a German museum of objects that had belonged to Witbooi to Namibia, which unfolded within a broader context of apologies and reparations. However, this case also illustrated that reconciliation efforts should extend beyond state-to-state processes to include affected communities, which were largely overlooked, resulting in an association of Nama leaders attempting to bring a restitution claim before a German court. This situation arose because Namibia sought to unify the nation, often at the expense of tribal identities, thereby controlling the return process of objects that had belonged to someone who had since become a national hero rather than being solely considered as a community leader.

Beyond the overarching issue of reconciliation, return processes have also offered opportunities to develop or strengthen relationships. For example, although local communities in Namibia were not directly involved in the process, the return of the Witbooi objects was nevertheless part of a broader initiative aimed at fostering new research partnerships between Germany and Namibia. Although such collaborations might appear to seek continued control and authority over returned objects, they often represent an important step towards rebalancing previously unequal relationships and provide a platform for mutually beneficial cooperation in the future.

In nearly all the cases analysed in this book, the parties engaged in negotiating the return of objects found themselves developing or strengthening their working relationships. This proximity often stemmed from the difficult conversations that were necessary to reach an agreement. These conversations often challenged long-held values such as those regarding conservation principles and the traditional role of museums focused on preserving the past. These negotiations also often stirred up complex and deep-seated emotions tied to the injustices that occurred when the objects were removed from their contexts. Indeed, negotiating the return of cultural objects can be a cathartic process.

However, regardless of how strong a newly formed relationship felt at the time an object was returned, that feeling often faded unless other arrangements, such as cooperation programmes, were established to sustain the connection. A prime example of this can be seen in the ongoing collaboration between the National Museum of Cambodia and the Guimet Museum in Paris, where experts have long worked together and continue to do so. Ultimately, while the return of cultural objects can provide a platform for developing future cooperation, a structural or institutional framework is necessary to ensure that the close relationships forged during negotiations evolve into longer-term partnerships, if that is desired by both parties. Otherwise, relationships are likely to dwindle, no matter how strong they felt at the time of a handover.

B. Steps towards a New Role for Museums

Each return process detailed in this volume is marked by its unique characteristics and specific challenges, underscoring the notion that a universal model does not exist. Nevertheless, despite the need for a flexible case-by-case approach, these processes highlight the necessity for a more institutionalised approach to guarantee fair and appropriate handling of return claims. Consequently, the experiences documented herein have influenced not only the guidance or policies adopted by the governments concerned but also the practices within the museum community.

In addition, museum professionals interviewed for this research frequently referred to returning cultural objects as work that is both essential and rewarding, albeit fraught with challenges. Therefore, museums should strive to adopt a proactive rather than reactive approach to the possible return of cultural artifacts in their collections. This does not imply that every item in a collection should inevitably be returned as, in the cases analysed, the claimants sought the return of specific objects rather than entire collections. But by embracing a proactive stance, museums can critically evaluate their collections, which can in turn contribute to knowledge exchanges through collaboration with experts and communities. Such an approach aligns with the recent definition of museums adopted by the International Council of Museums, which emphasises the importance of community participation and the role of museums in serving society, a society which also increasingly recognises the necessity of addressing historical injustices. A proactive approach to the potential return of cultural objects can thus be integrated into a decolonisation process, ensuring that museums remain relevant for contemporary societies.

While a museum may find itself with a vacant space following the return of an object, this presents an opportunity to consider how the narrative surrounding the object's return can be conveyed, despite its absence. When a tangible reminder of the returned object remains, this task becomes more straightforward. For example, in Leiden, although there is currently no reference of the past presence of the dagger that returned to Indonesia, the museum has entered the €1 coin received in exchange in its collection and intends to use it to narrate the story of the return. At the Guimet Museum, the Harihara head was exchanged for a foot piece that now completes another statue housed in Paris. Although the museum label indicates that the foot piece is on loan from Cambodia, it does not mention the head that was returned in exchange as part of the 'crossed deposits' model. In Wales, the Little Bell left behind serves as a tangible connection to the Santiago fire tragedy and the historical ties between Wales and Chile. Its display includes a panel recounting the story of the return of the other bells. In Sweden, the replica of the totem pole is also accompanied by an exhibit detailing the original pole's story and its return. While the narrative is not fully incorporated inside the museum's walls, there is a panel explaining that totem poles are traditionally meant to return to nature, an Indigenous principle made clear to the museum staff following the return of the G'psgolox pole.

It is evident that a tangible reminder aids in the storytelling of an object's journey and its return. However, the absence of any visible trace should not deter museums from discussing an object's past existence within their collection. As museums face a growing number of return claims, they should further explore how returning objects can enrich their narratives and contribute to their educational and societal missions. The cases examined here have revealed that, generally, this reflective practice has been rather limited, and sometimes entirely lacking, especially when no tangible evidence of the returned object remains.

Finally, several museum professionals noted in interviews that they now view their role as facilitators of return processes. Given their expertise, museums should be encouraged to play this intermediary function, which may include advising individuals approaching them with objects of uncertain provenance on the most appropriate course of action, in accordance with current ethical standards. In situations where provenance is not immediately clear, museums could serve as a 'safe haven' until provenance is established, preventing the object from disappearing into the marketplace.

IV. Some Final Observations

The cases explored in this volume illustrate that the return of cultural objects cannot be distilled into a singular event. Instead, these are ongoing processes that often lack a clear beginning and certainly a clear conclusion. While significant milestones, such as an official handover, did exist, it is overly simplistic to regard this as the end of a process. Therefore, the analysed cases reveal that cultural objects carry with them a continuous narrative, spanning from their origin to their presence in foreign collections, their return and beyond. Each phase of this journey holds significance and contributes to the object's overall story, adding layers of meaning and value thereto. For instance, the *keris* of Diponegoro was originally just one of the many daggers belonging to the prince. Its temporary residence in the Netherlands, the complexities surrounding its identification, and its return to Jakarta have infused it with a new depth of meaning.

Moreover, the duration between key milestones, such as from the initial claim for the object's return to its handover, can vary substantially. The factors contributing to a process's length are often multi-faceted and cannot be easily reduced to identifiable markers like the legal environment, financial constraints or willingness to return. The return of the Uma-Maheshwor to Nepal was particularly swift, as was the process for the Santiago bells, each taking less than a year to complete. In contrast, other cases, such as the return of the Makonde mask, spanned nearly 20 years, while the G'psgolox pole took 15 years to return for entirely different reasons. Several museum professionals deemed that allowing time for the return of an object can facilitate understanding among museum staff and the broader community on both sides regarding the rationale behind the return request, potentially supporting the process and enhancing satisfaction for all parties involved. Gaining insight into why an object is being claimed can significantly influence how other items in a museum's collection are managed. Furthermore, this understanding may impact the practices of other museums within the same jurisdiction or possibly further afield. The return of the G'psgolox pole, for example, has influenced museum practices with regard to similar claims and guided the adoption of new governmental guidance for museums.

Nevertheless, claimants deserve prompt attention be paid to their requests, particularly communities that may feel some urgency, as their elders often possess unique knowledge about objects that needs to be passed down to younger generations. Therefore, the necessity of avoiding undue delays must be balanced with ensuring rigorous processes that do not overlook any essential steps that could prevent mistakes being made along the way. The application of due process to these extra-judicial claims should entail adhering to established procedures in order to guarantee fair treatment for claimants. In light of a human rights approach, this should involve engagement or consultation with all relevant stakeholders from the country of origin, allowing for meaningful participation throughout the process. As processes may take time due to legal or other constraints, effective participation should be sought before reaching major milestones, such as a handover. Addressing a claim without undue delay and treating claimants fairly, in accordance with established processes, and facilitating meaningful stakeholder participation should all be integral components of the due process that should be applied to such returns.

The processes examined also reveal that determining the appropriate destination for a returned object – whether a national or regional museum, a community or another entity – and how it is subsequently re-integrated within that context is not a straightforward task. Even when objects are returned to their places of origin, those contexts have likely changed, along with the peoples connected to them, complicating the re-integration process. In many cases outlined in this volume, the initial location where the objects were returned did not ultimately serve as their 'final' resting place, with several still being housed in temporary locations at the time of writing. For example, the Makonde mask currently resides in storage at the National Museum of Tanzania, with staff expressing a desire for it to be exhibited once again. Similarly, the dagger that belonged to Diponegoro remained in storage at Indonesia's National Museum for over four years after its return, before eventually being put on display. In Namibia, objects once owned by Witbooi are still housed in national institutions, at least until a local museum can be established in Gibeon, where Witbooi was a leader. Furthermore, discussions about the Nepali idol are ongoing regarding its potential return to the community for worship, despite being currently displayed in a museum. A careful consideration of an object's re-integration, especially when it takes into account its intangible values, can in turn enable the fulfilment of human rights, including in particular cultural rights, through the practice of living traditions that may still be associated with the returned object.

Moreover, in several cases, objects have already been relocated multiple times since their return. For instance, the church bells returned by the parish community of Oystermouth were the object of the construction of three different memorials, with a permanent location established only after their return to Santiago. In the case of the totem pole, which was initially intended for conservation in a climate-controlled facility, it was ultimately returned to nature a few years after its return on Haisla traditional territory, following discussions within the community. This instance also underscored that differing viewpoints often exist within a community as some members of the Haisla community would have preferred that the pole be conserved for future generations. The context in Nepal also illustrated that communities may not unanimously support returning objects to the local level, outside of museum settings, with varying concerns expressed by different voices.

Therefore, returning cultural objects should not be perceived as processes that conclude with their handover, as the ways in which objects are re-integrated are likely to change over time. The vacant space they leave behind, or any tangible reminder of their past presence in an institution, also takes time to be filled again. Indeed, only a few of the institutions considered in this volume are telling the story of the objects they returned. This ongoing re-integration and retelling process should be understood as one in which the 'lives' of the objects continue to unfold alongside those of the communities invested in them. Beyond the various locations and displays to which objects may be subjected upon their return, the narratives surrounding them and their interpretation also evolve. The manner in which the stories of objects, including their returns, are told not only provides stakeholders with an insight into the objects themselves, but also contextualises their removal and return within a broader historical narrative. This should not be viewed as rewriting history in a manner that erases it, but rather as re-evaluating the past and re-interpreting stories through newly acquired knowledge and diverse perspectives. Consequently, both returning and receiving parties may regard the act of handover as a step in an ongoing journey, which could lead to further discussions and consultations regarding the re-integration of objects and the telling of their stories. Return processes can thus enrich the narratives surrounding those objects and, most importantly, the people associated with them.

BIBLIOGRAPHY

Abungu GO, '"Universal Museums": New Contestations, New Controversies' in M Gabriel and J Dahl (eds), *UTIMUT: Past Heritage – Future Partnerships* (Copenhagen, IWGIA/NKA, 2008)

Adviescommissie Nationaal Beleidskader Koloniale Collecties, 'koloniale collecties en erkenning van onrecht' (Raad Voor Cultuur, October 2020)

Aldrich R, 'France and the *Patrimoine* of the Empire: Heritage Policy under Colonial Rule' (2011) 4 *French History and Civilization* 202

Allgöwer R, 'Gericht macht den Weg frei: Land kann Witbooi-Bibel zurückgeben' *Stuttgarter Nachrichten* (21 February 2019) www.stuttgarter-zeitung.de/inhalt.gericht-macht-den-weg-frei-land-kann-witbooi-bibel-zurueckgeben.cd4b50aa-ffac-4071-88b3-5f71c730218b.html

Ani Casimir KC, Nwakego OS and Umezinwa E, 'Masking Traditions and Their Behavioral Functions in Accounting for Stability and Order: A Critical Exposition of Select Study of West, East and Central African Masks' (2015) 5 *Open Journal of Political Science* 115

Ardiyansyah P, 'Restitution and National Heritage: (Art) Historical Trajectories of Raden Saleh's Paintings' in L Tythacott and P Ardiyansyah (eds), *Returning Southeast Asia's Past: Objects, Museums and Restitution* (Singapore, NUS Press, 2018)

Arts Council England, 'Restitution and Repatriation: A Practical Guide for Museums in England' (September 2023)

Associated Press, 'Cambodia Welcomes the Met's Repatriation of Centuries-Old Statues Looted during Past Turmoil' *CNN Style* (5 July 2024) https://edition.cnn.com/2024/07/05/style/cambodia-statue-repatriation-met-museum/index.html

Aymonier E, *Le Cambodge I: Le Royaume actuel* (Paris, Ernest Leroux, 1900)

Baden-Württemberg.de, 'Baden-Württemberg bringt Witbooi-Bibel und Peitsche zurück nach Namibia' (baden-wuerttemberg.de, 22 February 2019) www.baden-wuerttemberg.de/de/service/presse/pressemitteilung/pid/baden-wuerttemberg-bringt-witbooi-bibel-und-peitsche-zurueck-nach-namibia-1

——. 'Witbooi-Bibel und Peitsche an Namibia übergeben' (baden-wuerttemberg.de, 28 February 2019) www.baden-wuerttemberg.de/de/service/presse/pressemitteilung/pid/witbooi-bibel-und-peitsche-an-namibia-uebergeben

Baird JR, Solanki A and Askren M (eds), *Returning the Past: Repatriation of First Nations Cultural Property* (Vancouver, UBC Museum of Anthropology, 2008)

Bandle AL, Chechi A, and Renold M, '20 Herero and Nama Skulls – Namibia and Charité Universitätsmedizin Berlin, Germany' (ArThemis Art-Law Centre University of Geneva) https://plone.unige.ch/art-adr/cases-affaires/20-skulls-of-colonial-victims-2013-namibia-and-charite-universitatsmedizin-berlin

Bandle AL, Contel R and Renold M, 'Affaire Masque Makondé – Tanzanie et Musée Barbier-Mueller' (ArThemis Art-Law Centre University of Geneva) https://plone.unige.ch/art-adr/cases-affaires/masque-makonde-tanzanie-et-musee-barbier-mueller

Bangdel LS, *Stolen Images of Nepal* (Kathmandu, Royal Nepal Academy, 1989)

Baptiste P and Zéphir T, 'L'Art khmer dans les collections du musée Guimet' (2008) MNAAG/Réunion des musées nationaux

Barkan E, *The Guilt of Nations: Restitution and Negotiating Historical Injustices* (New York, WW Norton & Company, 2000)

BBC, 'Church Bells May Return to Chile' *BBC News* (8 February 2010) http://news.bbc.co.uk/1/hi/wales/south_west/8504057.stm

——. 'Church Bells Ring in Mumbles for Rescued Chilean Miners' *BBC News* (14 October 2010) www.bbc.co.uk/news/uk-wales-south-west-wales-11543578
——. 'Swansea Clergy in Chilean Honour for Bells of Santiago' *BBC News* (2 March 2011) www.bbc.co.uk/news/uk-wales-south-west-wales-12607117
——. 'St Thomas's Church, Neath, Returns Bell to Chile' *BBC News* (24 September 2012) www.bbc.co.uk/news/uk-wales-19678810
——. 'Bell Salvaged from Disaster Returns to Santiago, Chile' *BBC News* (27 November 2013) www.bbc.co.uk/news/av/uk-wales-25131577
——. 'Santiago Bells: Swansea Service to Mark Chilean Cathedral Fire' *BBC News* (8 December 2013) www.bbc.co.uk/news/uk-wales-south-west-wales-25279970
——. 'Hindu God Statue's Head Returns to Cambodia' *BBC News* (21 January 2016) www.bbc.co.uk/news/world-asia-35378747#:~:text=The%20statue%2C%20a%20representation%20of,to%20the%20body%20on%20Thursday
——. 'Viewpoint: Why Germany's Namibia Genocide Apology is Not Enough' *BBC News* (1 June 2021) www.bbc.co.uk/news/world-africa-57306144
Bell CE and Paterson RK, 'International Movement of First Nations Cultural Heritage in Canadian Law' in CE Bell and RK Paterson (eds), *International Movement of First Nations Cultural Heritage in Canadian Law* (Vancouver, UBC Press, 2009)
Biard S, 'Réflexions sur l'histoire de l'exposition et de la restauration des effigies de culte anciennes au Cambodge' (2017) 30 *Recherche en sciences humaines sur l'Asie du Sud-Est* 131
Biblioteca del Congreso Nacional de Chile, 'Campanas del Congreso Nacional de Chile' (bcn.cl, 13 December 2010) www.bcn.cl/portal/noticias?id=campanas-congreso
——. 'Nueva Tradición en el Ex Congreso: Repique de las Campanas de la Compañía de Jesús' (bcn.cl, 11 March 2011) www.bcn.cl/portal/noticias?id=nueva-tradicion-repique-campanas-compania-de-jesus
Björklund A, *Hövdingens totempåle: Om konsten att utbyta gåvor* (Stockholm, Carlsson, 2016)
——. 'The Case of Chief G'psgolox's Totem Pole: "Rescuing", Keeping, and Returning' (2018) 11 *Baltic Worlds* 72
Brady K, 'Germany Refers to Herero Massacre as Genocide' *DW* (13 July 2016) www.dw.com/en/germany-officially-refers-to-herero-massacre-as-genocide/a-19396892
Brassem E, 'Indonesische experts: Nederland gaf de verkeerde kris terug' *Trouw* (21 April 2020) www.trouw.nl/gs-b42b3451
British Commonwealth Fire and Rescue Company 'J.A.S. Jackson', 'Ceremonias' (14.cl) www.14.cl/multimedia/videos/ceremonias
——. 'Nuestra Compañía Rinde Honores en el Momento del Funeral del Príncipe Felipe' (14.cl) www.14.cl/nuestra-compania-rinde-honores-en-el-momento-del-funeral-del-principe-felipe
Broderick C, 'The Discovery of "Zinj"' (The Leakey Foundation, 12 July 2019) https://leakeyfoundation.org/the-discovery-of-zinj
Brown K, 'People across the Globe Want Their Cultural Heritage Back. Canada May Offer a Blueprint for How to Get There' *Artnet* (24 June 2018) https://news.artnet.com/art-world/canada-restitution-indigenous-culture-1307060
Bursey L, 'Demokratia: Will the Greek Ideal Work in Greece's Favour to Return the Parthenon Marbles under International Law?' [2024] *Journal of International Humanitarian Legal Studies* 1
Bushozi PM, 'Towards Sustainable Cultural Heritage Management in Tanzania: A Case Study of Kalenga and Mlambalasi Sites in Iringa, Southern Tanzania' (2014) 69 *South African Archaeological Bulletin* 136
Cámara de Diputados de Chile, 'Entrega de Campanas de la Iglesia de la Compañía de Jesús' (YouTube, 7 December 2010) www.youtube.com/watch?v=GWx04Egb-pc&t=380s
Campfens E, *Cross-Border Claims to Cultural Objects* (Leiden, EM Meijers Instituut voor Rechtswetenschappelijk Onderzoek, 2021)
——. 'Cross-Border Claims to Looted Art' European Parliament's Policy Department for Citizens' Rights and Constitutional Affairs (October 2023)

Canadian Museums Association, 'More than Giving Back: Repatriation Toolkit. A Toolkit in Support of Moved to Action: Activating UNDRIP in Canadian Museums' (2022)
——. 'Moved to Action: Activating UNDRIP in Canadian Museums. A Response to the Truth and Reconciliation Commission's Call to Action #67' (2022)
Cannobbio J, 'cerem 01' (YouTube) www.youtube.com/watch?v=V6iQuYZaaLU
——. 'cerem 02' (YouTube) www.youtube.com/watch?v=_yQAJChSHE0
Cardinal G, 'Totem: The Return of the G'psgolox Pole' (nfb.ca, 2003) www.nfb.ca/film/totem_the_return_of_the_gpsgolox_pole
——. 'Totem: Return and Renewal' (nfb.ca, 2007) www.nfb.ca/film/totem_return_and_renewal
Carey P, 'Reflections on the Return of the Diponegoro's Dagger Kiai Nogo Siluman. Suluk Kebudayaan Indonesia' (Langgar.co Suluk Kebudayaan Indonesia, 2020) https://langgar.co/reflections-on-the-return-of-the-diponegoros-dragger-kiai-nogo-siluman
CBC News, 'Stolen Totem Pole Formally Welcomed Home to Nisga'a Territory after Nearly a Century in Scottish Museum' *CBC News* (28 September 2023) www.cbc.ca/news/canada/british-columbia/memorial-totem-pole-returned-1.6981891
CBS1863, 'Programa City Tour visita el Cuartel General de la Institución' (YouTube, 17 December 2012) www.youtube.com/watch?v=wy585GGk6YQ
Centro de Extensión del Senado, la Academia Parlamentaria de la Cámara de Diputados y la Biblioteca del Congreso Nacional at Biblioteca del Congreso Nacional de Chile, 'Coloquio sobre Rescate Patrimonial en el Congreso' (bcn.cl, 24 May 2019) www.bcn.cl/portal/noticias?id=video-segundo-coloquio-rescate-patrimonial-congreso
Chechi A, 'The Return of Cultural Objects Removed in Times of Colonial Domination and International Law: The Case of the Venus of Cyrene' (2008) 18 *Italian Yearbook of International Law* 159
——. *The Settlement of International Cultural Heritage Disputes* (Oxford, Oxford University Press, 2014)
Christian Today, 'Historic Church Bell Returns to Chile' (22 September 2012) www.christiantoday.com/article/historic.church.bell.returns.to.chile/30686.htm
Clément E, 'Musées, collections et les translocations du patrimoine culturel' (2022) 29 *La Vie des Musées* 18
Cole D, *Captured Heritage: The Scramble for Northwest Coast Artifacts* (Vancouver, UBC Press, 1995)
Collyns D, 'Chile Returns Looted Books to Peru' *BBC News* (7 November 2007) http://news.bbc.co.uk/1/hi/world/americas/7082436.stm
Consejo de Monumentos Nacionales de Chile, 'Las Campanas de la Iglesia de la Compañía Han Vuelto para Honrar a los Caídos' (monumentos.gob.cl, 29 September 2010) www.monumentos.gob.cl/prensa/noticias/campanas-iglesia-compania-han-vuelto-honrar-caidos
Cox D, '"Inalienable" Archives: Korean Royal Archives as French Property under International Law' (2011) 18 *International Journal of Cultural Property* 409
Cuerpo de Bomberos de Santiago, 'Historia' (cbs.cl) www.cbs.cl/historia
——. 'Institución' (cbs.cl) www.cbs.cl/Institucion/historia
Cultural Foundation, 'Launch of the Fondation Culturelle Musée Barbier-Mueller at the Musêe du Quai Branly in Paris on 24 March 2010' (fondation-culturelle-barbier-mueller.org) www.fondation-culturelle-barbier-mueller.org/en/launch-of-the-fondation-culturelle-musee-barbier-mueller-at-the-musee-du-quai-branly-in-paris-on-24-march-2010
Darling D and Cole D, 'Totem Pole Restoration on the Skeena, 1925–30: An Early Exercise in Heritage Conservation' (1980) 47 *BC Studies* 29
Database Peraturan, 'Peraturan Pemerintah (PP) No. 66 Tahun 2015' (peraturan.bpk.go.id) www.peraturan.bpk.go.id/Details/5642/pp-no-66-tahun-2015
Davies G, 'Clyne Chapel' *The Story of Mumbles* (22 May 2024) www.storyofmumbles.org.uk/stories/memories/20th-century/clyne-chapel-4
De Clippele M-S and Demarsin B, 'Pioneering Belgium: Parliamentary Legislation on the Restitution of Colonial Collections' (2022) 8 *Santander Art and Culture Law Review* 323

De Roux E, 'L'affaire du masque makondé du Musée Barbier-Mueller' *Le Monde* (14 February 1998) www.lemonde.fr/archives/article/1998/02/14/l-affaire-du-masque-makonde-du-musee-barbier-mueller_3655103_1819218.html

Delaporte L, *Voyage au Cambodge* (Paris, Maisonneuve et Larose, 1999)

Denk P, 'German Delegation in Namibia to Prepare for Hendrik Witbooi Bible Return' *NBC News* (2019) www.nbcnews.na/news/german-delegation-namibia-prepare-hendrik-witbooi-bible-return.19001

Department of International Law OAS, 'Multilateral Treaties. Signatories and Ratifications' www.oas.org/juridico/english/sigs/c-16.html

Desplat J, 'The Skull of Sultan Mkwawa' (*The National Archives*, 15 August 2019) https://blog.nationalarchives.gov.uk/the-skull-of-sultan-mkwawa

Dhakal A, 'The Enigma of Arrival of Nepal's Gods' *Nepali Times* (2 December 2021) www.nepalitimes.com/banner/the-enigma-of-arrival-of-nepals-gods

——. 'Laxmi-Narayan is Home' *Nepali Times* (4 December 2021) www.nepalitimes.com/banner/laxmi-narayan-is-home

Die Bundesregierung, 'Koalitionsvertrag zwischen CDU/CSU and SPD' (bundesregierung.de, 12 March 2018) www.bundesregierung.de/breg-de/themen/koalitionsvertrag-zwischen-cdu-csu-und-spd-195906

Dieden A, 'Stolen Soul: Africa's Looted Art' *DW* (2020) www.dw.com/en/stolen-soul-africas-looted-art/video-54792198

Dixit KM, 'Gods in Exile' *Himāl Southasian* (30 September 1999) www.himalmag.com/cover/gods-in-exile

Donald Luxton & Associates Inc, D Jensen & Associates Ltd. and Kinexus Consulting Inc, 'Shared Museum Cultural Facility Feasibility Study. Prepared for Kitimat Museum & Archives Haisla Nation Council District of Kitimat' (July 2023)

Duggan M, 'Fire Bell' *Church Times* (19 October 2012) www.churchtimes.co.uk/articles/2012/19-october/news/uk/fire-bell

Dupont P, *La Statuaire Préangkorienne* (Ascona, Artibus Asiae Publishers, 1955)

DW staff, 'Germany Asks for Namibians' "Forgiveness"' *DW* (14 August 2004) www.dw.com/en/germany-asks-for-namibians-forgiveness/a-1298060

EFE, 'Las Campanas que volverán a Santiago' *El Mostrador* (10 August 2019) www.campaners.com/php/textos.php?text=10467

Élysée, 'Emmanuel Macron's Speech at the University of Ouagadougou' (elysee.fr, 28 November 2017) www.elysee.fr/en/emmanuel-macron/2017/11/28/emmanuel-macrons-speech-at-the-university-of-ouagadougou

Erichsen C, 'German-Herero Conflict of 1904–07. African History' (Britannica) www.britannica.com/topic/German-Herero-conflict-of-1904-1907

Espinoza D, 'Campanas perdidas hace 150 años tras histórico incendio vuelven a la vida' *LT Latercera* (14 March 2019) www.latercera.com/cultura/noticia/campanas-perdidas-150-anos-tras-historico-incendio-vuelven-la-vida/570154

Evans C, 'Bell at Neath's St Thomas's Church Returned to Chile' *BBC News Wales* (24 September 2012) www.bbc.co.uk/news/uk-wales-19707617

Falser M, *Angkor Wat: A Transcultural History of Heritage (Volume 1 Angkor in France; Volume 2 Angkor in Cambodia)* (Berlin, De Gruyter, 2020)

Federal Foreign Office, 'Framework Principles for Dealing with Collections from Colonial Contexts Agreed by the Federal Government Commissioner for Culture and the Media, the Federal Foreign Office Minister of State for International Cultural Policy, the Cultural Affairs Ministers of the Länder and the Municipal Umbrella Organisations' (13 March 2019)

——. 'Concept on the Establishment and Organisation of a German Contact Point for Collections from Colonial Contexts' (auswaertiges-amt.de, 16 October 2019) www.auswaertiges-amt.de/blob/2262748/5450242f5fdd6b-343b32919aab9c11a6/191016-kol-kulturgueter-pdf-en-data.pdf (accessed July 2024)

——. 'Foreign Minister Maas on the Conclusion of Negotiations with Namibia' (auswaertiges-amt.de, 28 May 2021) www.auswaertiges-amt.de/en/newsroom/news/-/2463598

Federal Office of Culture Specialised Body for the International Transfer of Cultural Property, 'Bilateral Agreements' (bak.admin.ch) www.bak.admin.ch/bak/en/home/cultural-heritage/transfer-of-cultural-property/bilateral-agreements.html

Federal Office of Culture, 'Alternative Dispute Resolution' (bak.admin.ch) www.bak.admin.ch/bak/en/home/cultural-heritage/looted-art-from-the-nazi-period/alternative-dispute-resolution.html

——. 'Provenance Research in Switzerland' (bak.admin.ch) www.bak.admin.ch/bak/en/home/cultural-heritage/looted-art-from-the-nazi-period/provenance-research-in-switzerland.html

Fincham D, 'Cambodia and Musée Guimet Reunite Khmer Statue' (Illicit Cultural Property, 21 January 2016) http://illicitculturalproperty.com/cambodia-and-musee-guimet-reunite-khmer-statue

Foreign & Commonwealth Office, 'Fourth Bell of Historic Jesuit Church Returns to Chile' (gov.uk, 5 November 2013) www.gov.uk/government/news/fourth-bell-of-historic-jesuit-church-returns-to-chile

Foreign & Commonwealth Office and J Browne, 'From Swansea to Santiago – Historic Church Bells to Return Home' (gov.uk, 10 August 2010) www.gov.uk/government/news/from-swansea-to-santiago-historic-church-bells-to-return-home

Forkl H, *Von Kapstadt bis Windhuk. „Hottentotten" oder Khoisan? Die Rehabilitierung einer Völkergruppe* (Katalog zur gleichnamigen Ausstellung, Stuttgart, Linden-Museum)

Foundation Melina Mercouri, 'Oxford Union, June 12, 1986' (melinamercourifoundation.com) https://melinamercourifoundation.com/en/oxford-union-june-12-1986

Freiburger Institutionen, 'Koloniale Sammlungen im Adelhausermuseum Natur- und Völkerkunde' (freiburg-postkolonial.de) www.freiburg-postkolonial.de/Seiten/Adelhauser-Duerrenberger.htm

G Abbe, '"Decadence and Revival" in Cambodian Arts and the Role of George Groslier (1887–1945)' in M Falser (ed), *Cultural Heritage as Civilizing Mission: From Decay to Recovery* (Cham, Springer, 2015)

Gerda Henkel Stiftung, 'Confronting Colonial Pasts, Envisioning Creative Futures – Collaborative Conservation and Knowledge Production of the Historical Collections from Namibia Held at the Ethnological Museum Berlin and the National Museum of Namibia, Windhoek' (gerda-henkel-stiftung.de) www.gerda-henkel-stiftung.de/en/confronting-colonial-pasts-envisioning-creative-futures

German Museums Association, *Guidelines for German Museums: Care of Collections from Colonial Contexts*, 3rd edn (2021)

Gerstenblith P, 'Schultz and Barakat: Universal Recognition of National Ownership of Antiquities' (2009) 14 *Art Antiquity & Law* 21

——. 'The Meaning of 1970 for the Acquisition of Archaeological Objects' (2013) 38 *Journal of Field Archaeology* 364

Gobierno de Chile, 'Ceremonia de Entrega de Campanas de Iglesia de la Compañía' (YouTube, 20 September 2010) www.youtube.com/watch?v=wJiAghNcdgY

Gorham MV, 'Displaying the Nation: Museums and Nation-Building in Tanzania and Kenya' (2020) 63 *African Studies Review* 487

Government of Canada, 'Backgrounder: United Nations Declaration on the Rights of Indigenous Peoples Act' (justice.gc.ca) www.justice.gc.ca/eng/declaration/about-apropos.html

Green R and Green M, 'Haisla Nuuyum: Cultural Conservation and Regulation Methods within Traditional Fishing and Hunting' (2013) 2 *Decolonization: Indigeneity, Education & Society* 57

Greenfield J, *The Return of Cultural Treasures* (New York, Cambridge University Press, 1989)

Grimme G, 'Discomforting Heritage: Dealing with Colonial-Era Objects in Ethnological Museums: Final Report' (2018)

Grutters M and Muntefering M, 'Eine Lücke in unserem Gedächtnis' *Frankfurter Allgemeinen Zeitung* (15 December 2018) www.bundesregierung.de/breg-de/service/archiv/eine-luecke-in-unserem-gedaechtnis-1561942

Guidelines for the Deaccession of Museum Objects 'Leidraad afstoten museale objecten' (Museumvereniging, LAMO, 2023)

Gustafsson H, *Namibia, Bremen und Deutschland, ein steiniger Weg zur Freundschaft* (Berlin, Aschenbeck und Holstein, 2003)

Harring SL, 'German Reparations to the Herero Nation: An Assertion of Herero Nationhood in the Path of Namibian Development' (2002) 104 *West Virginia Law Review* 393

Hatton C, 'Cambodia: Returning the Gods' (The Documentary Podcast, 12 May 2022) www.bbc.co.uk/programmes/p0c67ghr

Hausler K, 'Les musées nationaux de Royaume-Uni face aux demandes de restitutions, ou l'exception qui confirme la règle' in C Bories et al (eds), *Demandes de restitution et avenir des collections muséales* (Paris, Mare et Martin, 2022)

Herman A, *The Parthenon Marbles Dispute: Heritage, Law, Politics* (London, Hart Publishing, 2023)

——. *Restitution: The Return of Cultural Artifacts* (London, Lund Humphries, 2021)

House of Commons Library, 'Briefing Paper. The Parthenon Sculptures' (9 June 2017) Number 02075

Humboldt Forum, 'Vinyago – Dancing beyond Colonial Biographies' (23 November 2022–8 January 2023)

ICOM Ethics Committee, 'Checklist on Ethics of Cultural Property Ownership Compiled by ICOM, the ICOM Ethics Committee, and the Koordinierungsstelle Magdeburg' (icom.museum) www.icom.museum/wp-content/uploads/2018/07/110825_Checklist_print.pdf

ICOM, 'Makonde Mask – Signing of an Agreement for the Donation of the Barbier-Mueller Museum of Geneva to the National Museum of Tanzania' (Press Release, 10 May 2010)

——. 'ICOM Approves a New Museum Definition' (icom.museum, 24 August 2022) https://icom.museum/en/news/icom-approves-a-new-museum-definition

Irwin R, 'Indian Agents in Canada' (The Canadian Encyclopedia, 25 October 2018) www.thecanadianencyclopedia.ca/en/article/indian-agents-in-canada

ITV Wales Tonight, 'Visit of Chilean Ambassador to All Saints Church Oystermouth, Swansea' (YouTube, 13 May 2011) www.youtube.com/watch?v=8P32pHJe924

Jakarta Globe, 'A Tribute to Indonesia's Prince Diponegoro' *Jakarta Globe* (22 January 2015) https://jakartaglobe.id/features/a-tribute-to-indonesias-prince

Javett-UP, 'The AngloGold Ashanti Barbier-Mueller Gold of Africa Collection' (24 September 2019–16 December 2025)

Jessiman S, 'The Repatriation of the G'psgolox Totem Pole: A Study of its Context, Process, and Outcome' (2011) 18 *International Journal of Cultural Property* 365

Jilala W, and Lwoga N, 'The Illicit Trade in Cultural Objects in Tanzania: An Investigative Report' (2024) 4 *Journal of the Kenya National Commission for UNESCO* 1

Kam Doum, 'Report on the Transfer of Buddha Statues and a Pedestal from Angkor Borei, Village of Prey Kabbas, Takeo Province' (1945) *Kampuchea Soriya* XVII(1): 1–14; XVII(2): 70–93; XVII(3): 137–55

Kashindi Ausiku, 'Gibeon: The Official Return of Kaptein Hendrik Witbooi's Bible and Whip from Germany' (YouTube, 2019) www.youtube.com/watch?v=Td4-v-3RQXw

Kitimat Northern Sentinel Staff, 'PROGRESS 2023: Elders Bless and Unveil Artwork at New Haisla Health Centre Building' *Northern Sentinel* (6 April 2023) www.northernsentinel.com/news/progress-2023-elders-bless-and-unveil-artwork-at-new-haisla-health-centre-building-6195659

Kößler R, 'Hendrik Witbooi's Bible' (africaisacountry.com) www.africasacountry.com/2019/09/hendrik-witboois-bible-and-the-humboldt-forum

——. 'The Bible and the Whip: Entanglements Surrounding the Restitution of Looted Heirlooms' (2019) 12 *ABI Working Paper* 1

——. 'The Restitution of Human Remains and Artefacts: Reflecting on Namibian-German Experiences' (2021)

Kuprecht K, 'Colonial Loot and its Restitution – Country Report: Switzerland' (2022) 8 *Santander Art and Culture Law Review* 457

Legêne S, *De bagage van Blomhoff en Van Breugel. Japan, Java, Tripoli en Suriname in de negentiende-eeuwse Nederlandse cultuur van het imperialisme* (Amsterdam, Koninklijk Instituut voor de Tropen, 1998)

Lidchi H and Brinkgreve F, 'Clues. Research into Provenance History and Significance of Cultural Objects and Collections Acquired in Colonial Situations. Final Report. Pilotproject Provenance Research on Objects of the Colonial Era' (2022) Institute for war, holocaust and genocide studies (NIOD)

Lighthouse Theatre Company, 'Bells of Santiago' (lighthouse-theatre.co.uk) www.lighthouse-theatre.co.uk/productions/bells-of-santiago

Linden Museum Stuttgart Collections Online, 'With Namibia: Engaging the Past, Sharing the Future' (lindenmuseum.de) https://sammlung-digital.lindenmuseum.de/en/topic/with-namibia-engaging-the-past-sharing-the-future_3181

Lopes Fabris A, 'South-South Cooperation on the Return of Cultural Property: The Case of South America' (2017) 49 *Case Western Reserve Journal of International Law* 173

Mace SR and Porte B, *Revealing Krishna: Essays on the History, Context, and Conservation of Krishna Lifting Mount Govardghan from Phnom Da* (Cleveland, D Giles Ltd, 2021)

MacMichael, Sir HA, KCMG, 'News and Views' (1937) 140 *Nature* 1003

Martinez J-L, 'Patrimoine partagé: universalité, restitutions et circulation des oeuvres d'art' (25 April 2023)

Maulipaksi D, 'Repatriasi, Upaya Indonesia Kembalikan Benda Cagar Budaya dari Belanda' (Kementerian Pendidikan dan Kebudayaan, 11 January 2021) www.kemdikbud.go.id/main/blog/2021/01/repatriasi-upaya-indonesia-kembalikan-benda-cagar-budaya-dari-belanda

Mbughuni L A, *The Cultural Policy of the United Republic of Tanzania* (Paris, UNESCO Press, 1974)

McGivern H, 'French Museum Reunites Head with Decapitated Khmer Statue' *The Art Newspaper* (20 January 2016) www.theartnewspaper.com/2016/01/20/french-museum-reunites-head-with-decapitated-khmer-statue

Melber H, 'Germany and Namibia: Negotiating Genocide' (2020) 22 *Journal of Genocide Research* 502

——. 'Germany and Reparations: The Reconciliation Agreement with *Namibia*' (2022) 111 *The Round Table: The Commonwealth Journal of International Affairs* 475

Michaels A, *Nepal: A History from the Earliest Times to the Present* (Oxford, Oxford University Press, 2024)

Mijlemans P, 'Nederland geeft verkeerde dolk terug aan Indonesië' *De Standaard* (23 April 2020) www.standaard.be/cnt/dmf20200423_04932234

Ministère de la Culture, 'Monuments & Sites. Un peu d'histoire' (culture.gouv.fr) www.culture.gouv.fr/Thematiques/monuments-sites/monuments-historiques-sites-patrimoniaux/un-peu-d-histoire

Ministerio de las Culturas, las Artes y el Patrimonio, 'Ministra Valdés Participa en Reinstalación de las Campanas de la Ex Iglesia de la Compañía de Jesús' (15 March 2019) www.cultura.gob.cl/ministra/ministra-valdes-participa-en-reinstalacion-de-las-campanas-de-la-ex-iglesia-de-la-compania-de-jesus

Ministerio de Relaciones Exteriores, 'Condecoraciones' (minrel.gob.cl) www.minrel.gob.cl/minrel/ministerio/ceremonial-y-protocolo/condecoraciones

——. 'Memoria del Ministerio de Relaciones Exteriores de Chile. Año 2009' (Archivo General Hisórico) www.minrel.gob.cl/biblioarchivo/site/artic/20131015/asocfile/20131015154606/memoria_2009__rev_abril_2014_.pdf

——. 'Memoria del Ministerio de Relaciones Exteriores de Chile. Año 2010' (Archivo General Histórico) www.minrel.gob.cl/biblioarchivo/site/artic/20131015/asocfile/20131015154606/memoria_2010__rev_abril_2014_.pdf

——. 'Piezas Patrimoniales Retornan a Chile para el Bicentenario' (chile.gob.cl, 10 August 2010) www.chile.gob.cl/chile/blog/reino-unido/londres/piezas-patrimoniales-retornan-a-chile-para-el-bicentenario

——. 'Ministro (s) Recibe Cuarta Campana de la Iglesia de la Compañía de Jesús' (minrel.gob.cl, 4 October 2013) www.minrel.gob.cl/ministro-s-recibe-cuarta-campana-de-la-iglesia-de-la-compania-de-jesus/minrel_old/2013-11-05/155924.html

Ministerium für Wissenschaft, Forschung und Kunst Baden-Württemberg, 'Aufarbeitung kolonialen Erbes mit der Namibia-Initiative' (mwk.baden-wuerttemberg.de) https://mwk.baden-wuerttemberg.de/de/kunst-kultur/namibia-initiative

Miura K, 'From Property to Heritage. Different Notions, Rules of Ownership and Practices of New and Old Actors in the Angkor World Heritage Site' in B Hauser-Schäublin (ed), *World Heritage Angkor and Beyond: Circumstances and Implications of UNESCO Listing in Cambodia* (Göttingen, Universitätsverlag Göttingen, 2017)

Morrell A, 'Press Release. Neath Church Returns Historic Bell to Earl of Wessex for Chilean Fire Service' (The Church in Wales, 20 September 2012) https://archive.is/20121223203445/http://www.churchinwales.org.uk/press/display_press_release.php?prid=5462

Mouhot H, *Travels in the Central Parts of Indo-China (Siam), Cambodia, and Laos*, in two volumes (London, William Clowes and Sons, 1864)

Museum-Digital, 'August Engelbert Wulff (1878–1952)' (museum-digital.org) https://global.museum-digital.org/?t=people_to_people&id=172940

Museums Association of Namibia, 'Activity-Based Annual Report' (1 April 2005–31 March 2006)

Namhila EN, 'Archives of Anti-colonial Resistance and the Liberation Struggle (AACRLS): An Integrated Programme to Fill the Colonial Gaps in the Archival Record of Namibia' (2015) 4 *Journal for Studies in Humanities and Social Sciences* 168

National Center for Truth and Reconciliation, 'Residential School History' (nctr.ca) https://nctr.ca/education/teaching-resources/residential-school-history

National Museum of Tanzania, 'Strategic Plan 2021/22–2025/26'

Nebe C, 'Namibia: A Timeline of Germany's Brutal Colonial History' *DW* (22 September 2021) www.dw.com/en/namibia-a-timeline-of-germanys-brutal-colonial-history/a-57729985

New York Times, 'Terrific Tragedy in Chili' (18 January 1864) www.nytimes.com/1864/01/18/archives/terrific-tragedy-in-chili-two-thousand-five-hundred-persons-roasted.html

News Desk, 'Prince Diponegoro Chamber Expected to Attract More History Buffs to Jakarta History Museum' *Jakarta Post* (7 April 2019) www.thejakartapost.com/news/2019/04/07/prince-diponegoro-chamber-expected-to-attract-more-history-buffs-to-jakarta-history-museum.html

NHRC, '[Press Note] Laxmi-Narayan's Return to Patko Tole, Patan' (4 December 2021) https://nepal-heritagerecoverycampaign.org/news/press-release-laxmi-narayans-return-to-patko-tole-patan

Nicolasen L and Maas M, 'Opwinding rond de Staf van Prins Diponegoro' *De Volkskrant* (25 March 2015) www.volkskrant.nl/nieuws-achtergrond/opwinding-rond-de-staf-van-prins-diponegoro~b82b40ed/?referrer=https%3A%2F%2Fwww.google.com%2F

NMVW, 'Research Report on the *Keris* of Prince Diponegoro' (27 February 2020)

Noce V, 'Jean-Paul Barbier-Mueller, Museum Founder and Collector Who Opposed the Return of Artefacts to Their Countries of Origin' *The Art Newspaper* (1 February 2017) www.theartnewspaper.com/2017/02/01/jean-paul-barbier-mueller-museum-founder-and-collector-who-opposed-the-return-of-artefacts-to-their-countries-of-origin

——. 'Masterpieces from the Barbier-Mueller African and Oceania Collection to Be Sold at Christie's in Paris' *The Art Newspaper* (6 February 2024) www.theartnewspaper.com/2024/02/06/christies-to-auction-masterpieces-from-the-barbier-mueller-african-and-oceanic-art-collection-in-paris

Observerid.com, 'A Prince's Legacy Part I: The Diponegoro Exhibition at the Indonesian National Museum' *Independent Observer* (21 November 2020) www.observerid.com/a-princes-legacy-part-i-the-diponegoro-exhibition-at-the-indonesian-national-museum

——. '395th Anniversary of the Former Batavia Stadhuis, Now the History of Jakarta Museum' *Independent Observer* (16 February 2022) https://observerid.com/395th-anniversary-of-the-former-batavia-town-hall-now-the-history-of-jakarta-museum

Opoku K, 'Do French Museums Still Need To Study Looted African Treasures?' *Modern Ghana* (26 May 2024) www.modernghana.com/news/1315012/do-french-museums-still-need-to-study-looted-afric.html

Orrin GR and Cowley FG, *A History of All Saints Church Oystermouth* (Llandysul, Gomer Press, 1990)

Overheid.nl Wettenbank, 'Uitvoeringswet UNESCO-verdrag 1970 inzake onrechtmatige invoer, uitvoer of eigendomsoverdracht van cultuurgoederen' (wetten.overheid.nl) https://wetten.overheid.nl/BWBR0025996/2013-01-01

——. 'Wet tot teruggave cultuurgoederen afkomstig uit bezet gebied' (wetten.overheid.nl) https://wetten.overheid.nl/BWBR0021656/2008-08-01

Paquette J, *Museum-Making in Vietnam, Laos, and Cambodia: Cultural Institutions and Policies from Colonial to Post-colonial Times* (New York, Routledge, 2022)

Parish Oystermouth, 'Flag Flying Days' (*oystermouthparish.com*) www.oystermouthparish.com/flag-flying-days (accessed July 2024)

——. 'The Bells of Santiago' (*oystermouthparish.com*) www.oystermouthparish.com/bells-of-santiago (accessed July 2024)

Pelz D, 'No Reconciliation without an Apology' *DW* (29 August 2018) www.dw.com/en/opinion-germany-must-apologize-for-its-genocide-in-namibia/a-45262584

——. 'Namibia: Dispute over Return of the Witbooi Bible' *DW* (27 February 2019) www.dw.com/en/namibia-dispute-over-return-of-the-witbooi-bible/a-47712784

Peters R, *Complementary and Alternative Mechanisms beyond Restitution: An Interest-Oriented Approach to Resolving International Cultural Heritage Disputes* (European University Institute, 2011)

——. 'La gestion des biens de collection issus de contextes coloniaux: les évolutions actuelles en Allemagne' in C Bories et al (eds), *Les restitutions des collections muséales* (Paris, Mare & Martin, 2021)

——. 'Dealing with Collections from Colonial Contexts: Current Developments in Germany' (2022) 8 *Santander Art and Culture Law Review* 371

Phelan S, 'Learn More: Makonde Mask 3' (*PLU/Pacific Lutheran University*, 2015)

Prabowo RS, 'Ini Wujud Keris Pangeran Diponegoro yang Dipamerkan di Museum Keris Solo' *Suara Surakarta* (22 November 2021) https://surakarta.suara.com/read/2021/11/22/142402/ini-wujud-keris-pangeran-diponegoro-yang-dipamerkan-di-museum-keris-solo

Praźmowska-Marcinowska K, 'Repatriation of Indigenous Peoples' Cultural Property: Could Alternative Dispute Resolution Be a Solution? Lessons Learned from the G'psgolox Totem Pole and the Maaso Kova Case' (2022) 8 *Santander Art and Culture Law Review* 135

Prott LV (ed), *Witnesses to History: A Compendium of Documents and Writings on the Return of Cultural Objects* (Paris, UNESCO, 2009)

Rayment C, 'Haisla Celebrate 14th Annual G'psgolox Day' *Northern Sentinel* (7 July 2020) www.northernsentinel.com/news/haisla-celebrate-14th-annual-gpsgolox-day-6170968

Regio TV, 'Witbooi-Bibel wird nochmal ausgestellt' (*regio-tv.de*, 12 December 2018) www.regio-tv.de/mediathek/video/witbooi-bibel-wird-nochmal-ausgestellt

Report of the Federal Office of Culture to the Science, Education and Culture Committee of the Council of States on the Work Undertaken in Relation to Cultural Property from a Colonial Context (2 March 2022)

Reuters, 'Hundreds Storm Namibia Parliament ahead of German Genocide Deal Vote' (22 September 2021) www.reuters.com/world/africa/hundreds-storm-namibia-parliament-ahead-german-genocide-deal-vote-2021-09-21

Rev Canon Evans K, *The Bells of Santiago* (Parish of Oystermouth, Swansea, 2013)

Rijksoverheid, 'Beleidsvisie collecties uit een koloniale context' (rijksoverheid.nl, 29 January 2021) www.rijksoverheid.nl/documenten/kamerstukken/2021/01/29/rapport-beleidsvisie-collecties-uit-een-koloniale-context

——. 'Nederland geeft dolk van Javaanse verzetsheld terug aan Indonesië' (rijksoverheid.nl, 4 March 2020) www.rijksoverheid.nl/actueel/nieuws/2020/03/04/nederland-geeft-dolk-van-javaanse-verzetsheld-terug-aan-indonesie

Sarr F and Savoy B, 'The Restitution of African Cultural Heritage: Toward a New Relational Ethics' (November 2018)

Savitri I et al, 'Kiai Naga Siluman. Dagger Cuts on Both Sides' (Tempo, 14 April 2020) https://magz.tempo.co/read/interlude/36576/kiai-naga-siluman-dagger-cuts-on-both-sides

Schick J, *The Gods are Leaving the Country: Art Theft from Nepal* (Bangkok, Orchid Press, 1997)

Schwarz SKW, 'Art Law in Germany' (Lexology) www.lexology.com/library/detail.aspx?g=9311edd6-803d-44a9-9814-111f7248c550

Scott C, *Cultural Diplomacy and the Heritage of Empire: Negotiating Post-colonial Returns* (Abingdon, Routledge, 2020)

Select Committee of the House of Commons on the Earl of Elgin's Collection of Sculptured Marbles &c (25 March 1816)

Selter E, 'Returning the Gods to the People: Heritage Restitution in Nepal' (2022) 2 *Santander Art and Culture Law Review* 95

Selter E and Weise K, 'Kathmandu Valley and the Management of Living Heritage Sites a Shifting Approach' (BIICL Blog, 30 May 2023) www.biicl.org/blog/61/kathmandu-valley-and-the-management-of-living-heritage-sites-a-shifting-approach

Servicio Nacional del Patrimonio Cultural, 'Mesa de lucha contra el tráfico Ilícito de Bienes patrimoniales' (patrimoniocultural.gob.cl) www.patrimoniocultural.gob.cl/asuntos-internacionales-y-trafico-ilicito-de-bienes-patrimoniales/mesa-de-lucha-contra-el-trafico

Shigwedha VA, 'The Homecoming of Ovaherero and Nama Skulls: Overriding Politics and Injustices' (2018) 4 *Human Remains and Violence: An Interdisciplinary Journal* 67

Shyllon F, 'Return of Makonde Mask from Switzerland to Tanzania: A Righteous Conclusion' (2011) 16 *Art Antiquity & Law* 79

Sijapati A, 'Nepal's Gods Return from Exile' (NHRC, 28 January 2021) https://nepalheritagerecovery-campaign.org/news/nepals-gods-return-from-exile

Small Z, 'Citizen Activists Lead the Hunt for Antiquities Looted from Nepal' *New York Times* (29 October 2021) www.nytimes.com/2021/10/29/arts/nepal-looted-antiquities-citizens.html

Smith E, Ristiawan R and Sudarmadi T, 'Protection and Repatriation of Cultural Heritage – Country Report: Indonesia' (2022) 8 *Santander Art and Culture Law Review* 383

Smith L, *Uses of Heritage* (New York, Routledge, 2006)

Spice M, 'The Valley Where the Gods Have Vanished (Book Review of "The Gods are Leaving the Country: Art Theft from Nepal" by J Schick)' *South China Morning Post* (3 September 2000)

——. 'Piece by Piece, Pillaged Art is Sent Home to Nepal' *The Guardian* (6 September 2000) www.theguardian.com/world/2000/sep/06/nepal

Staatliche Museen zu Berlin, 'Confronting Colonial Pasts, Envisioning Creative Futures' (smb.museum) www.smb.museum/en/museums-institutions/ethnologisches-museum/collection-research/research/confronting-colonial-pasts-envisioning-creative-futures

——. 'Ethnologisches Museum: Restitutions to Namibia and Tanzania' (smb.museum, 29 June 2022) www.smb.museum/en/whats-new/detail/ethnologisches-museum-restitutions-to-namibia-and-tanzania

Staff writer, 'Germany to Send Back All Artifacts it Stole during Maji-Maji Warfare' *Tanzania Times* (29 June 2022) https://tanzaniatimes.net/germany-sends-back-all-artifacts-it-stole-from-tanzania-during-maji-maji-warfare

Staff writer, 'Kwakwaka'wakw Pole Becomes Dutch Centrepiece' *North Island Gazette* (18 April 2013) www.northislandgazette.com/community/kwakwakawakw-pole-becomes-dutch-centrepiece-1367407

Staniforth A, 'Returning Zinj: Curating Human Origins in Twentieth-Century Tanzania' (2009) 3 *Journal of Eastern African Studies* 153

Stevens H, *Bitter Spice: Indonesia and the Netherlands from 1600* (Amsterdam, Rijksmuseum Collection in association with Vantilt Publishers, 2015)

Strebel FD, 'The Enforcement of Foreign Judgements and Foreign Public Law' (1999) 21 *Loyola of Los Angeles International and Comparative Law Review* 55

Swedish National Heritage Board, 'Good Collections Management. Guidance for Managing the Return of Cultural Objects' (2020)

Swiss Federal Council, 'Message for Culture for the Period 2021–2024', FF 2020 3037

Szeto W, 'Haisla Nation, School District Investigate after B.C. Teacher Allegedly Mocks Student for Traditional Regalia' *CBC News* (5 November 2021) www.cbc.ca/news/canada/british-columbia/haisla-nation-regalia-racism-1.6237893

Talmon S, 'The Genocide in Namibia: Genocide in a Historical-Political or in a Legal Sense?' (GPIL – German Practice in International Law, 23 September 2017) https://gpil.jura.uni-bonn.de/2017/09/genocide-namibia-genocide-historical-political-legal-sense

——. 'Reconciliation without Reparation: The German-Namibian Joint Declaration on Our Colonial Past' (GPIL – German Practice in International Law, 20 April 2023) https://gpil.jura.uni-bonn.de/2023/04/reconciliation-without-reparation-the-german-namibian-joint-declaration-on-our-colonial-past

Task Force on Museums and First Peoples, 'Turning the Page: Forging New Partnerships between Museums and First Peoples', 3rd edn (Ottawa, 1994)

Televisión Nacional de Chile, 'Campanas de la Iglesia de la Compañía Tienen Nuevo Memorial' (YouTube, 2018) www.youtube.com/watch?v=NuPzeUfnYfU

The Cambrian, Swansea, 5 February 1864 (copy with the author, courtesy of Susan Rees, member of the parish of All Saints Church)

Thompson EL, 'Returned to Nepal by the FBI, a Sculpture Becomes a God Again' (Hyperallergic.com, 17 December 2021) www.hyperallergic.com/700760/returned-to-nepal-by-the-fbi-a-sculpture-becomes-a-god-again

Titi C, *The Parthenon Marbles and International Law* (Cham, Springer, 2023)

Truth and Reconciliation Commission of Canada, 'Truth and Reconciliation Commission of Canada: Calls to Action' (2015)

Tuladhar S, 'Return of the Gods' *Nepali Times* (August 2000) https://archive.nepalitimes.com/news.php?id=11342

Turner R, 'How Swansea and Chile are Linked by the Bells of Santiago' *WalesOnline* (6 December 2013) www.walesonline.co.uk/lifestyle/nostalgia/swansea-chile-bells-santiago-6377327

Tythacott L and Arvanitis K (eds), *Museums and Restitution, New Practices, New Approaches* (Abingdon, Routledge, 2014)

Übersee-Museum Bremen, 'Provenance Research and Repatriations' (uebersee-museum.de) www.uebersee-museum.de/en/about-us/projekte-positionen/provenienzforschung-und-rueckfuehrungen

The Unesco Courier, 'An Appeal by Mr Amadou-Mahtar M'Bow Director-General of UNESCO' (July 1978)

US Embassy in Cambodia, 'United States Welcomes Return of Khmer Artifacts to Cambodia' (kh.usembassy.gov, 17 March 2023) www.kh.usembassy.gov/unitedstateswelcomesreturnofkhmerartifactstocambodia23

Va S, '$4.5 Million Given for Cambodia Heritage Work: Culture Minister' *Khmer Times* (18 March 2020) www.khmertimeskh.com/702747/4-5-million-given-for-cambodia-heritage-work-culture-minister

Vachon M, 'Statue's Head, Body Reunited after Generations' *The Cambodia Daily* (22 January 2016) https://english.cambodiadaily.com/lifestyle/106089-106089

Van Beurden J, *The Return of Cultural and Historical Treasures: The Case of the Netherlands* (Amsterdam, KIT Publishers, 2012)

——. *Treasures in Trusted Hands. Negotiating the Future of Colonial Cultural Objects, Interdisciplinary Studies in Culture, History and Heritage* (Leiden, Sidestone Press, 2017)

——. 'Hard and Soft Law Measures for the Restitution of Colonial Cultural Collections – Country Report: The Netherlands' (2022) 8 *Santander Art and Culture Law Review* 407

——. *Inconvenient Heritage. Colonial Collections and Restitution in the Netherlands and Belgium* (Amsterdam, University of Amsterdam Press, 2022)

Van Reybrouck D, *Revolusi. Indonesië en het Ontstaan van de Moderne Wereld*, (Amsterdam, De Bezige Bij, 2020)

Villa A, 'Albers Foundation to Launch New Museum in Senegal Aimed at Housing Restituted Artifacts' *ARTnews* (16 May 2022) www.artnews.com/art-news/news/albers-foundation-launch-new-museum-senegal-restitution-1234628808

——. 'Cambodia Receives over 70 Rare Gold Artifacts in Deal with Estate of Disgraced Antiquities Dealer' *ARTnews* (21 February 2023) www.artnews.com/art-news/news/cambodia-douglas-latchford-repatriation-1234658517

VMS AMS, 'Recherches de provenance dans les musées II: Collections liées aux contexts coloniaux. Notions de base et introduction à la pratique' (2022)

Walker D, *Saint James' Church Swansea 1867–1992*, revised and expanded edn (Cardiff, The Church in Wales, 1992)

Weber-Sinn K and Ivanov P, '"Collaborative" Provenance Research: About the (Im)Possibility of Smashing Colonial Frameworks' (2009) 18 *Museum and Society* 66

Weller M, '*Iran v. Barakat*: Some Observations on the Application of Foreign Public Law by Domestic Courts from a Comparative Perspective' (2007) *Art Antiquity & Law* 279

Welsh Icons News, 'Chile Honours Clergymen' (25 February 2011) www.welshicons.org/chile-honours-clergymen

Wijesuriya G, 'Living Heritage' in A Heritage and J Copithorne (eds), *Sharing Conservation Decisions. Current Issues and Future Strategies* (Rome, ICCROM, 2018)

Wira NN, 'National Cultural Week 2020 to Feature Exhibitions on Affandi, Prince Diponegoro' *Jakarta Post* (27 October 2020) www.thejakartapost.com/life/2020/10/27/national-cultural-week-2020-to-feature-exhibitions-on-affandi-prince-diponegoro.html

Zimmerer J and Zeller J, *Genocide in German South-West Africa: The Colonial War (1904–1908) in Namibia and its Aftermath* (London, Merlin Press, 2008)

INDEX

www.ingramcontent.com/pod-product-compliance
Ingram Content Group UK Ltd.
Pitfield, Milton Keynes, MK11 3LW, UK
UKHW020843290926
15470UKWH00004B/1530

9 781509 982523